The Illustrated Directory of the

UNITED STATES
STATES
AIR FORCE

The Illustrated Directory of the

UNITED STATES AIR FORCE

MICHAEL ROBERTS

Brian Trodd Publishing House Limited

Published in 1989 by
Brian Trodd Publishing House Limited
27 Swinton Street, London WC1X 9NW

ISBN 1 85361 032 1

Printed in Italy

Half-title page: Four F–16s of the 31st TFW based
at Homestead AFB, Florida.

Title page: The eerie glow from the cockpit of an
F–4 as the crew wait for take-off at George AFB in
the early morning light.

Right: An air crew prepare their flight plan before a
training flight.

CONTENTS

PHOTOGRAPHIC ACKNOWLEDGMENTS

The author and publisher would like to thank the United States Air Force, Department of Defense and the many companies who have helped in the preparation of this book. We have endeavoured to acknowledge all the different Air Forces photographers whose work appears in this book, and we are sorry if anyone's work has not been credited. We would also like to thank Ken Carter at DoD for all his help in supplying photographs often at very short notice so that the book is as up to date as possible.

USAF front cover (Aircraft, Bases, Commands, B–2 Bomber), back cover, 1, 4–5, 13b, 14b, 15t, 15b, 19, 22t, 23b, 24m, 24b, 25t, 25b, 28, 30t, 311, 31r, 32t, 35t, 35b, 37, 41tl, 41tr, 44, 54t, 61b, 66–67, 70t, 70b, 71, 72t, 72bl, 781, 81t, 81b, 84–85, 95, 96t, 100t, 100m, 101t, 103t, 103b, 104tl, 104tr, 104mr, 104bl, 104br, 111t, 111br, 117b, 122m, 1231, 123r, 128, 130m, 130b, 131tl, 133, 139t, 144 insert, 145, 146, 147, 148, 160tl, 168t, 168b, 169, 174t, 174m, 174b, 175, 176, 177t, 177br, 178–179, 181b, 186, 187b, 188t, 191b, 192, 193t, 195tr, 1961, 196r, 199t, 202, 205t, 205b, 209, 214b, 252t, 252b, 253b.
USAF photographers: SSgt Scott Stewart 2–3,

117t, 118t, 118b, 185b, 187t, 253m; CMSgt Don Sutherland 16–17, 27b, 137, 138b, 139b; MSgt Stephen Jones 18; SSgt Lono A Kollars 20t, 20bl, 20br, 21t, 21ml, 21mr, 21bl, 21br; SSgt Phil Schmitten 24t, 30b, 72mr, 72br, 88–89, 93, 94tl, 94tr, 94bl, 94br; SRA Keith Walker 29t; Garfield F Jones 29b; TSgt Jose Lopez Jr 40, 78r, 101b, 106t, 106b, 107, 108–109, 116; SSgt Fernando Serna 45tr, 60b, 163t, 163b, 164, 201; TSgt James Ferguson/Sgt Dean Wagner 48–49, 62–63, 63t, 63b, 252m; TSgt James Pearson 55t, 87, 141; TSgt James Ferguson 56–57; MSgt Patrick Nugent 59, 110t, 159; SSgt Valentino Gempis 60t; SSgt Gustavo A Garcia 60m; TSgt Kurt Vati 64, 126; SSgt Marv Lynchard 65t, 149, 203; E F Franz 68; Sr Airman Glenda Pellum 83; TSgt Vail 90; MSgt Ken Hammond 91t, 102tr, 102bl, 102br, 131b, 212–213, 250–251; TSgt Lou Hernandez 80t; SSgt David McLeod 91m, 200; AIC Al Labrado 102tl; TSgt Mau 111bl, 177bl; TSgt Michael Haggerty 112–113, 238; SSgt Bard Zimmerman 114; Bill Thompson 121; TSgt Lee Schading 130t, TSgt Herbert Cintron Jr 132b; Ken Hackman 145; SSgt David Nolan 154t, 154b, 155, 156t, 156b, 156bl, 156br, 157, 161t, 161b; TSgt Mike Haggarty 173; SSgt Steve McGill 184t; SSgt Bob Simons 185t,

198b; SSgt Bard Zimmerman 188b; AMN Marinez 214t; AIC Martin J Johanneck 253t; USAF/ASD, Wright-Patterson AFB 22b, 42r, 43b, 111m, 142t, 199t, 223.
Other sources: National Air & Space Museum 8–9, 10, 11t, 11m, 11b, 12t, 12b, 13t, 14m; Department of Defense 73, 92, 143, 191, 218t, 218b; McDonnell Douglas front cover (Missiles), 43t, 46, 53, 74, 76–77, 97, 1051, 115t, 115b, 124, 127, 132t, 138t, 152, 166–167, 189, 190t, 198t, 198m, 216b, 221; General Dynamics 14t, 82b, 134, 217t; Oshkosh 23t; LTV Corporation/DoD 38–39; Lockheed-Georgia/DoD 41b; Beech 45b; Boeing 72ml, 193, 216t; Westinghouse Corp. 110b, 150–151, 226; Cubic Corp. 80b, 80 insert, idd; Lockheed/DoD 96b; Grumman Corp. 142b, 211b, 222–223; Lockheed 182–3, 193b, 206–207, 208; Oates Learjet 190b; Boeing Vertol Company 194; Sikorsky 210; de Havilland Canada 211t; Hughes Aircraft Company 215, 229; Rockwell International 218t; British Aerospace 219; Alan Landau/TRH Pictures front cover (F–15), 32bl, 32br, 45tl, 91b, 131tr, 184b, Mike Roberts/TRH Pictures 122t, 122b, 160tr, 160b, 162, 170, 181t, 195tl, 197, 204.

HOW TO USE THIS BOOK

The book is divided into several sections. The first is a guide to the various Commands, Separate Operating Agencies and Direct Reporting Units and runs alphabetically. The second is the Bases guide in which the first symbol is always the Command operating the base followed by tenant Commands, etc. This guide is followed by the Aircraft and Missiles sections. Each command SOA and DRU has its own symbol which runs throughout the book, see below. So for example in the Bases section Davis-Monthan AFB will have ◆, ◕, ◪, representing Tactical Air Command, Air Force Logistics Command and Air National Guard units operational at the base. If you want to know which Commands operate the AGM-84 Harpoon missile, by looking at the missile entry you will see the ◆ and ▲ symbols representing Strategic Air Command and Pacific Air Forces. And this also applies to the Aircraft section. We hope that this system will allow quick and easy cross-referencing.

While every endeavor has been made to make this book as accurate as possible,

the Air Force is an ever-changing organization. The information we trust is accurate as at the middle of January 1989.

Strategic Air Command	◆
Tactical Air Command	◆
Military Airlift Command	◆
Pacific Air Forces United States Air Forces in Europe	▲
Air Force Space Command	▲
Alaskan Air Command	●
Air Force Logistics Command	◕
Air Force Communications Command	◑
Air Force Reserve	●
Air Force Systems Command	▮
Air National Guard	◪
Air Training Command	▪
All other units	▪

FOREWORD

'Over the last 36 years, I have traveled to nearly all of the major U.S. air bases in the world either as a pilot, staff officer, or inspector. For two years in the mid-1970's I participated in Air Staff planning, programming, and budgeting to improve the infrastructure of the U.S. Air Force. At another stage, I launched a ten-year base improvement master-plan for a large base in Germany that I commanded which is now approaching full development. As a result of my nearness to "basing", I respect this book's bold "footprint" and marvel at what we have achieved in our long-term improvement efforts to make our airfields the finest in the world. Those great modern bases are cornerstones to peace and monuments to a construction program which is the second-largest civil engineering effort in history.*

In Michael Roberts' new book, which I am privileged to introduce, he lists 222 of the most important bases of the Air Force, Air Reserve, and Air National Guard from which over 9.300 first-rate airplanes and aerospace systems are operated. He has provided a distilled look at those bases in a book which will prove interesting and useful to air enthusiasts. His 222 bases are the hardy "survivors" of buildups and cutbacks and will be the "hard points of power projection" well into the next century. Each base represents a costly investment toward deterrence. Capital expenditures at some of the best bases exceed a billion dollars, while replacement costs could easily triple the original costs. The inventory of big bases is indeed striking, but almost equally significant are several thousand small "places" that have not been cataloged which provide technical and logistical service to the global air force.

Those "two-hundred bases and two-thousand places" are work sites for a million skilled military and civilian technicians who generate thousands of flying sorties and operate the far-flung supply and logistics infrastructure that makes it all work. Complex aerospace systems require clean and secure servicing "environments" in which high-tech equipment can remain reliable and affordable to maintain. As General P.K. Carlton once told me: "If you want a first-class flying operation, you've got to go first-class in basing and support." That philosophy becomes even more vital as higher-tech systems come into service.

The years of air base planning and programming have paid off for the Air Force and for the world. Many of our great bases have become model communities with fine buildings, impressive support facilities and park-like grounds which shine with order and cleanliness. One of the most impressive man-made sights in the world is Dover Air Force Base in Delaware, where a mile-long line of C–5 "Galaxy" transports stretches along a heavy duty aircraft parking ramp. Supporting that two-billion dollar line of Galaxies is one of America's great bases which can transport air power to almost any point in the world. A close look at Dover and two hundred other main bases reveals much about the quality and strength of the United States Air Force. Those great bases are the bold footprint which makes air power truly global to help assure peace.'

Colonel Donald A. Walbrecht, USAF Retired

---

*The largest-ever construction effort in the history of the world is the U.S. federal highways program initiated by President Eisenhower in 1956 in which more than 40,000 miles of U.S. superhighways were built at a cost of over $66 billion.

INTRODUCTION

"The mission of the United States Air Force is to organize, train and equip aerospace forces to deter aggression and, if necessary, defeat aggressors across the spectrum of conflict. This supports the most fundamental national interest of the United States, the preservation of our free and independent nation with its institutions and values intact. In the first half of the 1980's, the support of the Administration, Congress and the American people enabled the Air Force to redress the shortfalls in readiness, sustainability and force structure that developed during the difficult times of the 1970's. As a result, today's Air Force is better manned, equipped and prepared than at any other time in history."

Larry D. Welch, General USAF, Chief of Staff, United States Air Force; E. C. Aldridge, Jr., Secretary of the Air Force. The United States Air Force Report to the 100th Congress of the United States of America.

With its roots going back to the start of powered flight, America has maintained an interest in the "High Frontier," the power to dominate the sky. From the founding of the Aeronautical Division of the US Army Signal Corps on 1 August 1907, through two world wars, and two conflicts in the Far East up to the present day, that goal of the High Frontier has not been allowed to fade.

Today as we look forward into the 21st century that goal remains. The pilots and staff of the Aeronautical Division could not have envisaged what they had a hand in starting, but they would have recognized the human element: However powerful the aircraft and space systems of today and tomorrow, you still have to have men to maintain, supply and fly these beasts of the air.

It was not long before the fledgling Aeronautical Division discovered what a war in the air was about. When America entered World War I it had a total of 266 aircraft. By the end of the war in November 1918 this figure had risen to 7,889 aircraft. When President Woodrow Wilson signed the 1917 Aviation Act providing $600 million for military aviation both the Aeronautical Division and American industry geared up for war. The problem was that three years of war had required the development of much more specialized aircraft than was being built in America. Colonel Raynal Bolling was sent to Europe to establish what was needed. It was obvious to him that American industry should concentrate on building trainers and reconnaissance aircraft and to buy Camels, Spads and Nieuports for the fighter element.

As the Army Air Service started to prove its worth over the battlefields of the Western Front, Major Billy Mitchell who was serving on the staff of General John Pershing, Commander of the American Expeditionary Forces, continually pushed for a more active role for the growing Air Service. This did not always go down well with the General who did not agree, feeling that air power could and should only be used in support of the land forces and that it had no potential as an offensive tool itself.

The inter-war years were hard for both the US Army Air Service formed on 24 May 1918 and then its successor the Army Air Corps which saw its aircraft inventory fall to a post-war low of 1,400 airframes. Billy Mitchell, now assistant Chief of the Air Service, felt that the Air Service should be strengthened and formed into an independent force. This did not go down well with the mainstream Army High Command and when he demonstrated the potential of using aircraft against naval targets his efforts were disregarded both by the Army and Navy Departments. The final straw for Mitchell came when the airship *Shenandoah* crashed in September 1925. He accused the various authorities of "criminal negligence." He had pushed his luck too hard with his earthbound seniors. He was court-martialed, found guilty and suspended from duty for five years. This was too much for him and he resigned his commission so that he could carry on the fight for a strong independent Air Force. He never gave up the struggle, working steadfastly on his vision until his death in 1936.

As war loomed yet again in Europe, America again found itself with only a small Air Force, which, for the most part, was made up of obsolescent aircraft. General H "Hap" Arnold, promoted to Chief of the USAAC on 29 September 1938 was given the task of building a modern Air Force. By 1940 the Air Corps had doubled in size and America's industrial might had been geared up to produce a new generation of aircraft to cope with the gathering threat. Arnold, unlike his predecessors, found in General Arnold an Army Chief of Staff who was prepared to listen. And on 20 June 1941, President Roosevelt authorized the formation of the US Army Air Force, General Arnold being its first Chief with the rank of Major General.

This was none too soon. On 7 December of the same year, the Japanese attacked Pearl Harbor and the air bases on Hawaii. The Army Air Force moved on to a war footing; the Far East Air Force which had evacuated the Philippines was reformed in Australia as the Fifth Air Force; and the Hawaiian Air Force was renamed the Seventh Air Force.

Very quickly USAAF aircraft started

Preceding pages: Curtiss P-36As of the 20th Pursuit Group operating from Moffett Field.

Below: One of over 4,800 license-built DH.4s delivered to the Army between 1918 and 1919. 1,538 were modified to DH.4B standard like this example.

to cross the Atlantic. The Eighth Air Force was formed in Great Britain and tasked alongside the RAF with taking the war into Europe. Each time the Army Air Force was presented with a new challenge it met it with vigor. At the same time, back in the States production lines rolled as industry turned out more and more aircraft, from fighters to transports – first the B-17 and then the B-29 strategic bombers.

At the start of World War II the Army Air Corps had a total of 23,455 men and less than four hundred aircraft. At the peak of the war in 1944 the Army Air Force had 78,757 aircraft and 2,373,292 personnel. This was the largest air force the world has ever known and will ever see.

As the war progressed new air forces were created to meet the new demands. In North Africa the Twelfth Air Force was formed out of elements of the Eighth Air Force. As the war moved into Europe, first into Sicily and then on to Italy, the Twelfth gave the vital air cover which the land forces needed, and its bombers attacked targets all over Southern Europe. The Ninth Air Force which along with the RAF Middle East Command had formed the Allied Middle East Air Forces was transferred to England to become an integral component of American air operations against mainland Europe.

To complement the strategic bombing missions of the Eighth Air Force and RAF Bomber Command, the Fifteenth Air Force was formed in Italy and tasked with hitting strategic sites in Austria, Southern France, Southern Germany, northern Italy and Rumania. The raid on the huge petroleum refinery at Ploesti in Rumania was a great success, denying vital fuel supplies to the Germany forces.

For the defense of the Panama Canal the Sixth Air Force was formed in February 1942 from the Caribbean Air Force. It became involved in an anti-submarine warfare campaign against

Germany U-Boats along America's south-eastern flanks. The Eleventh Air Force was formed in Alaska. In July 1943 the Eleventh launched the first land-based bomb raids on the Japanese Kurile Islands from the liberated Aleutians Islands. The bombing of mainland Japan was continued from the Marianas Islands by the Twentieth Air Force which was activated in April 1944. The goal set by General Arnold was to use strategic bombing to bring Japan to its knees without having to invade mainland Japan. He was able to supply the Twentieth with the Boeing B-29 Stratofortress to achieve this aim, the only Air Force to receive the

largest strategic bomber ever built.

In February 1942 the Tenth Air Force was formed for activities in the China/Burma/India theater. The Tenth was headed by Major General Lewis Brereton who arrived in Ceylon with just six aircraft but this number was quickly to grow. Its fighters and bombers took the war to Japanese positions deep in the jungle. It also supported the Air Transport Command which was flying supplies to China over the Himalayas "Hump", a vital airlink which was maintained whatever the weather.

In China itself, Brigadier General Claire Chennault and his American

Far left: Brig. Gen. Billy Mitchell talks to one of his pilots during a Pulitzer Air Race during the 1920's. Considered by many as a hero, his advanced concepts of a modern air force did not sit easily with senior military commanders of the period.

Center: America was forced to buy most of its World War I aircraft from France and Great Britain. This Nieuport 17 was one of the many types used by the American Expeditionary Force during the war.

Below: The war against the Japanese in China had been fought by Claire Chennault and his flying Tigers long before America entered World War II. Here a Flying Tigers Curtiss P–40 of the US Air Service Command passes Chinese works after repair.

Volunteer Group, the "Flying Tigers," had been supporting the Chinese against the Japanese invaders even before America had entered the war. With their P-40s decorated with shark-mouthed cowls the Flying Tigers conducted an aerial guerilla warfare campaign against the Japanese, inflicting heavy losses.

Several months after America entered the war the American Volunteer Group exchanged Chinese markings for American ones and became part of the Tenth Air Force's China Air Task Force. By March 1943 the Task Force had grown to such a size that it was converted into the Fourteenth Air Force and, flying from improvised airfields, its aircraft harried the enemy wherever it was found. And, although outnumbered, they were able to shoot down almost eight Japanese aircraft for each one they lost.

With the end of the war in Europe the focus of attention turned to the final defeat of the Japanese. The Twentieth with their B-29s had been inflicting considerable damage to the Japanese homeland. Unlike the fifteen other air forces which were under the control of the local theater commander, General Arnold had kept the Twentieth under his direct control and he used it as a training ground for ideas that could be

used in an independent American air force separate from the Army. On 6 August 1945 a single B-29 of the Twentieth Air Force with a single bomb completely changed the face of war when the aircraft dropped its load on the city of Hiroshima. The world had entered the Nuclear Age.

In April 1945 the Special Committee for the Reorganization of National Defense, which had been formed by the Joint Chiefs of Staff, reported back to the JCS with the recommendation that after the war a separate air force should be created on an equal basis with the Army and Navy. This horrified the Navy who saw a threat to its power and immediately set up its own committee to reappraise the situation. The plan backfired and

the Navy commission agreed with the Joint Chiefs of Staff which was the last thing the Navy Department wanted to hear.

For some time General Arnold had been a sick man and as 1945 drew to its close, General Spaatz was promoted to Major General and joined the Army Air Force headquarters where he was able to take over some of Arnold's workload. His main task was lobbying for an independent air force and creating a structure for when the great day arrived. General Spaatz was aided in the task by Brigadier General Laurence Kuter and General Ira Eaker who had both been brought to headquarters by General Arnold to build the framework for a new independent air force if it could be sold

Center: A North American P–51 of the 361st Fighter Group, 8th USAAF. Goering stated: "When I saw those Mustangs over Berlin I knew the war was lost."

Right: Consolidated B–24s of the 458th Bomb Group head towards Germany.

Above: A B–17 pilot winds up his engines as he prepares for a mission over Germany.

to the Joint Chiefs of Staff. With a solid team in place General Arnold retired on 28 February 1946 and General Spaatz took over the reins of the quickly diminishing Army Air Force. He now commanded 450,000 men and women, less than a quarter of the number of the previous year. Aircraft and equipment were being sold off at bargain-basement prices. You could buy a brand new P-51 Mustang for less than many post-war motor cars. The transport fleet was being bought up by airlines all over the world. And in America ex-pilots and flight engineers started up freight and passenger airlines, quite often buying the actual aircraft that they had flown for Uncle Sam.

Left: A pre-war Link trainer. The trainer was the first instrument flight training device. During the war over half a million men were trained on 10,000 "Blue Box" trainers.

The mainstay of the 8th Air Force's heavy bomber wings was the Boeing B–17 Fortress.

Convair's huge B–36 was first conceived in 1941, but it was not until 1946 that the first prototype flew. It had a span of 70m (230ft) and was powered by six Wasp Major piston engines which were backed up by four J47 booster turbojets.

Right: A sight which would not have seemed possible a few years ago. Admiral Crowe, Chairman of the JCS, and Marshall of the Soviet Union, Sergi F. Akhomeyer with a young Air Force officer during a visit to the B–1Bs stationed at Ellsworth AFB.

Arnold's team during the last stages of the war. The five main points laid down in Executive Order 9877 provided the organization to be able to train and equip the Air Force to operate on a global scale for both strategic and tactical missions, to supply aerial reconnaissance and to provide all airlift needs for the other services; to co-ordinate air defense with the other services; to develop new tactics and weapons, recognizing the effect that missiles, both nuclear and conventional and the jet engine, would have on the future of air combat; and finally to give assistance to the Army and Navy with supplies and joint operational services.

Forty years on, Arnold's dream goes from strength to strength. The "High Frontier" has been raised to new heights. The USAF's latest command, the Air Force Space Command, operates satellites deep in space, watching and listening and providing a secure global communications network. The concept of President Reagan's Space Defense Inititiative (SDI) moves ahead with research, co-ordinated by the Strategic Defense Initiative Organization, providing the necessary answers, so that one day an operational space-based shield may be able to take out enemy ICBMs before they can threaten America.

A complete type of nuclear missile is to be taken out of service following the signing of the Intermediate Nuclear Forces Treaty. The fielding of the Ground Launched Cruise Missile units in Europe forced the Soviet Union to sign an agreement that could not have happened if those missiles had not

The Strategic Air Command was formed on 21 March 1946 from the Second Air Force to which were added the Eighth and Fifteenth Air Forces. On 1 October the Eleventh Air Force was redesignated the Alaskan Air Command. The stage was being set for the birth of the new Air Force.

With the signing of the National Security Act on 26 July 1947 by President Truman, the United States Air Force was created. This Act called for three "Executive Departments," each headed by a civilian Secretary who would deal directly with his military Chief of Staff. At the same time the President signed Executive Order 9877, which outlined the roles of the three services. The Air Force role had been prepared by General

provide the ability to penetrate deep into Soviet territory if the need arose.

As the Soviet Air Forces continue to introduce more capable aircraft, like the Fulcrum A, Foxhound and Flanker B, with their improved avionics and armament systems, the USAF continues the upgrading of its front-line aircraft to maintain the vital technology gap between East and West. To increase the effectiveness of US theater air forces, the Air Force has to be able to suppress enemy defenses, disrupt their command and control capability, providing real-time warning and control. All these points are now being addressed by the tactical air firces as new weapons systems come on line and others are updated to meet the needs of air warfare into the 21st century.

The need for a larger airlift potential amounting to 66-million ton-miles per day is still some way off, but the arrival of the McDonnell Douglas C-17 will during the late 1990's provide the necessary airlift to approach this figure. Throughout the Air Force change is happening: A modern air force cannot rest on its laurels but must continually decide its priorities and goals and go all out to get them.

been fielded. The USAF is now in the middle of a major reshaping of its forces. 1987 saw the last Titan, Strategic Air Wing decommissioned as the Peacekeeper missile came on line. President George Bush in his first defense budget has called for the 50 MX missiles currently deployed in silos to be redeployed on rail cars, and to continue development of the Small ICBM. This mix would allow the Small ICBM to be used as a bargaining card with the Soviets. The B-1B reached its full strength during 1988 and the Northrop B-2, with its low-observable technology (stealth), is on line for service in the early 1990s, supplemented by the Short-Range Attack Missile (SRAM) II and the Advanced Cruise Missile which will

Northrop's B–2 bomber caused a storm when it was unveiled in November 1988. Its cost is formidable but so is its role.

COMMANDS, DIRECT REPORTING UNITS AND SEPARATE OPERATING AGENCIES

Note:
DRU = Direct Reporting Unit
MC = Major Command
SOA = Separate Operating Agency

AIR FORCE ACCOUNTING AND FINANCE CENTER

"Serving with honor . . . honored with trust."

The motto of the Air Force Accounting and Finance Center (AFAFC) well reflects the position of this organization. Charged with the vast task of paymaster for the Air Force, the AFAFC is located at Lowry AFB. Colorado is the central clearing house for 119 Air Force Accounting and Finance Offices (AFOs), situated around the world, plus a number of disbursing agent offices and 132 Air Reserve Forces pay offices.

AFAFC has a number of major roles: It develops and provides policy guidance on all Air Force financial matters. It oversees the flow of Air Force Funds from the time they are initially appropriated by Congress to final expenditure. It provides the technical support and advice needed to run the Air Force's global accounting and finance network.

The AFAFC is responsible for all funds that are granted to the Air Force by Congress in the annual defense budget which in the FY 1989 will be $97,224 million; this sum is greater than the gross national product of most countries. The AFAFC has a staff of 69 officers, 165 enlisted personnel and 2,200 civilians who are responsible for paying every member of the Air Force and pensions to more than 538,000 retirees and 32,000 annuitants. More than $21 billion from combined appropriations was paid out by the Center in 1987 for wages and pensions.

Computers are used to ease the mammoth task which the Center has in controlling all aspects of Air Force funding. The AFAFC has one of the largest banking organizations in the world and each of its offices is linked. Work continues on a centralized pay system to replace the current labor-intensive system operated at 100 locations worldwide.

During 1987, AFAFC handled funds in excess of $120 billion, which resulted in 31,000 major reports and processed 1,400,000 disbursement and collection vouchers.

Preceding pages: F–15 depot maintenance at the Warner Robins Air Logistics Center, Robins AFB, Georgia.

Right: The Air Force uses many civilians at bases both home and abroad. Here a South Korean meteorological expert Mr. Chan Pang Ko compares notes with his service colleague Staff Sgt. Martin Baroni during Team Spirit 88.

AIR FORCE AUDIT AGENCY

John W. Boddie, the Auditor General of the Air Force, and his staff are responsible directly to the Secretary of the Air Force and provide independent and objective appraisals of Air Force activities. The Agency not only deals with financial affairs but also with operational and support activities. The AFAA provides reports both to the major commands and to base level commanders. The Agency has its HQ at Norton AFB, California, and has a total strength of 250 military personnel and 750 civilians. The AFAA is divided into two staff and three line directorates. The staff directorates handle operations and resource management. The Line Directorates are:

The Acquisition and Logistics Systems Directorate

This is situated at Wright-Patterson AFB, Ohio, and handles the auditing matters relating to acquisitions, foreign military sales, installation logistics, maintenance, supply and weapon systems.

The Field Activities Directorate

This has its headquarters at Norton AFB and has a world-wide network of 67 area audit offices responsible for installation-level work. The audit offices are controlled from four regional offices at Andrews AFB, Md. (Eastern), Offutt AFB, Neb. (Central), McClellan AFB, Calif. (Western) and at Ramstein AB, West Germany (European).

The Forces and Support Management Directorate

Based at Norton AFB, it handles all aspects of audit work dealing with communications, comptroller, forces management, information technology, intelligence, personnel, non-appropriated funds, support services and transportation.

AIR FORCE CIVILIAN PERSONNEL MANAGEMENT CENTER

The Air Force employs more than a quarter of a million civilians at bases both at home and abroad. This civilian resource can be used at a time when the Air Force is having to reduce manning levels to release active duty personnel for other duties. To co-ordinate civilian employees, both American and foreign, is the responsibility of the Air Force Civilian Personnel Management Center located at Randolph AFB, Texas. The Center was created as a direct reporting unit on 1 January 1986. It reports to the Air Force Director of Civilian Management, which took over from the office of Civilian Personnel Operations which had been formed ten years before.

Today the center is divided into three divisions:

The Recruitment and Training Division has responsibility for ensuring that the AF is supplied with civilian staff who are trained to the highest standards. It carries out recruitment campaigns aimed at college leavers; in many instances new recruits need to have degree qualifications to obtain work in the Air Force and this need will increase as the work of the Air Force becomes more complex. It also oversees the in-service civilian education and training budget.

The Career Management Division is responsible for civilian executives and encourages career development in all professional, technical, management and administrative areas. Special career programs, which can combine academic, government and industrial training, encompass everything from manpower, personnel and engineering to historians and public relations personnel.

The Integrated Systems Management Division operates the civilian personnel information systems management program, which controls the world-wide network of civilian employees. The information which the system provides enables both long-term strategic planning and short-term tactical requirements to be met quickly and efficiently.

AIR FORCE COMMISSARY SERVICE

The men and women of the Commissary Service (AFCOMS) are dedicated to providing the Air Force both in peacetime and war with subsistence support. It ensures that food and rations are in the right place at the right time, both in the field and base dining facilities around the world. The Commissary Service sells its products at cost plus a 5 per cent surcharge. This surcharge is used to pay for the running of the service. AFCOMS is reckoned to be second only to medical benefits as the most important non-pay compensation reason that career airmen stay in the service.

The AFCOMS is based at Kelly

AFB, Texas and its 11,000 civilians and military personnel operate 113 troop support facilities plus 142 resale stores. With a turnover of $8.5 million per day, its facilities took $2.1 billion in 1986, making AFCOMS the twelfth largest food-retailing chain in America.

Like every other branch of the Air Force the AFCOMS is making greater use of computers to control its day-to-day running. 1988 saw the completion of the Automated Commissary Operations System. This project allows commissary officers to check on the movement of stock along the chain from warehouse to customer. The cash registers in the stores are directly linked to ACOS. This provides the commissary officers with vital information in what lines are selling and what is left sitting on the shelves.

At AFCOMS Headquarters at Kelly AFB the Commissary Automated Management Network is nearing completion. Once CAMNET comes on line, Headquarters will have a full real-time communications network, linking it with every store around the world. This system will allow AFCOMS to be able to plan and update its sales programs much quicker than before.

AFCOMS have been opening more Wee Serv stores which are open when their main stores are closed. The Wee Serv stores provide all the things you are always running out of, like bread and milk. And it is now possible for service personnel and their families to shop seven days a week. In many of the larger stores Salad Bars have been opened and more are on the way.

The Air Force Commissary Service provides a vital service to the Air Force community supplying comforts from home wherever service families are based.

AIR FORCE COMMUNICATIONS COMMAND

"Providing the Reins of Command"

*Motto of the Air Force
Communications Command*

Formed in 1961, the Air Force Communications Service was renamed

on 15 November 1979 as the Air Force Communications Command (AFCC). AFCC personnel can be found operating from more than 470 locations around the world. They are responsible for everything to do with communications in its widest sense. They handle and maintain communications – both voice and data – together with data processing, air traffic control and air traffic services. Each of the major commands is supported by a specific Communications Division. Strategic Communications Division at Offutt AFB, Nebraska handles SAC requirements. Pacific Communications is handled from Hickham AFB, Hawaii. Europe is controlled from the European Communications at Kapaun Barracks in West Germany.

There are three major communications nets available between bases: the Automatic Voice Network (AUTOVON), the Automatic Secure Voice Communications Network (AUTOSEVOCOM), and the Automatic Digital Network (AUTODIN). As the demand for swift, secure communications grows, AFCC has the capability to develop and install new equipment as the need arises. AFCC personnel operate at almost every Air Force location, and if a commander wants a communications net set up on a bare field site in support of an exercise such as Team Spirit then AFCC technicians will move swiftly into operation.

The AFCC provides all Air Force air-traffic controllers and runs the second largest air-traffic control in the world after the Soviet Union. It operates six facility-checking aircraft which test all aspects of air-traffic safety wherever Air Force aircraft operate.

The command is responsible for all Air Force air traffic movements.

AIR FORCE COMMUNICATIONS COMMAND

Headquarters, Scott AFB, Ill.

Commander
Maj. Gen. S. Cassity

Airlift Communications Division Scott AFB, Ill.	**Air Training Communications Division** Randolph AFB, Tex.	**Engineering and Installation Division** Tinker AFB, Okla.	**European Communications Division** Kapaun Adm. Annex. Germany
Logistics Communications Division Wright-Patterson AFB, Ohio.	**Pacific Communications Division** Hickam AFB, Hawaii	**Research and Acquisition Communications Division** Andrews AFB, Md.	**Strategic Communications Division** Offutt AFB, Neb.
Space Communications Division Colorado Springs, Colo.	**Tactical Communications Division** Langley AFB, Va.	**Standard Systems Center** Gunter AFB, Ala.	**Air Force Computer Acquisition Center** Hanscom AFB, Mass.
Air Force Frequency Management Center Washington, D.C.	**Air Force Communications-Computer Systems Doctrine Office** Keesler AFB, Miss.	**Air Force Central NOTAM Facility** Carswell AFB, Tex.	**1800th Communications Wing** Fort Myer. Va.

1931st Communications Wing
Elmendorf AFB, Alaska

One of the Air Force Communication Command's largest tasks is to run the Air Force Pentagon Telecommunications Center (AFPTC). The Center handles commercial and military phones through the Washington Tactical Switchboard. The Readiness Center, often called the nerve center is responsible for direct maintenance on secure phone, encryption devices, cameras and numerous special circuits. They also handle maintenance for all mainframe computers and 16,000 micro computers and word processors.

AIR FORCE DISTRICT OF WASHINGTON

The Air Force District of Washington (AFDW) is reponsible for all Air Force activities in the Washington, DC, area. It has its headquarters at Bolling AFB, DC, but it has control of a much larger area. It has units and detachments at Andrews AFB, Maryland, and the Pentagon. The two largest units in AFDW are the 1100th Air Base Group (ABG) which is host unit at Bolling AFB and the 1100th Resource Management Group (RMG). Other units within AFDW are the US Air Force Band and the US Air Force Honor Guard. The Air Force Band provides music for many special events in the District, and they can provide a wide range of music from the Concert Band through to the Ceremonial Band. Throughout the summer visitors to the Capital can see the Air Force Band and its sub-units at free concerts given around town. The Honor Guard is in regular attendance at the White House, the Pentagon and Andrews Air Force Base for official duties on behalf of the Air Force. It also mounts guard at military funerals held at Arlington Cemetery and at the Tomb of the Unknown.

The 1100th ABG supports the many tenant units at Bolling including the HQ Air Force Office of Special Investigations and the Air Force Office of Scientific Research. They also look after a number of Air Staff offices, including those of the Chief of Chaplains, the Office of Air Force History and the Surgeon General.

The 1100th RMGB among other roles provides command personnel, and runs education and military personnel offices at Bolling AFB, Fort Meade and the Pentagon. Two sub-units, the 1100th Contracting Squadron and the AFDW Accounting Office, provide contracting and financial services for the AF in the District.

AIR FORCE ENGINEERING AND SERVICES CENTER

Based at Tynall AFB, Florida, the Air Force Engineering and Services Center (AFESC) supports the Air Force Director of Engineering and Services by developing programs and recommending technical policies. It is also responsible as a separate operating agency for providing direct aid to all the major commands and base-level engineering and services organizations all over the world. Its teaching programs provide wartime training for an average of 13,000 active-duty and reserve engineering and services personnel each year. The Center is also home for the Engineering and Services Laboratory which conducts civil engineering and environmental research, development, testing and evaluation.

AFESC staff provide global support in the areas of readiness which include all Prime BEEF, Prime RIBS and Red Horse Forces. They deal with fire protection, base power supply, civil and environmental engineering, housing and community services. AFESC handles all matters relating to the overall operation and maintenance of facilities at all Air Force installations world-wide.

Its staff can tackle anything, from

Right: Silver-suited fire fighters tackle an aircraft fire during training. AFESC is responsible for fire fighting training and equipment.

Right: An artist's impression of a new generation fire fighting tender developed by the AFESC.

programs, its staff teach all US armed forces the techniques of accident investigation. Every AF accident or mishap is investigated and if possible any lessons learnt are acted on to provide positive corrective measures.

The Directorate of Inspection

The operational readiness status in the major commands is monitored by the Directorate. Its staff monitor all the Operational Readiness Inspection (ORI) reports and conduct Assistance and Evaluation Inspections while the ORI reports are being undertaken. They continually work with the command's own inspector general teams to maintain a clear picture of the efficiency of the unit under examination. It maintains checks on all Air Force management systems and can recommend any changes which come to light during Function Management Inspections.

The Directorate of Medical Inspection

The readiness of all the Air Force's medical units and the Air Force and Air Reserve Forces Biennial Health Services Management Inspections are undertaken and checked by the Directorate. The health of Air Force personnel and dependents is a vital obligation and the Directorate Inspections ensure that all medical resources are effectively maintained in both peace and war.

The Directorate of Nuclear Safety

Located at the heart of the Air Force's nuclear forces and other government nuclear agencies at Kirkland AFB, New Mexico, the Directorate of Nuclear Safety co-ordinates Air Force

Left: Pride of the fire fighting teams are their Oshkosh Crash/Vehicles developed by the Air Force Engineering and Services Center.

surveys into things like vehicle shortages and the impact these can have on service efficiency, to site surveys at AF installations. On the power supply side they rebuilt four generators at Thule AB, Greenland, in 1986 which provided the AF with a saving of $3.0 million, and they are continually providing support maintenance and modernization for all power supplies.

On the firefighting and prevention front, AFESC staff design and develop all aspects of firefighting equipment and tacts which enable the Air Force to increase firefighting skills. Each year AFESC runs the Readiness Challenge competition which tests the skills of Prime BEEF (Base Engineer Emergency Force) and Prime RIBS (Readiness in Base Service) teams from all the major commands.

commanders with an assessment of the Air Force's fighting capabilities and resource management effectiveness. Its commander is also Deputy Inspector General for Inspection and Safety at HQ USAF in Washington, DC.

Although the Center has only 356 military personnel and 111 civilian staff it has a vast impact on the operation of the Air Force. It is based at Norton AFB, California and is divided up into four directorates and two offices.

The Directorate of Aerospace Safety

Responsible for all flight, ground, missile, explosives and systems-safety

AIR FORCE INSPECTION AND SAFETY CENTER

The men and women of the Air Force Inspection and Safety Center (AFISC) have a wealth of experience in many AF specialties. These various talents provide the Secretary of the Air Force, the Chief of Staff and Air Force

A badly damaged F–15 which was able to make a safe landing. It is the responsibility of the inspection and safety Center to determine the cause of any accident and to suggest preventive measures.

The Directorate of Nuclear Safety, a division of the Air Force Inspection and Safety Center, is responsible for checking the handling of all nuclear materials.

nuclear safety programs. If it is nuclear the Directorate has a role to play from original design to operational service. It manages the Air Force Nuclear Surety Program and checks that all safety checks are carried out at Air Force establishments all over the world. It is responsible for maintaining checks and inspections on nuclear weapons and nuclear power reactors both on Earth and on satellites.

The Office of Computer Systems
Operates the AFISC computer which supports the agencies' activities globally. It is also responsible for the design and development of computer software for use by the Center. It also maintains and manages the priceless Air Force flight records collection, which has been logged since 1911.

The Office of Management Support
To co-ordinate the vast amount of work the Center undertakes each year, the Office manages the running of AFISC dealing with manpower and budget. It also controls the very complex schedule of Inspections in which the AFISC is involved.

Above right: On 14 April 1986 Air Force and Navy bombers hit Libya. This photograph was taken by an F–111F air crew and shows an IL–76 transport just before it was destroyed by a 500–lb bomb. The Pave Tack laser-guided delivery system provided the AFIS with a detailed blow by blow account of the mission.

Right: As the F–111s were attacking Tripoli, Navy A–6 crews attacked the Benina airfield. This infra-red photo of the field was taken by an Air Force SR–71 which provided confirmation of the heavy damage that had been inflicted.

AIR FORCE INTELLIGENCE SERVICE

From its headquarters in Washington, DC the Air Force Intelligence Service (AFIS) maintains and provides a vast

data base of information which is continually updated. Its Commander is also the Deputy Assistance Chief of Staff Intelligence, HQ USAF. It is his and his staff's job to provide accurate and reliable intelligence to the Chief of Staff and major command and separate operating agency commanders. This covers everything from Soviet studies, target analysis, operational intelligence and the security of telecommunications.

The 2,200 personnel who make up the AFIS are divided into a number of separate divisions. Major Directorates and offices include:

Air Force Special Activities Center
With offices in CONUS, Europe and the Pacific, the Center co-ordinates all Air Force information-gathering from human resources.

Attache Affairs Directorate
Liaises with Air Attaches at all American Embassies around the world.

Intelligence Data Management Directorate
The Directorate manages all of the Air Forces global intelligence data handling systems.

BENINA AIRFIELD
15 APR 86

DESTROYED MIG-23/FLOGGER

MIG-23/FLOGGER PIECES

Left: Two lieutenants work on a detailed plan of a Tu–22 Backfire. Using data collected from a wide range of sources allows the AFIS and AFSC's Foreign Technology Division to piece together vital details of Soviet equipment.

Intelligence Reserve Forces Directorate

Through the Intelligence Reserve Program, it manages the recruiting and training of Reserve personnel in all aspects of Air Force intelligence work. This provides the AF with a large corp of trained personnel who can be quickly mobilized in the event of an emergency.

Operational Intelligence Directorate

It provides the Secretary of the Air Force, the Chief of Staff and other senior officers with all intelligence information that they require for the planning of operations and warnings of all possible threats. As directed it is also able to provide photo interpretation and signals analysis experts to the Air Staff.

Soviet Affairs Directorate

The Soviet Affairs personnel monitor all Soviet-produced information including newspapers, magazines and broadcasts in which it gathers in and analyses. It issues a number of publications, including the *Soviet Military Thought* and *Studies in Communist Affairs* series. It also produces a regular synopsis of Soviet press reports.

Special Studies Division

This Division reports on all foreign denial and deception activities which are identified from all sources of information.

Target Intelligence Directorate

To support the Air Staff the TID handles all aspects of target intelligence. It includes mission planning, targeting and mapping.

AIR FORCE LEGAL SERVICES CENTER

With its headquarters in Washington, DC, the Legal Services Center handles a wide range of legal matters and looks after the interests of the Air Force and its personnel throughout the world. Its Commander also serves as the Air Force Judge Advocate General. Its staff of nearly 600 operate a number of special offices dedicated to the service of military justice.

The Civil Law Center

The Center handles all aspects of civil law which relate to contracts, general litigation, legal assistance, patents, etc.

The Claims and Tort Litigation Staff

The Staff of this department handle claims which arise from the Air Force's operations around the world. It acts on behalf of the Air Force in any claim it issues or with which it is served.

The Contract Law Division

Tasked with all legal matters dealing with contracts, it handles claims for monetary damages filed by and against contracts. Actions are brought through the award of contracts and bankruptcies filed by the Air Force. The Judge Advocate General is supported by the Division in all cases which involve abuse, fraud and waste. In the past few years it has gained a high profile in actions against a number of major aerospace companies following action in Congress.

The Court of Military Review

Established in 1968 the Court is responsible for reviewing any court-martial which finds the defendant guilty and sentenced to be dismissed from the service, confined for more than one year or discharged with a dishonorable or bad conduct sentence. Appeals over the decision of Court of Military Review can in some cases be taken to the US Court of Military Appeal or to the US Supreme Court.

The Defense Services Division

It provides legal representation for Air Force personnel who are broguht before any court of law, including the Court of Military Review, the US Court of Military Appeals and the United States Supreme Court.

Left: The use of photographs will be phased out as new video imaging equipment is brought into service during the 1990's.

The Environmental Law Division
It acts in all cases which involve the Air Force in environmental issues.

The General Litigation Division
The Division acts on behalf of the Air Force in domestic cases – for example, administration labor law, general litigation and personnel cases.

The Government Trial and Appellate Counsel Division
The Division acts for the prosecution on behalf of the Air Force in the Court of Military Review and the US Court of Military Appeal and acts in support of the Solicitor General in the Supreme Court. It has a team of 21 full-time circuit trial prosecutors for normal court appearances.

The Patents Division
The Air Force is involved in a vast amount of research and production of equipment and it is the Patents Division's task to protect this vast investment. It also assists the Department of Justice when any action is brought against the Air Force involving copyrights, patents and trade secrets.

The Preventive Law and Legal Assistance Office
It manages the Air Force Preventive Law and Legal Assistance Program wherever the Air Force operates throughout the world. Its installation legal officers assist Air Force personnel with legal matters.

The Special Assistant for Clemency and Rehabilitation Matters
This office can recommend clemency and reduction of sentence for individual cases. It also provides information for the Judge Advocate General on matters concerning imprisonment, sentences and rehabilitation programs.

AIR FORCE LOGISTICS COMMAND

"Keeping the fleet flying through innovative maintenance and spare-parts programs is our main job"

Gen. Earl T. O'Loughin, CINCAFLC

With 102,000 civil and military staff Air Force Logistics Command (AFLC) is third in size after Strategic Air Command and Tactical Air Command. This vast network of talent is used to maintain the aircraft, missiles and other equipment used by the Air Force. It is such a large organization that it is the largest single site employer in all but one of seven states that have a Logistics Center, the exception being California. It is very aware that its personnel are a valuable asset and is continually looking to improve procedures and operating practices as the demand on the Command grows.

Its Logistics Centers handle a variety of maintenance schemes. Based at Hill AFB, the Ogden Air Logistics Center provides everything needed to support the entire fleet of F-4s, RF-4s, F-16s and ICBMs. It also handles both air-to-air and air-to-ground missiles, explosives and solid propellants and rocket motors and carries a wide range of spare parts for aircraft and photographic equipment.

The maintenance hangar at the Oklahoma City Air Logistics Center, Kelly AFB, is so large that it can accommodate six C-5s or fourteen B-52s at one time. It also handles a wide range of aircraft engines and all fuels and lubricants used by the Air Force and NASA.

At McClellan AFB, Calif., the Sacramento Air Logistics Center is running an on-going Avionics Modernization Program for F-111 bombers. This was the first time that the Air Force was prime contractor on a major project. The program is upgrading the bomb navigation system for all the F-111 and FB-111 aircraft. The first one to be upgraded was an FB-111 which left the Center in December 1986. By 1994 the entire fleet will have all been converted and F-111s will be in service until at least

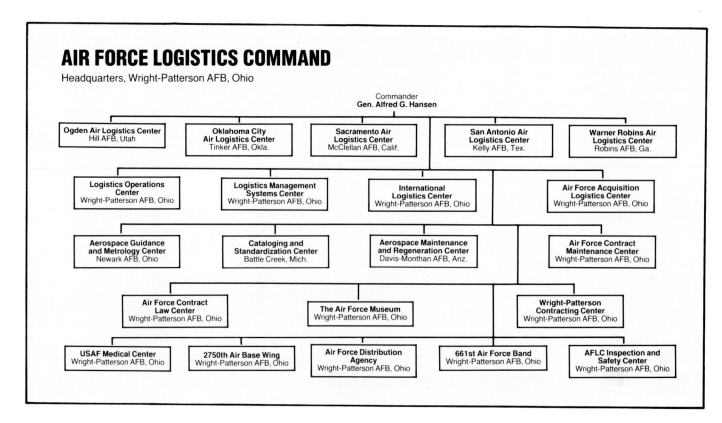

2010. The Center also handles the Fairchild A-10, the Air Force Satellite Communications system (AFSATCOM) and maintains and modifies local F-4s.

The Warner Robins Air Logistics Center is the System Program Manager for JSTARS (Joint Surveillance and Target Radar System) and also Source of Repair for the project. On behalf of the US Navy it maintains their C-130 fleet. It also manages the Air Force F-15, C-130, C-141 and helicopter fleets, plus missile systems.

One of the command's most interesting centers for aircraft historians is the vast Military Aerospace Maintenance and Regeneration Center (MAMRC) located at Davis Monthan AFB in Arizona. The dry atmosphere is kind to the thousands of aircraft that are mothballed there, aircraft are protected by a plastic film waiting for the day that it might be needed again. Commonly known as the Boneyard, it is a unique resource for spare parts that are no longer manufactured.

The AFLC is working on a range of advanced composite materials which may be used in future aircraft like the Advanced Tactical Fighter.

To assist in all aspects of AFLC life new generations of computers and software are coming into service with Logistics Command. Under its modernization program, the DMMIS (Depot Maintenance Management Information System) will by 1990 replace 41 of AFLCs 56 maintenance computer systems. The new computers are able to process a greater amount of information much more quickly. The Contracting Information Data System (CIDS) now provides Logistics Command customers with information on spare parts and suppliers. When it is fully operational it will provide a paperless contracting system. The power of modern computers is having a revolutionary effect on all areas of Air Force life: The pen might be mightier than the sword but the microchip is faster.

AIR FORCE MANAGEMENT ENGINEERING AGENCY

The need to make the best use of manpower at a time when the birth rate is falling, industry is able to offer large incentives to gather the best people and the military budget is being reduced, places a great pressure on the military.

"The future capability of the Air Force will depend in large measure, on how well we recruit and retain quality people today. . . . There are, however, downward trends in retaining pilots, engineers and some enlisted specialists. These trends are cause for serious concern."

USAF Report to the 100th Congress.

For example MAC is faced with a fall-off in pilots which in 1988 amounted to 40 per cent. To tackle this major problem of manpower management is the responsibility of the Air Force Management Engineering Agency (AFMEA).

The AFMEA sets the manpower standards required by the Air Force, these standards being determined by use of the Functional Review Process (FRP) which has three main objectives:

1 To develop the most efficient and effective organization without reducing readiness.
2 To develop manpower standards.
3 To develop manpower decision packages.

The FRP allows the AFMEA and Air Force Commanders to decide what manpower would be required during a war. The AFMEA also sets down the officer/enlisted personnel manning levels and distribution. Based at Randolph AFB, Texas, the AFMEA is able through its ten subordinate units to advise the Command Management Engineering Teams who operate at almost every Air Force base around the world. Each sub-unit has a special area of responsibility, there are eight Functional Management Engineering Teams (FMETs) and two special teams:

> Comptroller Management
>   Engineering Team
>   (AFCOMPMET)
>   Lowry AFB, Colorado
> Engineering and Services
>   Management Engineering Team
>   (AFESMET)
>   Tyndall AFB, Florida
> Intelligence Management
>   Engineering Team
>   (AFINTELMET)
>   Fort Belvoir, Virginia

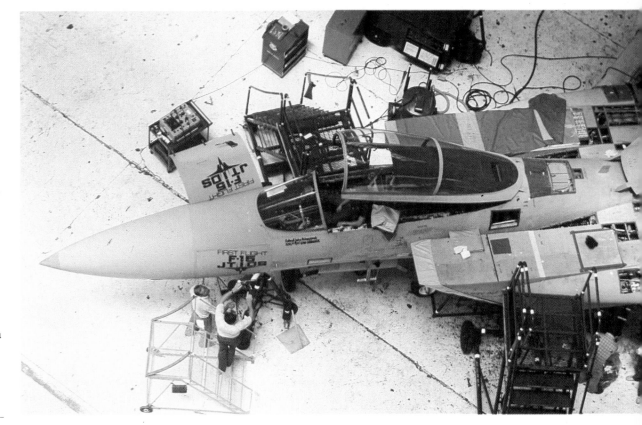

The Warner Robins Air Logistics Center at Robins AFB is responsible for major maintenance on Air Force F-15s as well as a number of transport aircraft.

Logistics Management
Engineering Team
(AFLOGMET)
Dover AFB, Delaware
Manpower And Personnel
Management Engineering Team
(AFMPMET)
Randolph AFB, Texas
Medical Management Engineering
Team (AFMEDMET)
Maxwell AFB, Alabama
Security Police Management
Engineering Team (AFSPMET)
Kirkland AFB, New Mexico
Special Staff Management
Engineering Team (AFSSMET)
Peterson AFB, Colorado
Plus OL-A at the Pentagon,
Washington, DC, and the Air
Force Wartime Manpower and
Personnel Readiness Team
(AFWMPRT) at Fort Richie,
Maryland.

They are able to make use of the
AFMEA's computer simulations to
examine the most efficient use of
manpower in any given situation – for
example, the Logistics Composite
Model, an advanced software program
which shows what level of maintenance
manpower is required for any weapon
system. Another of their programs, the
Manpower Standards Development
System, which runs on both mainframe
and desktop computers, offers
automated support for the manpower
engineering teams of the MAJCOMS to
determine manpower standards for any
individual base location.

AFMEA is also responsible for
getting the best productivity from Air
Force personnel, which allows a better
return on investment and frees
manpower to be redeployed where it is
needed most.

AIR FORCE MILITARY PERSONNEL CENTER

The Air Force's most valuable resource
is its people. To look after the Air
Force's 600,000 plus active duty men
and women and approximately the
same number of retired personnel is
the task of the Air Force Military

Personnel Center based at Randolph
AFB, Texas. Its staff of 2,126 military
and civilian staff is commanded by
Maj. Gen. Billy J. Boles, who is also
the Assistant Deputy Chief of Staff for
Personnel, HQ USAF.

The Center is responsible for many
aspects of Air Force life. It runs
promotion programs for officers and
other ranks. It looks after morale,
welfare and recreation through a series
of MWR programs. These programs are
not only restricted to Air Force
personnel but their families as well. It
also runs the Air Force Casualty
Service Program, which aids the
families of active-duty casualties and
still cares for the families of 906
unaccounted-for Air Force personnel
in South-east Asia.

It is responsible for running a
number of initiatives aimed at
persuading service personnel to re-
enlist. This is an important task, which
can allow the Air Force to keep
valuable men and women in the
service. Special bonus schemes are
run by the AFMPC – the Selective
Enlistment Bonus operated by the

Center was awarded to 16,365
personnel in Fiscal Year 1986. They
can also guide airmen in both
voluntary and selective retraining
schemes.

As in every other branch of the Air
Force, computers are being used to
provide vital information resources to
the Center. Personnel information is
fed into the system from over a
thousand remote terminals situated in
personnel offices throughout USAF
and minicomputers at the headquarters
of the various commands. During 1987
the Advanced Personnel Data System
II was completed, further enhancing
the system. And in 1992 the Personnel
Concept III computer automation
program will provide enhanced support
by replacing old paper-based
personnel systems with a full
electronic office system. It will also
provide access to other Air Force data
bases, assuring vital interoperability
for the Air Force.

The growing role of the AFMPC is
very important if the Air Force is to
cope with the challenges it faces as it
enters the 1990's.

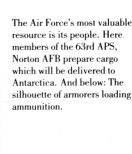
Opposite page: The F–15 was designed with maintenance in mind, allowing easy access to the interior.

The Air Force's most valuable resource is its people. Here members of the 63rd APS, Norton AFB prepare cargo which will be delivered to Antarctica. And below: The silhouette of armorers loading ammunition.

TSgt. Robert Walker, a medical technician from the 32nd AES, assists 1st Lt Pamela Spaulding, 146th AES, to load patients onto a C–130 aircraft during a medical evacuation exercise.

Maintaining the good health of the Air Force personnel is the main priority of the Air Force Office of Medical Support.

AIR FORCE OFFICE OF MEDICAL SUPPORT

The 269 military and civilian personnel of the Air Force Office of Medical Support (AFOMS) support the Air Force Surgeon General in all areas of health care both in war and peace. The Office is located at Brooks AFB, Texas, and consists of the Directorate of Health Care Support and a number of Professional Affairs Activities.

The Directorate of Health Care Support is split into four divisions and one office:

The Biometrics Division

Processes and monitors information covering all aspects of the medical services including services, administrations, clinical and outpatient records and patient affairs at all medical centers.

The Medical Facilities Division

The Division looks after all aspects of building and maintenance of medical facilities within the Air Force.

The Medical Service Information Systems Division

Controls the development, acquisition, installation and running of computer-based medical information handling and retrieval systems.

The Medical Logistics Division

The Division is accountable for all plans and policies relating to the supply of medical materials and equipment, maintenance and repair of equipment and medical material support during wartime. Part of AFOMS, the Air Force Medical Logistics Office based at Fort Detrick, Maryland, is responsible under the Medical Logistics Division umbrella as an operational control center for all Air Force commands. It is the single manager of medical resources and advises on technical activities involving medical material maintenance.

The Medical Service Innovation Office

As its title suggests this office is continually monitoring and cataloging new medical practices and distributing relevant information throughout the Air Force medical system. Professional Affairs Activities control two major programs and the USAF Radioisotope Committee. The Family Advocacy Program handles a number of Air Force programs which deal with all aspects of child health care. It also reports directly to the AF Surgeon General on matters relating to social welfare and the family. The Health Promotion Program is accountable for activities which relate to good-health activities including preventive medicine and public relations activities aimed at informing service personnel and their families about good health.

AIR FORCE OFFICE OF SECURITY POLICE

The smallest of the Separate Operating Agencies, the Air Force Office of Security Police (AFOSP) based at Kirkland AFB, New Mexico, has approximately 150 staff. Its commander, Brig. Gen. Frank K. Martin, is also the Air Force Chief of Security Police and the Assistant Inspector General for Security Police. The Office controls the activities of over 50,000 security personnel both military and civilian.

Its activities include programs relating to the physical defense of air bases up to the perimeter fence (the army is responsible for area defense beyond the perimeter), secure communications, information security, maintenance of law and order and prisoner rehabilitation and correction.

The Air Force Security Education Council, which is made up of representatives from the MAJCOMS, is chaired by AFOSP. The Council produces guidelines and promotes security awareness at all levels of the Air Force.

In conjunction with the Air Force System Command's Electronics Systems Division, AFOSP has developed the Scope Shield radio program. This provides security forces with secure communications using a variety of radios depending on operational requirements.

AIR FORCE OFFICE OF SPECIAL INVESTIGATIONS

With its headquarters at Bolling AFB, DC, the Air Force Office of Special Investigations (AFOSI) is the Air Force's chief criminal investigative organization. Formed in 1948, the Office is tasked with providing service chiefs with the information required to undertake judicial or administrative action when dealing with cases of a criminal or fraudulent nature. It also deals with a variety of anti-terrorism, counter-intelligence and personnel protective operations (Key Air Force, DoD, Government officials and foreign VIPs). It is the USAF's central organization for running polygraph tests and in 1987 it conducted over 6,000 polygraph examinations.

Today the Office is headed by Brig. Gen. Francis R. Dillon and totals some 3,000 personnel of whom 90 per cent are military personnel and the remaining 10 per cent are civilians. Its personnel operate around the world and can call on an impressive array of technical support during the course of investigations. They regularly use a mixture of computers, electronics, forensics and human behavioral science experts to aid their inquiries.

Each year the AFOSI runs a Special Investigators course at its own Special Investigations Academy situated at Bolling AFB. The course is attended by some 240 officers, non-commissioned officers and civilians and lasts three months. It also conducts specialist courses for its staff and members of the Air Force and runs regular courses for AF Reserve and Individual Mobilization Augmentees who are assigned to AFOSI.

Almost 40 per cent of the agency's time is taken up with the investigation of major crimes such as assault, drug trafficking, murder and rape. The organization has continued to make headlines in the civilian press by its fight against irregularities and fraudulent misuse of Air Force funds. It has certainly worked hard for its funding over the past few years and in FY 1987 it recovered or saved almost $68 million of which some $30 million was recovered from contract frauds.

AIR FORCE OPERATIONAL TEST AND EVALUATION CENTER

With its headquarters at Kirkland AFB, New Mexico, the military and civilian staff of the Air Force Operational Test and Evaluation Center (AFOTEC) are responsible for testing new generations and modifications of weapons systems and components which might be or are fielded by the Air Force and the other services. It is their responsibility to advise the Air Force, the Department of Defense, and finally Congress as and when new projects lead to production status.

There are approximately 533 personnel at Kirkland AFB plus 165 staff divided between five detachments and 24 test teams; at any one time AFOTEC has about 2,400 people under its control. The five major attachments are at Colorado Springs, Eglin AFB, Edwards AFB, and Nellis AFB, plus the Kapaun Administrative Annex, West Germany. AFOTEC personnel head up the management teams for test programs, the rest of the teams being brought together from the relevant major commands.

Over the past few years, AFOTEC teams have worked on the Joint Tactical Information Distribution System (JTIDS), the High-Speed Antiradiation Missile, and are continuing work on the Advanced Medium-Range Air-to-Air Missile (AMRAAM). Other current projects include the B-1B strategic Bomber,

Far left: The Office of Security Police is responsible for all security training.

Below: The Armament Division at Eglin Air Force Base has been conducting test firing of the Advanced Medium Range Air-to-Air Missile. Here a 3246th Test Wing F-15 armed with an AMRAAM receives fuel from a KC-135 while a 3246th TW F-16 chase plane looks on.

A KC–10 refuels A–10s; the Air Force Reserve took delivery of the McDonnell Douglas KC–10 at the same time as the regulars.

Consolidated Space Operations Center, MX missile and the Next Generation Weather Radar. Future projects to be undertaken include the Advanced Tactical Fighter and new generations of flight simulators. Each of the projects that is examined by AFOTEC is tested under operationally realistic conditions which provide information not only on how the system will work, but how it can be maintained so that it is ready for use. Over the years the center has been responsible for identifying a number of problems that might have arisen and corrected them before the project went into full production.

AIR FORCE RESERVE

●

"The Reservist is twice the citizen"

Winston Churchill

"I think that we often do the job better than the full timers because they do it everyday, and it's a routine for them. For us it remains a novelty . . . it's so different from our other jobs and we try that bit harder."

A Reservist

Right: The distinctive emblem of the 89th Tactical Fighter Squadron.

Far right: An F–4D of the 89th TFS based at Wright Patterson AFB, Ohio.

The Air Force Reserve (AFRES) has since 1983 been a Separate Operating Agency (SOA), having been until then a Direct Reporting Unit, and consists of 58 flying squadrons and 450 mission support units. Its mission is training reserve Air Force Personnel to be ready for mobilization, both as complete units and as individuals who would report direct to regular units. It has its headquarters at Robins AFB, Georgia and is divided into three numbered Air Forces; the Fourth whose headquarters is at McClellan AFB, California and the Fourteenth whose headquarters is at Dobbins AFB, Georgia, MAC is the gaining command for all their units. The Tenth AF headquartered at Bergstrom AFB, Texas has squadrons assigned to both SAC and TAC. During the 1980's the Air Force Reserve has continued to grow in numbers of personnel; in 1980 the AFRES numbered 60,000; that figure had risen to 80,000 in 1987 and is due to rise to 86,000 during FY 1989. AFRES provides 50 per cent of Military Airlift Commands C-5 and C-141 crews, 47 per cent of aerial port personnel, 40 per cent of its strategic airlift maintenance force, almost 75 per cent of MAC medical crews, 50 per cent of AC-130 crews and 25 per cent of all Air Force C-130 crews.

Since World War II both the AFRES and Air National Guard (ANG) have been called in to action because of national emergencies on a regular basis. During the Berlin crisis in 1961 both AFRES and ANG units were ordered into service by the President. A total of 36 Air National Guard and AFRES flying squadron and an Air National Guard tactical control unit, totalling 27,000 Reservists, were brought into service.

A year later in October 1962 ANG and AFRES units were called up in support of President Kennedy's response to Soviet attempts to establish nuclear missiles in Cuba. Five days after the President had told the world about the missiles, 24 Air Force Reserve airlift squadrons with 400 aircraft manned and serviced by 15,000 personnel had been called up for active duty. Within 24 hours 93 per cent of the personnel had reported for duty. It had been a tremendous achievement and Secretary of Defense McNamara called it "a Fantastic performance." Although not called up, many reserve units went into service on a voluntary basis, which meant that regular units could be freed for service in support of the Cuban mission. In particular ANG and AFRES airlift units took over MAC missions around the world.

In 1965 reserve units were again in action, assisting in "Power Pack" flying out of US and other foreign nationals from the Dominican Republic. In total they flew 1,747 missions, logging nearly 16,000 flying hours. They evacuated 5,115 people and carried 4,000 plus tons of cargo.

Throughout the Vietnam War Reserve units supported MAC and CINCPAC. And in 1973 the Air Force Reserve was in action again, flying 300 missions in support of Israel during the Israeli–Egyptian war. Since then both AFRES and ANG units have been involved in many humanitarian missions both in America and around the world. In 1986 A C-141 from the 459th MAW and two C-5s from the 512th MAW flew humanitarian missions to El Salvador following a major earthquake.

During 1987 the 446th MAW sent a unit to Puerto Rico to evacuate eight

Air Force Reserve Flying Wings and Assigned Units

Fourth Air Force
HQ McClellan AFB
California
Commander
Major General C, Wahleithner

Wing	Group	Squadron	Aircraft	Location	Gaining command
		71st SOS	HH-3E, CH-3E	Davis-Monthan AFB, Ariz.	MAC
	919th SOG	711th SOS	AC-130A	Eglin AFB, Fla.	MAC
	939th ARRG	304th ARRs	HC-130H/HH-1H HH-3E/CH-3E	Portland IAP, Ore.	MAC
		301st ARRs	HC-130H/N, HH-3E	Homestead AFB, Fla.	MAC
		305th ARRS	HC-130H/N, HH-3E	Selfridge ANGB, Mich.	MAC
349th MAW*		301st MAS*	C-5A	Travis AFB, Calif.	MAC
		312th MAS*	C-5A	Travis AFB, Calif.	MAC
		708th MAS*	C-141B	Travis AFB, Calif.	MAC
		710th MAS*	C-141B	Travis AFB, Calif.	MAC
403rd TAW		815th TAS	C-130E, WC-130E/H	Keesler AFB, Miss.	MAC
	934th TAG	96th TAS	C-130E	Minneapolis-St Paul IAP, Minn	MAC
433rd MAW		68th MAS	C-5A	Kelly AFB, Tex.	MAC
302nd TAW		731st TAS	C-130B	Peterson AFB, Colo.	MAC
	943rd TAG	303rd TAS	C-130B	March AFB, Calif.	MAC
440th TAW		95th TAS	C-130A	General Mitchell IAP. WIS**	MAC
	927th TAG	63rd TAS	C-130E	Selfridge ANGB, Mich	MAC
	928th TAG	64th TAS	C-130A/H	O'Hare ARFF, Ill	MAC
445th MAW*		728th MAS*	C-141B	Norton AFB, Calif.	MAC
		729th MAS*	C-141B	Norton AFB, Calif.	MAC
		730th MAS*	C-141B	Norton AFB, Calif.	MAC
446th MAW*		97th MAS*	C-141B	McChord AFB, Wash.	MAC
		313th MAS*	C-141B	McChord AFB, Wash.	MAC

Tenth Air Force
HQ Bergstrom AFB
Texas
Commander
Brigadier General John J. Closner III

Wing	Group	Squadron	Aircraft	Location	Gaining command
301st TFW		457th TFS	F-4D/E	Carswell AFB, Tex.	TAC
	924th TFG	704th TFS	F-4D	Bergstrom AFB, Tex.	TAC
419th TFW		466th TFS	F-16A/B	Hill AFB, Utah	TAC
	507th TFG	465th TFS	F-4D	Tinker AFB, Okla.	TAC
	944th TFG	302nd TFS	F-16C/D	Luke AFB, Ariz.	TAC
434th AREFW(H)		72nd AREFS(H)	KC-135	Grissom AFB, Ind.	SAC
	98th AREFG(H)	78th AREFS(H)*	KC-10A	Barksdale AFB, La.	SAC
	916th AREFG(H)	77th AREFS(H)*	KC-10A	Seymour Johnson AFB, N.C.	SAC
442nd TFW		303rd TFS	A-10A	Richards Gebaur AFB, Mo**	TAC
	930th TFG	45th TFS	A-10A	Grissom AFB, Ind.	TAC
917th		47th TFS	A-10A	Barksdale AFB, La.	TAC
		46th TFTS	A-10A	Barksdale AFB, La.	TAC
	926th TFG	706th TFS	A-10A	NAS New Orleans, La.	TAC
452nd AFREFW(H)		336th AREFS(H)	KC-135	March AFB, Calif.	SAC
		79th AREFS(H)*	KC-10A	March AFB, Calif.	SAC
	940th AREFG(H)	314th AREFS(H)	KC-135	Mather AFB, Calif.	SAC
	482nd TFW	93rd TFS	F-4D	Homestead AFB, Fla.	TAC
	906th TFG	89th TFS	F-4D	Wright-Patterson AFB, Ohio	TAC

Fourteenth Air Force
HQ Dobbins AFB
Georgia
Commander
Brigadier General Dale R. Baumler

Wing	Group	Squadron	Aircraft	Location	Gaining command
	932nd AAG*	73rd AAS*	C-9A	Scott AFB, Ill.	MAC
94th TAW		700th TAS	C-130H	Dobbins AFB, Ga.**	MAC
	907th TAG	356th TAS	C-130A	Rickenbacker ANGB, Ohio	MAC
	908th TAG	357th TAS	C-130H	Maxwell AFB, Ala.	MAC
315th MAW*		300th MAS*	C-141B	Charleston AFB, S.C.	MAC
		701st MAS*	C-141B	Charleston AFB, S.C.	MAC
		707th MAS*	C-141B	Charleston AFB, S.C.	MAC
439th TAW		337th TAS	C-130E	Westover AFB, Mass.**	MAC
	911th TAG	758th TAS	C-130A	Greater Pittsburgh IAP, PA**	MAC
	914th TAG	328th TAS	C-130A	Niagara Falls IAP, N.Y.**	MAC
459th MAW		756th MAS	C-141B	Andrews AFB, Md.	MAC
	910th TAG	757th TAS	C-130B	Youngstown MAP, Ohio**	MAC
	913th TAG	327th TAS	C-130E	Willow Grove ARF, Pa.**	MAC
512th MAW*		326th MAS*	C-5A	Dover AFB, Del.	MAC
		709th MAS*	C-5A	Dover AFB, Del.	MAC
514th MAW*		335th MAS*	C-141B	McGuire AFB, N.J.	MAC
		702nd MAS*	C-141B	McGuire AFB, N.J.	MAC
		732nd MAS*	C-141B	McGuire AFB, N.J.	MAC

* = Associate unit
** = AFRES base

victims of a major fire. Reservists from the 315th MAW, Charleston AFB, S.C. and the 914th Tactical Airlift Group, Niagara Falls IAP, N.Y. flew emergency supplies into Ecuador following a series of earthquakes. Later on, the 907th Tactical Airlift Group from Rickenbacker ANGB, Ohio flew to San Juan to help suppress a possible epidemic. Their specially equipped C-130s were able to spray areas infested by mosquitos and prevent any illness.

For years the Air Force Reserve and Air National Guard had been the poor relations of the regular Air Force, being equipped with aircraft that had finished service with regular units. Today the story is very different, with units receiving aircraft straight off the production line. In 1981 Strategic Air Command (SAC) started to take delivery of the McDonnell Douglas KC-10 Extender and AFRES was tasked to supply 50 per cent of the aircrews. As many AFRES pilots were flying the DC-10 on a commercial basis, this was a very practical answer for SAC's crewing requirement.

While SAC has established three AFRES maintenance squadrons at March AFB, California, Barksdale AFB, Louisiana and Seymour Johnson AFB, North Carolina, AFRES has been undergoing a rapid change in its aircraft during the past few years. In 1986 AFRES started to receive its own C-141s when the 459th Military Airlift Wing took delivery of its first Starlifters, and the 934th Tactical Airlift Group converted from C-130As to the C-130E, while the C-130Es of the 908th TAG were replaced by C-130Hs. During 1986/87 it also upgraded 24 of its KC-135As to KC-135E standard. In 1987/88 this process has continued with the 944th Tactical Fighter Group receiving new F-16Cs and Ds. To enlarge AFRES airlift capability the 337th MAS at Westover AFB is continuing to convert from the C-130 to the C-5A and the 911th TAG has exchanged its 30-year-old C-130As for new C-130Hs.

The 302nd Special Operations Squadron was raised at Davis-Monthan AFB to operate the HH-3E and CH-3E, while the 434th Air Refueling Wing was established at Grissom AFB to provide control for AFRES KC-10s and KC-135s operating along the eastern side of America. The 917th Tactical Fighter Group based at Barksdale was uprated to Wing status to provide local control of its A-10s.

AFRES units regularly take part in Air Force competitions and major exercises. In 1987 the 403rd Rescue and Reconnaissance Wing from Keeler AFB won at SAREX against other teams from the Air Force and Canada. The competition tests teams in all search-and-rescue skills. At Gunsmoke '87, the Air Force's fighter gunnery competition, top honors went to the AFRES's 419th TFW: They gained the first individual place, plus second and fifth place. They were also placed second overall in the team competition. Also at Gunsmoke AFRES units from the 926th Tactical Fighter Group won the maintenance team crown and achieved second place in the weapons load section. AFRES units consistently achieve high placings in competitions against their regular Air Force colleagues. I started this section with a quote from a serving Reservist and while the Regulars might disagree with some of the sentiments, AFRES personnel are proud that "their standards are our standards."

AIR FORCE SERVICE INFORMATION AND NEWS CENTER

To provide Air Force personnel and their families with up-to-date information about the Service is the responsibility of the Air Force Service Information and News Center. It also supplies news stories about the Air Force personnel to their home-town media outlets including television, radio and newspapers. The Center, commanded by Col. Paul Heye, which reports to the Air Force Director of Public Relations, operates both home and abroad, with 728 military and 198 civilian staff. It is broken into four areas of concern:

Air Force Broadcasting Service
With three broadcast squadrons, the Arctic Broadcasting Squadron,

Television keeps service personnel in touch with what's going on around the world and back home.

A1C Robert Hawkins, 1352 AVS checks out his video camera.

Opposite: A Titan III launch vehicle stands on its pad at Vandenberg waiting for launch. The Titan is currently the Air Force's largest expendable launch system.

Overleaf: An LTV concept of an SDI space based Boost Phase Interceptor using chemically propelled missiles.

European Broadcasting Squadron and the Pacific Broadcasting Squadron, it operates a total of 164 television and radio outlets around the world as part of the Armed Forces Radio and Television Services. This is a vital service as it brings the home news and entertainment to troops wherever they are stationed. The use of satellites has meant that news stories can now be beamed to bases on the other side of the world and be viewed almost at the same time that it is seen in America.

Army and Air Force Hometown News Service

The Hometown News Service provides stories on individual military personnel to their local news services, in both the print and broadcast media. Over 1,800,000 stories were filed with the media in 1987 plus 3,900 news releases to the broadcast media.

Internal Information

This is responsible for providing channels of communication for the distribution of information down the Air Force chain of command. Outlets include the *Airman* magazine, the *Air Force Policy Letter for Commanders* and the *Family News*. It also produces films and the Air Force News Service.

Air Force Office of Youth Relations

The office is the point of contact between the Air Force and 30 national youth organizations. Its aim is to promote community relations events that can promote Air Force awareness among the young.

AIR FORCE SPACE COMMAND

The junior command in the Air Force, it truly occupies the "High Frontier" of the Air Force aerospace defense system. Established in September 1982, AFSPACECOM is a widely deployed command, with its headquarters at Peterson AFB, Colorado, and operating from sites in both the Northern and Southern Hemispheres. All aspects of US military operations are becoming increasingly dependent on space-based systems from tracking missile flight paths to providing secure, survivable means of collecting and transmitting information. As part of the all-services United States Space Command, AFSPACECOM is tasked with the equipping, organization, operation and training of the Air Forces space forces.

The problem of launchers that beset all aspects of the American space effort during 1986 are being tackled, but it will not be until the early 1990's that the problems are ironed out. The current inventory consists of three shuttles (one of which is mothballed) and approximately 25 expendable launch vehicles. Following the tragic loss of the Challenger in January 1986 the entire shuttle program was halted. Thirty-two months later in October 1988 Discovery took off with a civilian payload.

Because of changes in design of the shuttle propulsion system, the shuttle launch pad at Vandenburg AFB can no longer be used to place satellites into polar orbit and the shuttle launch pad has been mothballed. This has caused a major headache for mission planners because of the need to launch missions over water: flights from the Kennedy Space Center in Florida have to be launched either to the north-east or north-west to avoid the adjacent land mass and cannot reach polar orbit.

The first military mission STS 27 lifted off from the Kennedy Space Center 2 December 1988. The Atlantis shuttle was used to deploy the world's most advanced military space craft code-named Lacrosse. Built by Martin Marietta the satellite is a radar reconnaissance satellite which allows the Air Force and other defense intelligence services to monitor Soviet and Warsaw Pact ground forces and mobile nuclear missiles both day and night. It is so powerful it is thought to be able to penetrate dense foliage, creating a major headache for Soviet military planners. The mission was also used to test certain aspects of the Space Defense Initiative.

Expendable Launch Vehicles

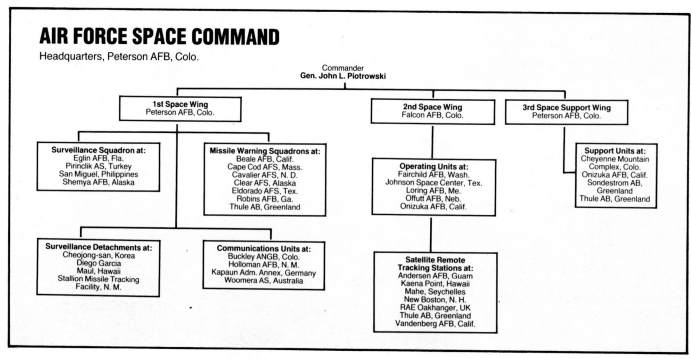

AIR FORCE SPACE COMMAND
Headquarters, Peterson AFB, Colo.

Commander
Gen. John L. Piotrowski

1st Space Wing
Peterson AFB, Colo.

2nd Space Wing
Falcon AFB, Colo.

3rd Space Support Wing
Peterson AFB, Colo.

Surveillance Squadron at:
Eglin AFB, Fla.
Pirinclik AS, Turkey
San Miguel, Philippines
Shemya AFB, Alaska

Missile Warning Squadrons at:
Beale AFB, Calif.
Cape Cod AFS, Mass.
Cavalier AFS, N. D.
Clear AFS, Alaska
Eldorado AFS, Tex.
Robins AFB, Ga.
Thule AB, Greenland

Operating Units at:
Fairchild AFB, Wash.
Johnson Space Center, Tex.
Loring AFB, Me.
Offutt AFB, Neb.
Onizuka AFB, Calif.

Support Units at:
Cheyenne Mountain Complex, Colo.
Onizuka AFB, Calif.
Sondestrom AB, Greenland
Thule AB, Greenland

Surveillance Detachments at:
Cheojong-san, Korea
Diego Garcia
Maul, Hawaii
Stallion Missile Tracking Facility, N. M.

Communications Units at:
Buckley ANGB, Colo.
Holloman AFB, N. M.
Kapaun Adm. Annex, Germany
Woomera AS, Australia

Satellite Remote Tracking Stations at:
Andersen AFB, Guam
Kaena Point, Hawaii
Mahe, Seychelles
New Boston, N. H.
RAE Oakhanger, UK
Thule AB, Greenland
Vandenberg AFB, Calif.

U. S. AIR FORCE
TITAN III COMPLEX

An artist's impression of a DSCSIII satellite. The Defense Satellite Communication Systems provide the main DoD network for long distance high-volume communications.

(ELVs) include the last Titan 34D, Atlas, Delta and Scout launchers. The Titan 34D program resumed operations in October 1987. To combat loss of launch capability by the Shuttle fleet, production enhancements and dual pads at Cape Canaverel and Vandenburg AFB will provide up to 10 Titan IV launchers per year by 1994. The first batch of 20 Delta IIs will launch Navstar Global Positioning System satellites; additional Delta IIs will be obtained to launch Navstar replenishments.

1st Space Wing with its headquarters at Peterson AFB operates the Air Force missile warning and space surveillance systems at locations around the world. It also operates the phased-array radars at Robins AFB, Georgia, which came on line in 1986 and Eldorado AFS, Texas, which was activated in 1987. These two radars are designed to track incoming Soviet submarine-launched ballistic missiles. The BMEWS radar at Thule AB, Greenland, has undergone a major overhaul which was completed during 1987. The final task of the 1st Space Wing is the continual monitoring of the 6,000 plus man-made objects which circle the planet.

The 2nd Space Wing at Falcon AFS in Colorado has a number of sub-units based around America. The heart of the 2nd SW is the Consolidated Space Operations Center (CSOC) at Falcon AFS, which controls a network of ground stations. It has taken over prime authority for the operational and resource management responsibility of the Air Force Satellite Control Network from Air Force Systems Command. These resources include Navstar Global Positioning satellites, Satellite Early Warning System (SEWS),

Right: A DSCS ground station at Falcon AFB, Colorado.

Defense Satellite Communications System (DSCS), Fleet Satellite Communications System (FLTSATCOM) plus the Milstar next-generation military communications web of satellites. It has a large contingent of 1st Manned Spaceflight Control Squadron at the Johnson Space Center at Houston, which are responsible for AF space launches. Operating from Loring AFB, Me., and Fairchild AFB, Wash., the 1,000th Satellite Operations Group has its headquarters at Offutt AFB, Nebraska: The unit controls the weather satellite network, the main type being the Defense Meteorological Satellite Program (DMSP), a DoD Joint service program.

Formed in October 1986, the 3rd Space Support Wing provides technical support for the command's installations around the world.

Space Command runs two major training schemes: the ATC Undergraduate Space Training (UST), which provides the AF with officers who can fully understand the intricacies of space operations, and the 1013th Combat Crew Training Squadron which offers specific crews positional training for locations assigned to or supported by Air Force Space Command.

1. Meet the users' needs.
2. Maintain acquisition excellence.
3. Enhance Air Force technological superiority.

The three major goals set down for AFSC by its commander, General Bernard P. Randolph

With its roots going back to the Airplane Engineering Department established at McCook Field near Dayton, Ohio in December 1917, Air Force Systems Command (AFSC) and its predecessors have been involved with the development of new aircraft and systems for the Air Force almost since the beginning of powered light. AFSC was renamed from the Air Research and Development Command on 1 April 1961.

Today AFSC has a budget of $30 billion, almost a third of the entire current Air Force Budget. Its staff is made up of 10,700 officers, 13,400 enlisted men and women, and 28,700 civilian staff. In total AFSC is responsible for the current issuing and administrating of in excess of 48,000 contracts, with a total value of approximately $305 billion. This figure shows a rise of nearly $110 billion over the FY 1987 figure. To try to describe all of AFSC's activities would require a book of its own. Therefore the list below can only give a taste of the Command's activities.

The Command is divided into 5 test centers, 5 product divisions, 3 support divisions and 14 laboratories, each with a special area of interest, and is controlled from its headquarters at Andrews AFB.

The largest of the divisions is the Aeronautical Systems Division (ASD) at Wright-Patterson AFB. It is responsible for aircraft, aircraft systems, missiles and flight simulators. Among other programs it has been running the B-1B acquisition program. The B-1B under joint AFSC and SAC crews has broken 13 different world records in the course of its development. The Division is still investigating problems with the defensive avionics of the aircraft and although this is not considered to be a problem today if it is not corrected it

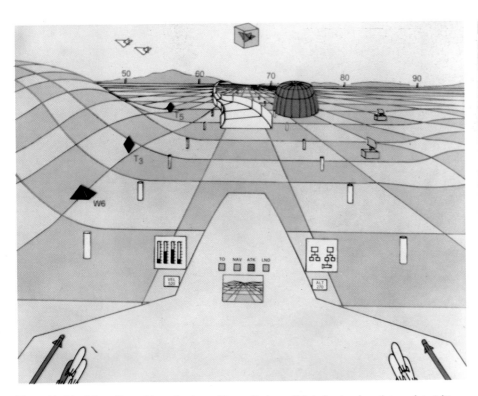

The world of the fighter pilot could soon be changed in a radical way. This is the view that a future pilot might have of the world both in and out of the cockpit. The foreground shows the weapons available, the next symbols show the aircraft status. The flight plan is shown as a corridor in red while two friendly aircraft are shown in white.

The Project Forecast II looked at many ways that technology could be used to push forward the Air Force. This artist's concept, created from ideas developed, shows a future battle management work center. In the foreground is a three-dimensional graphic representation of the battle in real time using holographic and laser imaging.

To enable future pilots to handle all the information being fed to them, work is being carried out on the pilot's Associate System (PAS). This advanced artificial intelligence computer system is graphically represented as a ghost image in the rear cockpit. It is programmed to understand verbal commands and can also respond verbally. It thinks along with the pilot, and handles all the routine tasks allowing the pilot to concentrate on the critical mission tasks.

Far right: Engineers in the Harry G. Armstrong Medical Research Laboratory are developing a cockpit that enables pilots to fly through a cartoon-like world using an instrument panel they cannot touch. The visually Coupled Airborne System simulator (VCASS) is composed of miniaturized electronics that allow a pilot to fly a plane by moving his hands in the air, select weapons by looking at the device that controls access to them, arm them with a turn of his head, and fire them by using voice command. All without looking out of the cockpit or pushing a button.

could cause problems into the 1990's.

It is also deeply involved with the Advanced Tactical Fighter. The ATF has been designed to provide an air-superiority fighter for the 1990's and beyond. The two competing teams led by Lockheed (YF-22A) and Northrop (YF-23A) are due to have their first flights in late 1988 or early 1999. After intensive testing one of the designs will be taken up by the Air Force and placed into full-scale production.

ASD is also overseeing the upgrading of 270 F-16As under an air defense fighter program. This program is designed to replace the F-4s currently used to defend North American airspace.

It is also working on the development of the AC-130U special operations/unconventional gunship. The basic C-130 airframes are being procured from Lockheed Georgia and the avionics integration is being done by Rockwell International. The first prototype is due to have finished testing by July 1992 and initial deliveries will follow later in the year with deliveries to Hurburt Field.

AFSC's National Aerospace Plane Joint Program Office has overseen the program move into Phase II. This phase will begin the ground testing of engine and special airframe parts and will finalize the preliminary designs for the X-30 spaceplane. At the Arnold Engineering Development Center work has started on hypersonic tests of the

airframe's aerodynamics. The NASP Joint Program Office is the project manager on behalf of DoD and NASA.

Situated at Los Angeles AFS, the Space Division has close links with AFSPACECOM and the AFSC's Space Divisions Commander is also AFSPACECOM's Vice-Commander.

The Space Division has the responsibility of managing all DoD space systems, including launchers and satellites. It also works in close consultation with NASA. It operates a number of units which include the Air Force Satellite Control Facility situated at Sunnyvale AFS, California,

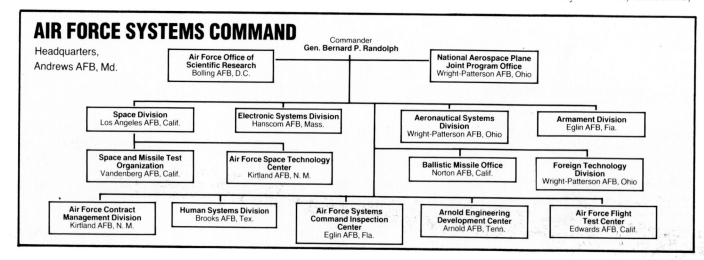

and controls a world network of satellite tracking stations. The Manned Space Flight Support Group at the Johnson Space Center and at Vandenburg AFB is the Space and Missile Test Organization (SAMTO), which manages flight tests for Dod ballistic and space programs. It operates two separate test centers.

The first at Vandenburg itself is the Western Space and Missile Test Center (WSMC), which covers a flight area from the Pacific to the Indian Ocean and the Eastern Space and Missile Test Center which is jointly based at Patrick AFB and at Cape Canaveral for operations over the Atlantic.

The Electronics Systems Division (ESD) at Hanscom AFB, Mass. has at last finished its 13-year Pave Paws Radar program. The last of the four radar sites was handed over to AFSPACECOM in May 1987 and completes a radar network that can detect the launch of intercontinental and submarine launched ballistics missiles. It is also working on the Over-the-Horizon Backscatter (OTH-B) network. To test this system, high-speed drones have been launched from C-130s to simulate Soviet cruise missiles. ESD is also the primary Air Force agency for command-control, communications and intelligence (C31) systems. In total it is presently involved with over a hundred different projects.

Eglin AFB is the home of the Command's Armament Division which develops tests and procures all aspects of non-nuclear air weapons. The two major systems it is involved with at the present time are the Advanced Medium-Range Air-to-Air Missile (AMRAAM) and the GBU-15 precision-guided missile. The AMRAAM has now entered low-rate initial production while the GBU-15/IR has now entered full-scale production.

The Ballistic Missile Office at Norton AFB manages the MX missile system and the Peacekeeper Rail Garrison program. As of the end of May 1988 the latter was to be put into full-scale development. It also manages the Small ICBM, a single warhead ICBM which will be transported on a tractor trailer. Initial deployment is scheduled for 1992 when it will enter service at Malmstrom AFB. In the longer term it is working on the Advanced Strategic Missiles Systems (ASMS), this project is to

maintain a quantitative edge for the Air Forces ballistic missiles.

The Human Systems Division, Brooks AFB, Texas is involved with all aspects of the man–machine interface. It has produced the first fully integrated life-support system, which tackles the human physiological requirements when flying in future high-performance aircraft. The Division was responsible for the Project Forecast II study into new technologies and systems concepts during 1986. This study is already having a profound effect on new designs for future Air Force systems involving things like the Super Cockpit and Robotic Telepresence.

The Air Force Flight Test Center (AFFTC) is situated at Edwards AFB. If it can fly it has probably been tested at the AFSC Test Center in the Mojave Desert, which has been used to test military aircraft for over fifty years and now has over 38,850 sq. km (15,000 sq. miles) of unrestricted airspace. It was the site for a number of early

Space Shuttle landings, and is still an emergency landing site.

The world's greatest collection of flight simulators can be found at the Arnold Engineering Development Center (AEDC) at Arnold AFS. They can simulate conditions from sea level up to 1,000 miles and speeds from subsonic up to speeds in excess of Mach 20. The center is not only used by the Air Force. It handles work for the other services, NASA, private corporations and a select group of foreign government agencies.

An F–15 modified by McDonnell Douglas began test flights in September 1988. It is designed to take off and land in very small areas. Although there is no plan to retrofit existing aircraft with the new system, the ideas which are being tested may well influence future aircraft design.

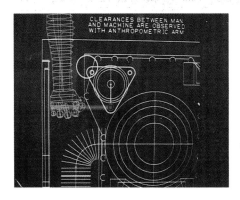

Computer-aided design and manufacture have played a major part in the design and building of the Northrop B–2.

AIR FORCE TECHNICAL APPLICATIONS CENTER

The Air Force Technical Applications Center (AFTAC) monitors the world for nuclear explosions and reports any activity to the HQ Air Force who then pass the information on to the relevant government departments. It maintains through the US Atomic Energy Detection System (USAEDS), a world-wide chain of satellite, electromagnetic pulse, hydro-acoustic, seismic and airborne operations facilities situated in more than 35 countries.

With its headquarters at Patrick AFB, Florida, AFTAC operates 12 detachments, 5 operating locations, and 70 equipment sites. The Technical Operations Division is situated at McClellan AFB in California, where it runs the McClellan Central Laboratory which is the central clearing house for the USAEDS system. AFTAC also has major units in the Pacific and Europe. The HQ Pacific Technical Operations is situated at Wheeler AFB, Hawaii and the HQ European Technical Operations Area is at Lindsey AB, West Germany.

In 1947 the Army Air Force was ordered by Gen. Dwight D. Eisenhower to establish a unit to "detect atomic explosions anywhere in the world." Two years later AFTAC was to prove its worth, B-29 using AFTAC equipment to fly from Alaska to Japan and identify contamination from the Russians first atomic explosion. With the signing of the 1963 Limited Test Ban Treaty in 1963, it fell to AFTAC to provide the personnel and equipment to enforce the Treaty. Two other major treaties that are enforced by the Center are the 1974 Threshold Test Ban Treaty and the 1976 Peaceful Nuclear Explosions Treaty.

AIR NATIONAL GUARD

"The Air Force thinks of the Air National Guard and the Air Force Reserve in the same manner as it does of its regular units. As nearly as possible, we expect the same rapid response from them. They are subjected to identical readiness tests. We need a 'Ready Now' combat capability in the Air Reserve Forces because we depend on them to augment the active force in times of crisis."

General LeMay, Speech to Congress in 1964

Unlike any other Air Force unit, the control of the Air National Guard during peacetime is invested in the governors of each of the fifty states, the Commonwealth of Puerto Rico, the Territories of Guam and the Virgin Islands and the Commanding General of the District of Columbia. Only in times of crisis or war can the President call up Air Guard units. ANG units do have a stake in the Air Forces in that each unit is assigned to one of the major commands. Like the AFRES the ANG is continuing to grow as the regular Air Force is slowly slimmed. It provides 86 per cent of fighter interceptors, 50 per cent of reconnaissance aircraft, 39 per cent of tactical air support, 35 per cent of tactical airlift, a quarter of TAC's tactical fighters, 18 per cent of SACs

air refuelling capability and 17 per cent of rescue and recovery capability. The Air National Guard also provides 239 mission support units dedicated to combat communications, fixed communications computer support, engineering installation support and air base ground defense to USAF.

National Guard units saw action during the two world wars but it was not until the end of World War II that the Aviation Group, National Guard Bureau was formed. When the USAF was created the Aviation Group was renamed the Air Force Division, National Guard Bureau, and then finally the Air National Guard.

As with the AFRES it was originally given cast-off equipment that the regular Air Force no longer needed. As each new generation of aircraft was brought into service, the ANG was provided with the older mark or generation; for example, when the regulars started to receive F-15s and had a good supply of F-4s so the ANG was provided with the older F-106s. This process changed when the South Carolina ANGs 169th Tactical Fighter Group started to receive brand new F-16s straight off the factory line. It is true that the average age of ANG aircraft is 17.4 years old compared with the regular's average age of 13.9 years and this has risen by 1.4 years since 1984. The figure should come down quite sharply over the next few years as the ANG trades in a number of its aircraft that have some thirty-odd years in their logbooks.

A pilot of the 112th TFS, Ohio ANG waits in his A–7 for take-off. It is likely that the ANG's A–7s will undergo major refitting to carry them into the 21st century.

Right: ANG units regularly carry out training exercises around the world. This KC–135 of the Utah ANG was photographed over the English Channel while operating in support of RAF Upper Heyford F–111s.

A Beechcraft C–12J of the 127th TFS from McConnell AFB, Kansas. The C–12J is operated by a number of ANG units as a supply aircraft.

This F–4E from the Missouri ANG's 131st Tactical Fighter Wing in St. Louis was specifically painted to commemorate the 30th anniversary of the F–4's first flight, 27 May 1958.

The ANG started to receive the F-15A/B in 1985 and now there are four units operating them. The 116th Tactical Fighter Wing Dobbins AFB, Georgia and the 159th Tactical Fighter Group, New Orleans, Louisiana were the first two F-15 operators, followed by the 154th Composite Group, Hickham AFB, Hawaii which converted from the F-4C in 1987, and the 102nd Fighter Interceptor Wing, Otis ANGB, Massachusetts, which converted from the F-106 in 1988.

The Air National Guard is increasing its F-16 units, and 1988 saw four units convert to the F-16 with two to come in 1989. The 184th TFG converted from the F-4E, 187th TFG from the F-4D, 188th TFG from the F-4C and the 177th Fighter Interceptor Group from the F-106 Delta Dart. This meant the end of the line for the Air National Guard's F-106s which have been used for the defense of America's air space for thirty years. But it will not be the end of the F-106 story: The airframes will convert to QF-106 aerial target drones.

ANG units carry a heavy responsibility for air defense activities, and the Hawaiian ANG is solely responsible for the island's air defense. To meet this vital task the ANG's F-4Es are now being converted to carry AIM9-L and M missiles. In the ground attack mission ANG A-7, A-10, F-4E and F-16s will operate the Maverick AGM-65D which has an imaging infrared seeker head and the CBU-87/89 area-denial submunition.

It is not just in fighters that ANG units are seeing change. At the same time as the F-15 was introduced in 1985, the 105th Military Airlift Group took delivery of the Lockheed C-5A Galaxy, the Western world's largest airlift aircraft. The following year the 172nd Military Airlift Group received the C-141B Starlifter. Other ANG airlift units are replacing their old C-130s with new C-130H Hercules. The C-130H is similar to the C-130E in specification but with uprated T56-A-15 turboprop engines, upgraded avionics, redesigned outer wings and a number of other improvements.

The 109th Tactical Airlift Group with their four unique LC-130Hs which are fitted with wheel-ski gear are preparing to take over from the US Navy resupply missions to Antarctica when the Navy's supply aircraft undergo major scheduled maintenance. They made their first familiarization deployment in January 1988 and will again return in 1989 before they take over from the Navy for two years in 1990 and 1991. They are well equipped for this vital mission. Each year they are tasked by the Air Force to Greenland where they fly resupply missions to remote radar stations which require operating from snow- and ice-covered airfields.

The Air National Guard is growing in size and talent; in FY 1987 the Guard achieved its highest manning level ever with a total of 114,600 men and women and this level is due to rise still further. Each year they regularly compete with regular AF and reserve units in competitions covering all aspects of AF activities and they can beat the best. It is this desire to excel that has created a vital force in the Total Air Force.

The Air National Guard by Major Command Assignment

Strategic Air Command
KC-135

101st Air Refueling Wing	*Bangor, Me.*
126th Air Refueling Wing	*Chicago, Ill.*
141st Air Refueling Wing	*Fairchild AFB, Wash.*
171st Air Refueling Wing	*Pittsburgh, Pa.*
128th Air Refueling Group	*Milwaukee, Wis.*
134th Air Refueling Group	*Knoxville, Tenn.*
151st Air Refueling Group	*Salt Lake City, Utah*
157th Air Refueling Group	*Pease AFB, N.H.*
160th Air Refueling Group	*Rickenbacker ANG Base, Ohio*
161st Air Refueling Group	*Phoenix, Ariz.*
170th Air Refueling Group	*McGuire AFB, N.J.*
190th Air Refueling Group	*Forbes Field, Kan.*

Tactical Air Command

A-7D/K

121st Tactical Fighter Wing	*Rickenbacker ANG Base, Ohio*
127th Tactical Fighter Wing	*Selfridge ANG Base, Mich.*
132nd Tactical Fighter Wing	*Des Moines, Iowa*
140th Tactical Fighter Wing	*Buckley ANG Base, Colo.*
112th Tactical Fighter Group	*Pittsburgh, Pa.*
114th Tactical Fighter Group	*Sioux Falls, S.D.*
138th Tactical Fighter Group	*Tulsa, Okla.*
150th Tactical Fighter Group	*Kirtland AFB, N.M.*
156th Tactical Fighter Group	*San Juan, Puerto Rico*
162nd Tactical Fighter Group	*Tucson, Ariz.*
178th Tactical Fighter Group	*Springfield, Ohio*
180th Tactical Fighter Group	*Toledo, Ohio*
185th Tactical Fighter Group	*Sioux City, Iowa*
192nd Tactical Fighter Group	*Richmond, Va.*

F-16A/B

149th Tactical Fighter Group	*Kelly AFB, Tex.*
158th Tactical Fighter Group	*Burlington, Vt.*
169th Tactical Fighter Group	*McEntire ANG Base, S.C.*

A-10A

128th Tactical Fighter Wing	*Truax Field, Wis.*
174th Tactical Fighter Wing	*Syracuse, N.Y.*
103rd Tactical Fighter Group	*Bradley, Conn.*
104th Tactical Fighter Group	*Barnes, Mass.*
175th Tactical Fighter Group	*Baltimore, Md.*

F-4C

188th Tactical Fighter Group	*Fort Smith, Ark.*

F-4D

113th Tactical Fighter Wing	*Andrews AFB, Md.*
183rd Tactical Fighter Group	*Springfield, Ill.*
184th Tactical Fighter Group	*McConnell AFB, Kan.*
187th Tactical Fighter Group	*Montgomery, Ala.*

F-4E

108th Tactical Fighter Wing	*McGuire AFB, N.J.*
122nd Tactical Fighter Wing	*Fort Wayne, Ind.*
131st Tactical Fighter Wing	*St. Louis, Mo.*
163rd Tactical Fighter Group	*March AFB, Calif.*
181st Tactical Fighter Group	*Terre Haute, Ind.*

RF-4C

117th Tactical Reconnaissance Wing	*Birmingham, Ala.*
123rd Tactical Reconnaissance Wing	*Louisville, Ky.*
124th Tactical Reconnaissance Group	*Boise, Idaho*
152nd Tactical Reconnaissance Group	*Reno, Nev.*
155th Tactical Reconnaissance Group	*Lincoln, Neb.*
186th Tactical Reconnaissance Group	*Meridian, Miss.*

OA-37

110th Tactical Air Support Group	*Battle Creek ANG Base, Mich.*
111th Tactical Air Support Group	*Willow Grove ARF, Pa.*
182nd Tactical Air Support Group	*Peoria, Ill.*

F-15A/B

116th Tactical Fighter Wing	*Dobbins AFB, Ga.*
159th Tactical Fighter Group	*NAS New Orleans, La.*

Air Defense Units (TAC)
F-4C

142nd Fighter Interceptor Group	*Portland, Ore.*

F-4D

144th Fighter Interceptor Wing	*Fresno, Calif.*
107th Fighter Interceptor Group	*Niagara Falls, N.Y.*
119th Fighter Interceptor Group	*Fargo, N.D.*
147th Fighter Interceptor Group	*Ellington ANG Base, Tex.*
148th Fighter Interceptor Group	*Duluth, Minn.*
191st Fighter Interceptor Group	*Selfridge ANG Base, Mich.*

F-16A/B

120th Fighter Interceptor Group	*Great Falls, Mont.*
125th Fighter Interceptor Group	*Jacksonville, Fla.*

Military Airlift Command
C-130

118th Tactical Airlift Wing	*Nashville, Tenn.*
133rd Tactical Airlift Wing	*Minneapolis/St. Paul, Minn.*
136th Tactical Airlift Wing	*Dallas, Tex.*
137th Tactical Airlift Wing	*Oklahoma City, Okla.*
146th Tactical Airlift Wing	*Van Nuys, Calif.*
109th Tactical Airlift Group	*Schenectady, N.Y.*
130th Tactical Airlift Group	*Charleston, W. Va.*
135th Tactical Airlift Group	*Baltimore, Md.*
139th Tactical Airlift Group	*St. Joseph, Mo.*
143rd Tactical Airlift Group	*Quonset Point, R.I.*
145th Tactical Airlift Group	*Charlotte, N.C.*
153rd Tactical Airlift Group	*Cheyenne, Wyo.*
164th Tactical Airlift Group	*Memphis, Tenn.*
165th Tactical Airlift Group	*Savannah, Ga.*
166th Tactical Airlift Group	*Wilmington, Del.*
167th Tactical Airlift Group	*Martinsburg, W. Va.*
179th Tactical Airlift Group	*Mansfield, Ohio*
189th Tactical Airlift Group	*Little Rock AFB, Ark.*

HC-130 and HH-3

106th Aerospace Rescue & Recovery Group	*Suffolk, N.Y.*
129th Aerospace Rescue & Recovery Group	*NAS Moffett, Calif.*

C-141

172nd Military Airlift Group	*Jackson, Miss.*

C-5A

105th Military Airlift Group	*Newburgh, N.Y.*

EC-130E

193rd Special Operations Group	*Middletown, Pa.*

Pacific Air Forces
F-15A/B

154th Composite Group	*Hickham AFB, Hawaii*

A–7s of the 132 TFS and 124
(Arizona Air National Guard)
during deployment for Cope
North 88.

AIR RESERVE PERSONNEL CENTER

Col. Joseph C. Ramsey and his staff of over 800 military and civilian staff based at the Air Reserve Personnel Center are responsible for over 250,000 Air National Guard and Air Force Reserve personnel. They provide support during peacetime, are responsible for mobilization readiness in time of crisis, and maintain records of all members who are not on extended service. Since the inception of the Center it has handled three mobilizations when called upon because of national emergencies.

In 1987 ARPC undertook the first nationwide screening of the Individual Ready Reserve (IRR). This reserve is made up of former Air Force personnel who are not active in either the reserve or ANG, but who still have a remaining military service duty and can be recalled for active duty. They were able to assist 114 regular and reserve installations in calling 13,000 IRR personnel for duty. Another group that the Center deals with are Individual Mobilization Augmentees who, because they train directly with active duty units, have no reserve unit assignment.

As the regular forces are being cut back, Air National Guard and Air Force Reserve Units are being increased, which has placed new importance on the activities of the Air Reserve Personnel Center.

AIR TRAINING COMMAND

Commanded by Lt. Gen. Robert C. Oaks, the world's largest training organization, the Air Training Command, has its HQ at Randolph AFB, Texas. ATC is the fourth largest Command in terms of personnel with 69,477 military personnel and 14,035 civilian staff and operates from 13 installations across the country. Although a major part of ATC is designated to the teaching of flying and technical skills, it is also involved in recruiting, basic military training, and specialized education. It offers over 6,300 training courses covering more than 350 specialties.

Before World War II training was carried out by the various sections of the service, but the rapid growth of the Army Air Force and the need for thousands of trained pilots demanded swift action. On 7 July 1943, the Army Air Forces Training Command was formed. The new Command rapidly grew with a million-plus personnel and the construction of 375 flying training bases and 234 technical training

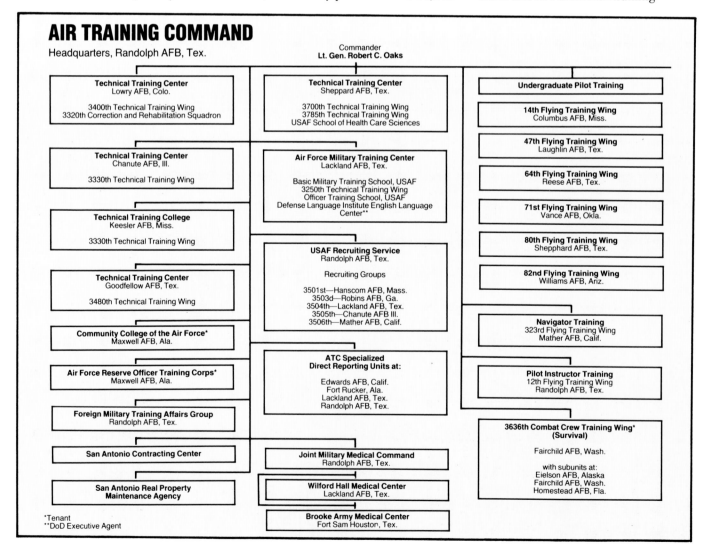

AIR TRAINING COMMAND
Headquarters, Randolph AFB, Tex.

Commander
Lt. Gen. Robert C. Oaks

Technical Training Center
Lowry AFB, Colo.

3400th Technical Training Wing
3320th Correction and Rehabilitation Squadron

Technical Training Center
Chanute AFB, Ill.

3330th Technical Training Wing

Technical Training College
Keesler AFB, Miss.

3330th Technical Training Wing

Technical Training Center
Goodfellow AFB, Tex.

3480th Technical Training Wing

Community College of the Air Force*
Maxwell AFB, Ala.

Air Force Reserve Officer Training Corps*
Maxwell AFB, Ala.

Foreign Military Training Affairs Group
Randolph AFB, Tex.

San Antonio Contracting Center

San Antonio Real Property Maintenance Agency

*Tenant
**DoD Executive Agent

Technical Training Center
Sheppard AFB, Tex.

3700th Technical Training Wing
3785th Technical Training Wing
USAF School of Health Care Sciences

Air Force Military Training Center
Lackland AFB, Tex.

Basic Military Training School, USAF
3250th Technical Training Wing
Officer Training School, USAF
Defense Language Institute English Language Center**

USAF Recruiting Service
Randolph AFB, Tex.

Recruiting Groups

3501st—Hanscom AFB, Mass.
3503d—Robins AFB, Ga.
3504th—Lackland AFB, Tex.
3505th—Chanute AFB Ill.
3506th—Mather AFB, Calif.

ATC Specialized Direct Reporting Units at:

Edwards AFB, Calif.
Fort Rucker, Ala.
Lackland AFB, Tex.
Randolph AFB, Tex.

Joint Military Medical Command
Randolph AFB, Tex.

Wilford Hall Medical Center
Lackland AFB, Tex.

Brooke Army Medical Center
Fort Sam Houston, Tex.

Undergraduate Pilot Training

14th Flying Training Wing
Columbus AFB, Miss.

47th Flying Training Wing
Laughlin AFB, Tex.

64th Flying Training Wing
Reese AFB, Tex.

71st Flying Training Wing
Vance AFB, Okla.

80th Flying Training Wing
Shepphard AFB, Tex.

82nd Flying Training Wing
Williams AFB, Ariz.

Navigator Training
323rd Flying Training Wing
Mather AFB, Calif.

Pilot Instructor Training
12th Flying Training Wing
Randolph AFB, Tex.

3636th Combat Crew Training Wing*
(Survival)

Fairchild AFB, Wash.

with subunits at:
Eielson AFB, Alaska
Fairchild AFB, Wash.
Homestead AFB, Fla.

bases. Following the war most of the bases were handed over to other Commands, and the Command was redesignated Air Training Command on 15 April 1946.

The first introduction that most prospective recruits to the Air Force get is by members of the United States Air Recruiting Service. The USARS, with its HQ at Randolph AFB, is divided into five Recruiting Groups and 35 squadrons. The five Recruiting Groups are the 3501st RG at Hanscom AFB, Mass., 3503rd RG at Robins AFB, Ga., 3504th RG Lackland AFB, Tex., and 3506th RG Mather AFB, Calif. The Recruiting Service operates a network of 1,350 recruiting offices in America and around the world wherever there is a large concentration of expatriate Americans.

New recruits, both enlisted personnel and officer cadets, report to Lackland AFB for basic training and will then move on for more specialized training in whichever branch of the service for which they are destined. Those that are going on to flying training have 52 weeks of training in front of them. They will have already conducted a period of basic flying at Hondo Municipal Airport, Tex. in the T-41 Mescalero. Here prospective pilots are screened for adaptability. The Air Force is due to bring in Specialized Undergraduate Pilot Training (SUPT) which will see all students learning their basic flying skills on the Cessna T-37, progressing on to the T-38 Talon and then specializing in either Bomber-Fighter or Tanker-Transport training.

The ATC is due to decide on an aircraft for the Tanker Transport Training System. This large contract, due to be awarded in January 1989, will involve the purchase of 211 modified business jets. It will be awarded to one of the following teams or individual companies: Beech, British Aerospace and Rockwell, Cessna and Singer, Learjet and FlightSafety Services Corporation and finally McDonnel Douglas and FlightSafety International.

Undergraduate Pilot Training is conducted by the 14th Flying Training Wing, Columbus AFB, Miss.: 47th FTW, Laughlin AFB, Tex.; 64th FTW, Reese AFB, Tex.; 71st FTW, Vance AFB, Okla.; 80th FTW, Sheppard AFB, Tex.; and the 82nd FTW, Williams AFB, Ariz. ATC also provides flying training through the Euro-NATO Joint Jet Pilot Training Program at Sheppard AFB.

Navigators are also put through a similar pattern of training; the first part of the course is undertaken by everyone and then they move into one of three disciplines: Fighter/Attack/Reconnaissance, Tanker/Transport/Bomber or Electronic Warfare. Training is provided by the 323rd FTW at Mather AFB, Calif.

During their training all aircrew personnel undertake survival training which is organized by the 3636th Combat Crew Training Wing. Training is provided in basic survival at Fairchild AFB, Wash.; water survival at Homestead AFB, Fla.; and Arctic survival at Eielson AFB, Alaska.

For Air Force personnel joining one of the technical services their training is conducted at one of the five ATC Technical Training Centers at Chanute, Goodfellow, Keesler, Lowery and Sheppard AFBs.

The USAF School of Health Care Science at Sheppard AFB is where all Medical Service officers begin their Air Force careers. It runs courses in medicine, nursing, dentistry and all other aspects of health care. The ATC is also responsible for the DoD's Joint Military Medical Command which provides a consolidated health care program. It also offers graduate medical training. Established in 1972 the Community College of the Air Force provides both on- and off-duty courses on academic and technical subjects.

The role of the Air Training Command will continue to expand to cope with the ever more complex needs of the Air Force. This is illustrated well by the development of the Undergraduate Space Training course at the Lowery Technical Training Center. This course is designed to provide Space Command with the specialists needed to challenge the High Frontier.

AIR UNIVERSITY

The Air University was formed in 1946 and operated as a Major Command unit. It was amalgamated into the Air Training Command in 1978 and regained Major Command status in 1983. From its formation it has trained officers and senior non-commissioned officers (NCO) for command and staff duties.

Most of the University's professional military education faculties are established on Chennault Circle at Maxwell AFB with the exceptions of the USAF Senior NCO Academy and the Extension Course at Gunter AFB and the Air Force Institute of Technology at Wright-Patterson AFB, Ohio. The University runs courses for

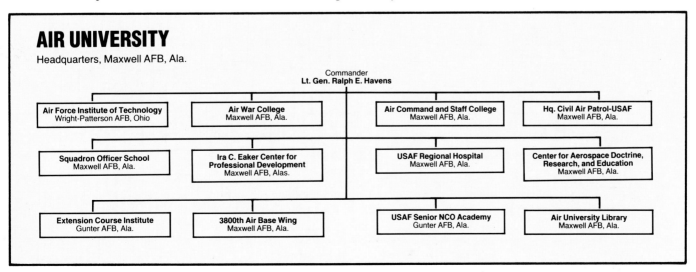

AIR UNIVERSITY
Headquarters, Maxwell AFB, Ala.

Commander
Lt. Gen. Ralph E. Havens

Air Force Institute of Technology Wright-Patterson AFB, Ohio	**Air War College** Maxwell AFB, Ala.	**Air Command and Staff College** Maxwell AFB, Ala.	**Hq. Civil Air Patrol-USAF** Maxwell AFB, Ala.
Squadron Officer School Maxwell AFB, Ala.	**Ira C. Eaker Center for Professional Development** Maxwell AFB, Alas.	**USAF Regional Hospital** Maxwell AFB, Ala.	**Center for Aerospace Doctrine, Research, and Education** Maxwell AFB, Ala.
Extension Course Institute Gunter AFB, Ala.	**3800th Air Base Wing** Maxwell AFB, Ala.	**USAF Senior NCO Academy** Gunter AFB, Ala.	**Air University Library** Maxwell AFB, Ala.

all levels of the Air Force command structure from senior staff who attend the Air War College (AWC), middle-ranking officers who study at the Air Command and Staff College (ACSC) and the Squadron Officer School (SOS) for company level officers. Senior NCOs attend their own Academy at the nearby Gunter AFB.

Over the past few years the number of people who have attended residential courses at the University has more than doubled, with nearly 25,000 military and civilians having completed courses between 1987 and 1988. The Center for Aerospace Doctrine, Research and Education, which was established in January 1983, is dedicated to its title; it consists of the Airpower Research Institute which among other tasks launched the new Airpower Journal which is to become the AF's in-house professional publication. It is also home to the Air Force Wargaming Center. The Center was started in June 1983 to provide professional wargaming studies just for the University but is now linked into the DoD, Army and Navy wargaming

centers. This facility adds new dimensions to inter-service war training at all levels.

The Air University Library (AUL) is the largest and most comprehensive military library in the Western world. The index can be logged into by students using computers connected into the system by modems. This means that wherever a student lives throughout the world he or she may gain access to the library.

The Ira C. Eaker Center for Professional Development provides courses in eight schools covering a wide variety of professional fields and offering 55 courses. Courses cover everything from aircraft maintenance through chaplaincy to systems information.

ALASKAN AIR COMMAND

The men and women who make up the Alaskan Air Command know more than most that they are at the forefront of North America's defense. The 826 officers, 6,628 enlisted personnel and 1,437 civilians of the command admirably fulfil their motto "Top Cover for America." And it is not only a human enemy they have to guard against. The weather is just as dangerous and extreme: The temperature can be up in the 80s Fahrenheit during the summer and drop to −30°F in winter. The daylight range is just as extreme with 22 hours of sun during the summer and down to

less than 4 hours of light when winter sets in. The Alaskan Air Command was formed on 18 December 1945 from the World War II Eleventh Air Force and tasked with maintaining American sovereignty along the border with Russia. They have come to know their Soviet counterparts very well over the last forty-odd years.

Only 44 miles separates Alaska from the Soviet Union. And if you stand on Little Diomede Island you are only separated from Russia by 2 miles and this distance can be greatly reduced by the ice pack during the winter months. Along the border the F-15s of the 43rd Tactical Fighter Squadron maintain a continual patrol to discourage any Soviet "Bear" that might stray over the border into American air space. Alaska is also the forward area of operations for Strategic Air Command's 6th Strategic Wing, which undertakes regular reconnaissance missions along the Russian, Kamchatka Peninsular with RC-135 aircraft. It is also responsible for operating the Alaskan Tanker Force which maintains the KC-135A aircraft which undertake duties in the region. The tankers are supplied by regular Air Force, Air Force Reserve and Air National Guard units posted from the continental United States. Alaska is represented in this

Opposite: An F–15 of the 21st TFW from Elmendorf AFB armed with four AIM–7 Sparrows and four AIM–9 Sidewinders climbs skyward over one of Alaska's glaciers.

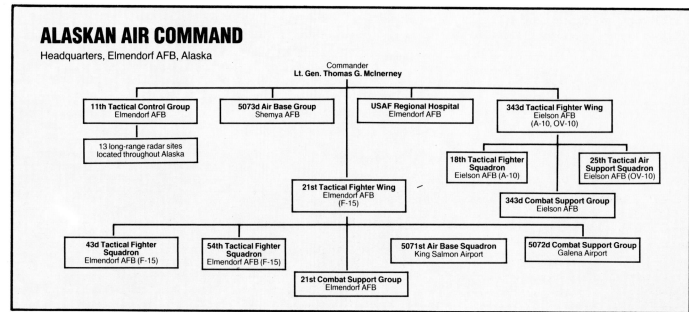

ALASKAN AIR COMMAND
Headquarters, Elmendorf AFB, Alaska

Commander
Lt. Gen. Thomas G. McInerney

- 11th Tactical Control Group — Elmendorf AFB
  - 13 long-range radar sites located throughout Alaska
- 5073d Air Base Group — Shemya AFB
- USAF Regional Hospital — Elmendorf AFB
- 343d Tactical Fighter Wing — Eielson AFB (A-10, OV-10)
  - 18th Tactical Fighter Squadron — Eielson AFB (A-10)
  - 25th Tactical Air Support Squadron — Eielson AFB (OV-10)
  - 343d Combat Support Group — Eielson AFB
- 21st Tactical Fighter Wing — Elmendorf AFB (F-15)
  - 43d Tactical Fighter Squadron — Elmendorf AFB (F-15)
  - 54th Tactical Fighter Squadron — Elmendorf AFB (F-15)
  - 5071st Air Base Squadron — King Salmon Airport
  - 5072d Combat Support Group — Galena Airport
  - 21st Combat Support Group — Elmendorf AFB

task force by the 168th Air Refueling Squadron, ANG, based at Eielson AFB.

The 343rd Tactical Fighter Wing based at Eielson AFB operates the Fairchild A-10 Thunderbolt II flown by the 18th Tactical Fighter Squadron and the OV-10 Broncos of the 25th Tactical Air Support Squadron. The Wing's task is to provide air support for army units by supplying ground and airborne forward air controllers. It is also tasked with visual reconnaissance, artillery adjustment and cold weather testing.

It is not only aircraft that monitor the Soviet Union. A chain of 13 long-range radars, operated by the 11th Tactical Control Group whose headquarters are at Elmendorf AFB, constantly watch for any sign of aircraft or missile that might be "inbound." The radar system has been operating 24 hours a day since 27 June 1950. The radar system during this period has undergone a number of changes.

In 1957 the joint US–Canadian, North American Air Defense Command (NORAD) was formed and the following year the Alaskan NORAD Region came into service, providing vital warning cover for the western flank of North America. In the mid-1970's USAF Chief of Staff John Ryan commissioned a report on the need to update the system. And in 1979 the Air Force awarded General Electric a contract to build a new generation of radar systems. Codenamed "SEEK IGLOO," the AN/FPS Minimally Attended Radar meant that radar sites could be operated automatically. This was much appreciated by the personnel who had to control the old manually operated radar chain.

The "SEEK IGLOO" program was completed in 1984 and forms a chain of radar stations from Cape Lisburne AFS in the north down to Cold Bay AFS in the south. This modernization has provided the Air Force with a saving of $108 million in running costs compared with the 1970's. The 13 radar sites feed raw information into both the Region Operations Center and direct into the NORAD headquarters in Cheyenne Mountain. Also fed into NORAD are signals from the "Cobra Dane" AN/FPS-108 Phased Array Radar facility at Shemya AFB which provides detailed information about Soviet space and missile operations in eastern Siberia and Kamchatka. To communicate with the rest of USAF,

A Distant Early Warning Station in Alaska's permanent snow; it feeds its information through to NORAD.

AAC uses – in addition to a single-channel satellite link – Meteor Burst Communciations to provide secure communications with the outside world and its own aircraft.

The Alaskan Air Command also provides search-and-rescue facilities in the region. The Elmendorf Rescue Coordination Center (RCC) brings together both military and civilian services to provide SAR cover for the region. Since its conception in 1961 the RCC has been credited with providing aid to well over 10,000 people.

Lt. Gen. Thomas G. McInerney, who commands the AAC, has to wear a number of other hats. As senior officer in the region, he is the co-ordinating chief for all joint military and logistics matters and is the pivot for military/civilian contacts. He is also responsible to CINCNORAD as Commander, Alaskan North American Aerospace Defense Command Region for the aerial defense of North America and for accomplishing all assigned operational missions. And finally, in the event of an emergency (as in time of war, or heightened international tension), the AAC Commander becomes Commander, Joint Task Force—Alaska (JTF–AK) whose responsibility is the unified defense of Alaska.

ELECTRONIC SECURITY COMMAND

Although the use of jamming and listening to enemy communications had been in use since the turn of the century, the war in Vietnam produced a reawakening in the use of electronic counter measures in combat. The Electronic Security Command has both an offensive and defensive role in the modern Air Force. It is faced by the most comprehensive air defense system in the world. The Soviet Union has a highly integrated network of radar and other electromagnetic sensors, command, control and communications and electromagnetically guided weapons ranged against the West. Electronic warfare has for a long time been a very high Soviet priority.

To counter these threats the USAF has some of the most advanced electronics aircraft and systems ever devised. In place of the F-100s and F-105s of the Vietnam era, today's

ELECTRONIC SECURITY COMMAND

Headquarters, San Antonio, Tex.

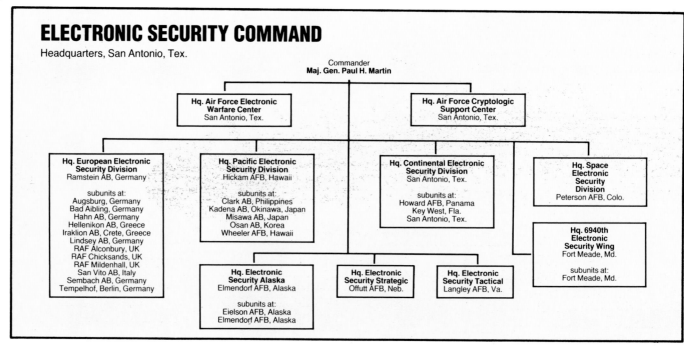

Commander
Maj. Gen. Paul H. Martin

Hq. Air Force Electronic Warfare Center
San Antonio, Tex.

Hq. Air Force Cryptologic Support Center
San Antonio, Tex.

Hq. European Electronic Security Division
Ramstein AB, Germany

subunits at:
Augsburg, Germany
Bad Aibling, Germany
Hahn AB, Germany
Hellenikon AB, Greece
Iraklion AB, Crete, Greece
Lindsey AB, Germany
RAF Alconbury, UK
RAF Chicksands, UK
RAF Mildenhall, UK
San Vito AB, Italy
Sembach AB, Germany
Tempelhof, Berlin, Germany

Hq. Pacific Electronic Security Division
Hickam AFB, Hawaii

subunits at:
Clark AB, Philippines
Kadena AB, Okinawa, Japan
Misawa AB, Japan
Osan AB, Korea
Wheeler AFB, Hawaii

Hq. Continental Electronic Security Division
San Antonio, Tex.

subunits at:
Howard AFB, Panama
Key West, Fla.
San Antonio, Tex.

Hq. Space Electronic Security Division
Peterson AFB, Colo.

Hq. 6940th Electronic Security Wing
Fort Meade, Md.

subunits at:
Fort Meade, Md.

Hq. Electronic Security Alaska
Elmendorf AFB, Alaska

subunits at:
Eielson AFB, Alaska
Elmendorf AFB, Alaska

Hq. Electronic Security Strategic
Offutt AFB, Neb.

Hq. Electronic Security Tactical
Langley AFB, Va.

Wild Weasels – the F-4G supported by F-16s – have far more complex electronics and missiles. Their main armaments are the AGM-88 High Speed Anti-Radiation Missile (HARM) and AGM-45A Shrike. These missiles are designed both to destroy and intimidate individual threat radar surface-to-air and air-to-air missile systems. And they will in the future be supported by the Northrop Tacit Rainbow missile. The AGM-136A is an air-launched, autonomous, loitering, lethal, emitter attack unmanned air vehicle. Designed to destroy and suppress ground-based GBCI, SAM and AA radars, it will be fired hundreds of miles from its target. Once on target over a hostile area it will fly a holding pattern until it homes in on a target. If the enemy radar switches off it will climb back into a holding pattern until it has a new target. It enters initial production during Fiscal Year 1989.

MILITARY AIRLIFT COMMAND

"Today's world situation and the delicate balance of power which exists in many regions necessitate readily deployable US forces. The primary objective of force projection is to get a sufficient quantity of personnel and equipment to the right place at the right time. Proper and timely use of force projection can be crucial in escalation control, limiting the intensity and scope of a conflict at the lowest manageable level."

FY 1989 Air Force Acquisition Statement

Renamed Military Airlift Command on 1 January 1966, it has a direct line back to the Air Corps Ferrying Command raised on 29 May 1941. The Ferrying Command came into existence to support the Anglo-American Land Lease agreement and on 20 June 1942 was renamed Air Transport Command. Throughout the war ATC was to be found around the world, shipping men and equipment to where they were needed most. To keep the American war effort moving, ATC was split into eight wings, each with a specific area of concern: Domestic Transportation Wing, North Atlantic, South Atlantic, Alaska, Africa/Middle East, Caribbean, India/China and South Pacific. As the war progressed ATC was used by all the departments of War Department as the major source of flights to anywhere that Americans were fighting. Today Military Airlift Command carries more DoD and military personnel than any other branch of the military.

With the formation of the USAF in 1947, it was felt that the Air Force and navy airlift capabilities should be amalgamated. And the task of organizing the new command was given to Major General Laurence Kuter who had worked on the concept of a single Air Force under General Arnold. On 1 May 1948, Kuter became head of the new Military Air Transport Service (MATS). The new commander was given no time to reflect on his new command.

A month later all ground routes to Berlin were closed by the Russians, and the city was under siege. The Allies at once started to fly in all supplies needed by the American, British and French forces stationed in West Berlin. President Truman decided that more were needed; he

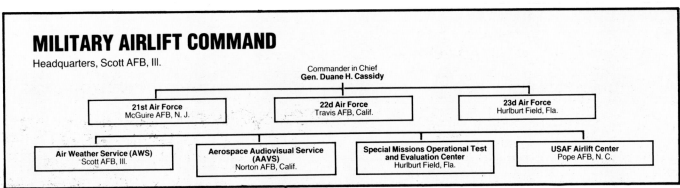

MILITARY AIRLIFT COMMAND

Headquarters, Scott AFB, Ill.

Commander in Chief
Gen. Duane H. Cassidy

21st Air Force McGuire AFB, N. J.	**22d Air Force** Travis AFB, Calif.	**23d Air Force** Hurlburt Field, Fla.

Air Weather Service (AWS) Scott AFB, Ill.	**Aerospace Audiovisual Service (AAVS)** Norton AFB, Calif.	**Special Missions Operational Test and Evaluation Center** Hurlburt Field, Fla.	**USAF Airlift Center** Pope AFB, N. C.

An evocative shot of a Lockheed C-130 silhouetted against a low sun.

TWENTY-FIRST AIR FORCE (MAC)

Headquarters, McGuire AFB, N. J.

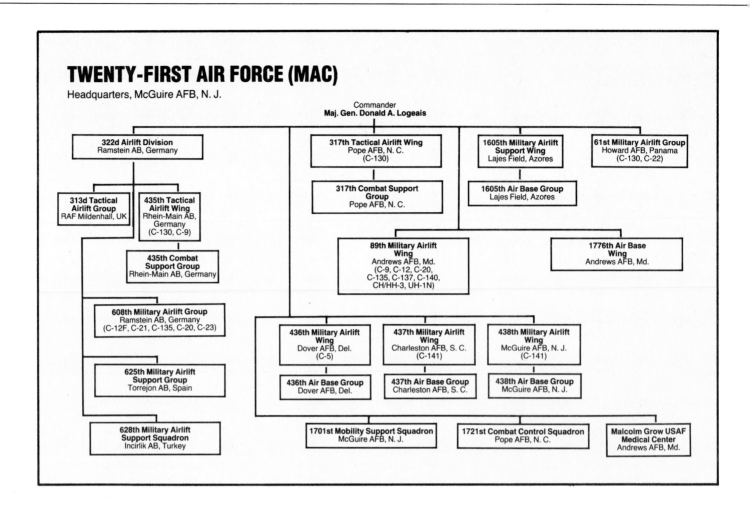

Commander
Maj. Gen. Donald A. Logeais

322d Airlift Division
Ramstein AB, Germany

313d Tactical Airlift Group
RAF Mildenhall, UK

435th Tactical Airlift Wing
Rhein-Main AB, Germany
(C-130, C-9)

435th Combat Support Group
Rhein-Main AB, Germany

608th Military Airlift Group
Ramstein AB, Germany
(C-12F, C-21, C-135, C-20, C-23)

625th Military Airlift Support Group
Torrejon AB, Spain

628th Military Airlift Support Squadron
Incirlik AB, Turkey

317th Tactical Airlift Wing
Pope AFB, N. C.
(C-130)

317th Combat Support Group
Pope AFB, N. C.

1605th Military Airlift Support Wing
Lajes Field, Azores

1605th Air Base Group
Lajes Field, Azores

61st Military Airlift Group
Howard AFB, Panama
(C-130, C-22)

89th Military Airlift Wing
Andrews AFB, Md.
(C-9, C-12, C-20, C-135, C-137, C-140, CH/HH-3, UH-1N)

1776th Air Base Wing
Andrews AFB, Md.

436th Military Airlift Wing
Dover AFB, Del.
(C-5)

436th Air Base Group
Dover AFB, Del.

437th Military Airlift Wing
Charleston AFB, S. C.
(C-141)

437th Air Base Group
Charleston AFB, S. C.

438th Military Airlift Wing
McGuire AFB, N. J.
(C-141)

438th Air Base Group
McGuire AFB, N. J.

1701st Mobility Support Squadron
McGuire AFB, N. J.

1721st Combat Control Squadron
Pope AFB, N. C.

Malcolm Grow USAF Medical Center
Andrews AFB, Md.

TWENTY-SECOND AIR FORCE (MAC)

Headquarters, Travis AFB, Calif.

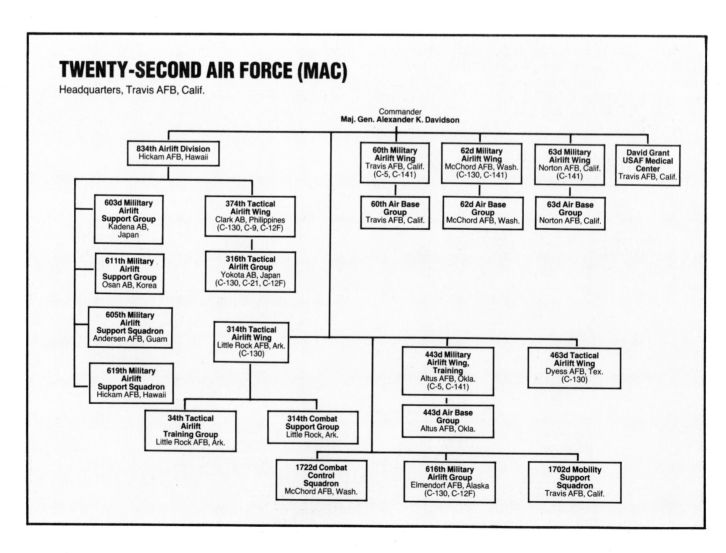

Commander
Maj. Gen. Alexander K. Davidson

834th Airlift Division
Hickam AFB, Hawaii

60th Military Airlift Wing
Travis AFB, Calif.
(C-5, C-141)

60th Air Base Group
Travis AFB, Calif.

62d Military Airlift Wing
McChord AFB, Wash.
(C-130, C-141)

62d Air Base Group
McChord AFB, Wash.

63d Military Airlift Wing
Norton AFB, Calif.
(C-141)

63d Air Base Group
Norton AFB, Calif.

David Grant USAF Medical Center
Travis AFB, Calif.

603d Military Airlift Support Group
Kadena AB, Japan

611th Military Airlift Support Group
Osan AB, Korea

605th Military Airlift Support Squadron
Andersen AFB, Guam

619th Military Airlift Support Squadron
Hickam AFB, Hawaii

374th Tactical Airlift Wing
Clark AB, Philippines
(C-130, C-9, C-12F)

316th Tactical Airlift Group
Yokota AB, Japan
(C-130, C-21, C-12F)

314th Tactical Airlift Wing
Little Rock AFB, Ark.
(C-130)

34th Tactical Airlift Training Group
Little Rock AFB, Ark.

314th Combat Support Group
Little Rock, Ark.

443d Military Airlift Wing, Training
Altus AFB, Okla.
(C-5, C-141)

443d Air Base Group
Altus AFB, Okla.

463d Tactical Airlift Wing
Dyess AFB, Tex.
(C-130)

1722d Combat Control Squadron
McChord AFB, Wash.

616th Military Airlift Group
Elmendorf AFB, Alaska
(C-130, C-12F)

1702d Mobility Support Squadron
Travis AFB, Calif.

ordered the Air Force to deliver enough food and materials to keep the entire western sector of the city supplied. For almost a year an air bridge connected British and American bases in the west and the besieged city deep in East Germany. During Operation Vittles, the Combined Airlift Task Force controlled by MATS Major General William Tunner was to fly over 150,000 sorties both by day and night. The Russians might have extended an Iron Curtain across Europe, but the new command was able to gain a major victory for freedom.

The war in Korea provided new tasks for MATS this time the lines of communication being much longer than the Berlin Airlift. It took over 30 hours to ferry men and materials from America to Korea across the Pacific and General Tunner was again chosen to organize the airlift. He divided the route into two: the first stage started from aerial parts on the West Coast of America and ended in Japan. The aircraft were then refuelled and the crews changed for the second stage on to Korea.

General Tunner became commander of MATS in July 1958 and he pushed hard his ideas of the role of airlift forces, seeing their task as a force which must have the resources to be able to move into action at the first sign of trouble. The late 1950's and early 1960's saw MATS in operation around

the globe, flying men and materials into the Lebanon (1958), Taiwan (1958) and the Congo (1960 and 1964). MATS also took part in a number of large-scale overseas readiness exercises to Puerto Rico and Europe to test the viability of strategic airlift capabilities.

With war again threatening, this time in South-east Asia, MATS was upgraded and renamed Military Airlift Command on 1 January 1966. With a new name came a new plane, both of which were to prove their worth. For years MATS had been after a long-range jet transport to improve both its lift capability and to cut flight times. Lockheed came up with the C-141 Starlifter, and it quickly proved its worth. It took the Lockheed C-130 Hercules over 30 hours to fly to Tan Son Nhut, South Vietnam; the Starlifter was able to fly the route, with a heavier cargo, in just over 18 hours. In total MAC carried two million-plus passengers and two million tons of equipment during the war. Its Air Rescue Service rescued 2,780 personnel trapped during combat missions.

In 1983 MAC was again in combat, ferrying troops and equipment. This time it was to the island of Grenada where the Cubans were increasing their presence. MAC C-141s dropped the first wave of paratroops on to the airport at Point Salines at the south of the island, while US Marines landed at

The Commander-in-Chief of MAC, Maj. Gen. Duane H. Cassidy meets Air Force officers on a visit to Europe.

Pearls Airport in the north. The army started to ferry in more troops by helicopter into Point Salines but several of the helicopters were hit by Cuban anti-aircraft fire from several points. MAC AC-130 gunships were quickly on the scene and laid down a heavy fire screen against the enemy positions. The effect was devastating and within hours C-130s and C-141s were landing at the airfield bringing in re-enforcements. The AC-130s were used throughout the island, providing heavy fire power wherever needed.

Today Military Airlift Command has over 78,000 active-duty military and 15,000 civilian staff working for it. They operate more than a thousand aircraft from 24 different countries. MAC also has on call another 70,100 personnel and 400 aircraft assigned to it from ANG and AFRES units, and it has responsibility for the Civil Reserve Air Fleet (CRAF). This reserve consists of 393 cargo and passenger aircraft operated by 29 commercial carriers. CRAF aircraft are equipped with extra communications equipment

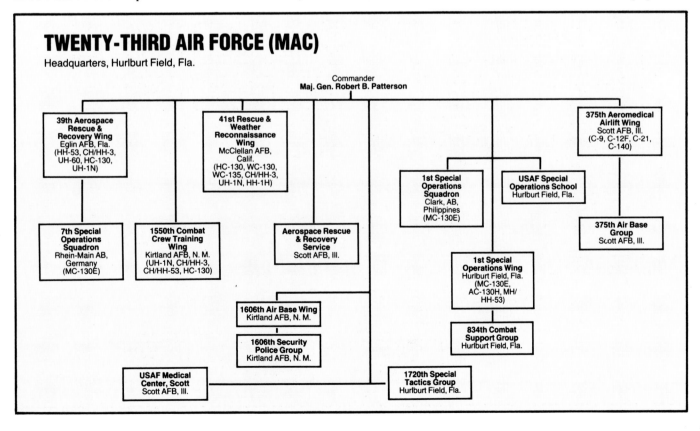

and an ongoing program is to fit cargo facilities to standard passenger aircraft, including the strengthening of the deck of the planes and fitting a cargo door. During 1988 MAC was involved in 71 of the Joint Chiefs of Staff's exercises out of a total of 80 exercises. This is more than any other command in any service. It will have undertaken in excess of 65,000 flying hours and will represent 12 per cent of MAC's allocation of flying hours.

MAC is divided into three numbered Air Forces: the Twenty-First with its headquarters at McGuire AFB, the Twenty-Second with its headquarters at Travis AFB and the Twenty-Third based at Hurlburt Field. The Twenty-First is tasked with Trans-Atlantic operations while the Twenty-Second operates through the Pacific Basin. The Twenty-Third Air Force provides the Air Force part of the recently formed US Special Operations Command.

Like any commercial airline MAC operates a world-wide network of aircraft on regular passenger and cargo schedules, flying from 21 intertheater aerial ports and 22 intertheater

operating locations. These are backed up by commercial gateway operating locations at 13 commercial airports across the globe. And like any commercial airline it has a set of fares and freight tariffs which users pay. All the commands and outside agencies who use the system — and that includes official Presidential flights — are charged according to a set of charges laid down by an Assistant Secretary of Defense. The charges reflect operating costs and all funds raised are paid into the Airlift Service Industrial Fund (ASIF). During 1987 MAC carried 2,137,031 passengers and 462,274 tons of cargo on a combination of military and commercial flights on behalf of the Department of Defense.

MAC operates a wide variety of aircraft from small aircraft like the C-21A up to the mighty C-5 Galaxy. It has a number of aircraft with specific roles like the C-9 Nightingale, used for aeromedical airlift and the Shorts C-23 Sherpa which is used exclusively in Europe.

The C-130 Hercules is operated in a number of roles over and above that of a simple transporter. First introduced in 1956 it has operated all over the world. Variants include the HC-130 which has an extended range with up-rated T56-A-15 engines. It also incorporates advanced direction-finding equipment and an air-to-air recovery system. The MC-130E is used by Special Operations Squadrons for low-level deep-penetration missions. These are due to be supplemented by 24 improved MC-130Hs by 1991. The AC-130A gunships were first brought

Right: Three ages of flight can be seen in this picture. A MAC C-5 unloads a US Army UH-60 Blackhawk while a Honduran DC-3 takes off. The C-5 delivered three UH-60s for medivac use during Ex. Ahuas Tara III.

Below: MAC aircraft regularly deploy to allied bases. Here C-130s of the 37th TAS exercise with the Portuguese Air Force.

into service during the Vietnam War and are equipped with two 40 mm (1.6 in) cannon, two 20 mm (0.8 in) Vulcan cannon and two 7.62 mm (0.3 in) Miniguns. They are flown today by the Air Force Reserve's 711st SOS. The AC-130H flown by the 16th SOS is similar to the AC-130A but has had one of its 40 mm (1.6 in) cannon replaced by a 105 mm (26.6 in) howitzer and the miniguns removed. In July 1987 Rockwell gained the contract to develop a new generation of gunship to replace the AC-130s. Six of the new AC-130U have been requested in the FY 1989 budget.

The latest airlifter to join MAC will be the McDonnell Douglas C-17 which is due to make its first flight in FY 1990 and to enter initial service with 12 aircraft in FY 1992. A total of 210 C-17s are due to be procured by the year 2000. The C-17 will provide MAC with an aircraft that can cover trans-ocean distances right into the forward battle area. It will be able to carry outsize cargos and will also have the ability to airdrop them.

The two main Presidential aircraft based on the Boeing 707, which are designated Air Force One when the President is aboard, are both now over 15 years old and are due to be replaced. They do not meet Federal Aviation Administration (FAA) noise level standards, and they also need comprehensive avionics and communications updates. They are due to be replaced by two new Boeing 747-200Bs, designated VC-25A. The first is to be delivered on 30 November 1988 and the second on 31 May 1989.

The Air Force will begin the procurement of the CV-22 tilt-rotor aircraft in FY 1994. These aircraft will be used for long-range penetration by MAC's Twenty-Third AF. MAC uses a variety of helicopters for Aerospace

Rescue and Recovery missions. The latest addition to the helicopter fleet is the MH-53J Pave Low III "Enhanced," which has been developed from the C/HH-53 B/C deliveries started at the end of 1987. It is equipped with an integrated digital avionics suite and will be capable of refueling from the upgraded MC-130E and HC-130P/N tanker aircraft. All the existing H-53s will be upgraded to PAVE LOW standard by the middle of 1991.

PACIFIC AIR FORCES

The Pacific Air Forces (PACAF) is divided into three numbered air forces, the Fifth which operates from Japan, the Seventh in South Korea and the Thirteenth in the Philippines. It is tasked with the air defense of the vast Pacific basin and the Indian Ocean and covers more than 100 million square miles. Originally called the Far East Air Forces (FEAF), it was renamed on 1 July 1957. At that time it

had only two numbered air forces, the Fifth in Japan and the Thirteenth in the Philippines. Both FEAF and PACAF have been involved in large-scale war. The Far East Air Forces was formed during World War II from the Fifth and Thirteenth Air Forces. It was later expanded to include the Seventh Air Force and finally the Twentieth Air Force. When the war in Korea erupted in 1950 FEAF was the largest of the United Nations Air Forces and it saw service throughout the war, gaining a bomber command from SAC resources. Korea saw the first all-jet dogfights. On 8 November 1950 Lieutenant Russell Brown, flying an F-80 of the 51st Fighter Interceptor Wing, shot down a Chinese MiG-15.

With the formation of PACAF in 1957 the new Command's

General Dynamics F–16s of the 35th Tactical Fighter Squadron (Wolf Pack) prepare for take-off from Kunsan,AB.

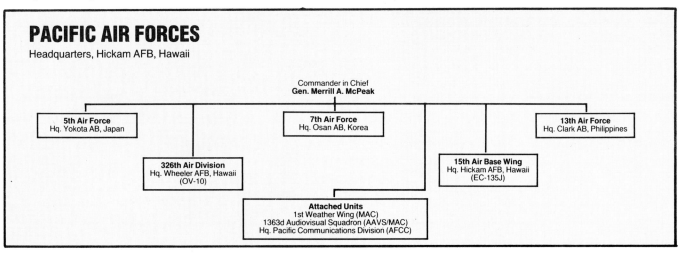

PACIFIC AIR FORCES
Headquarters, Hickam AFB, Hawaii

Commander in Chief
Gen. Merrill A. McPeak

| **5th Air Force** Hq. Yokota AB, Japan | **7th Air Force** Hq. Osan AB, Korea | **13th Air Force** Hq. Clark AB, Philippines |

326th Air Division
Hq. Wheeler AFB, Hawaii
(OV-10)

15th Air Base Wing
Hq. Hickam AFB, Hawaii
(EC-135J)

Attached Units
1st Weather Wing (MAC)
1363d Audiovisual Squadron (AAVS/MAC)
Hq. Pacific Communications Division (AFCC)

Above: Amn. Tony Hoffman, 12th AMU gathering tools for an inspection of an F–15.

Left: 432nd TFW F–16s flying in formation with JASDF F–15s during Cope North 88–3.

Below: SSgt. Richard Pennington follows a maintenance manual for the A–7 post-flight inspections.

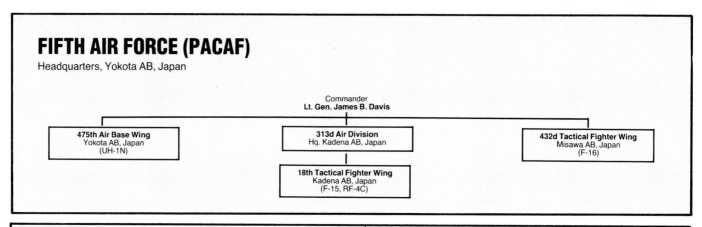

FIFTH AIR FORCE (PACAF)
Headquarters, Yokota AB, Japan

Commander
Lt. Gen. James B. Davis

475th Air Base Wing
Yokota AB, Japan
(UH-1N)

313d Air Division
Hq. Kadena AB, Japan

432d Tactical Fighter Wing
Misawa AB, Japan
(F-16)

18th Tactical Fighter Wing
Kadena AB, Japan
(F-15, RF-4C)

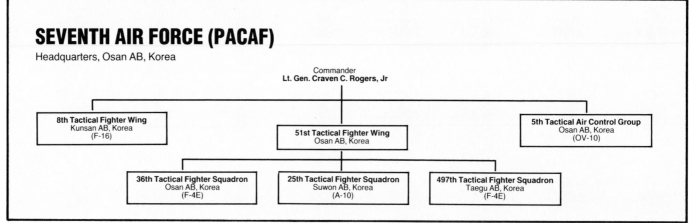

SEVENTH AIR FORCE (PACAF)
Headquarters, Osan AB, Korea

Commander
Lt. Gen. Craven C. Rogers, Jr

8th Tactical Fighter Wing
Kunsan AB, Korea
(F-16)

51st Tactical Fighter Wing
Osan AB, Korea

5th Tactical Air Control Group
Osan AB, Korea
(OV-10)

36th Tactical Fighter Squadron
Osan AB, Korea
(F-4E)

25th Tactical Fighter Squadron
Suwon AB, Korea
(A-10)

497th Tactical Fighter Squadron
Taegu AB, Korea
(F-4E)

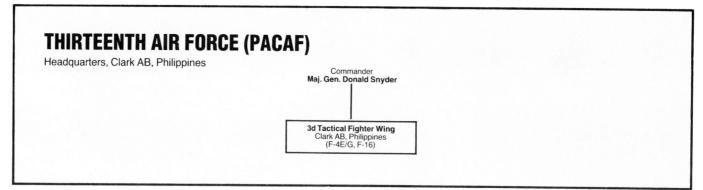

THIRTEENTH AIR FORCE (PACAF)
Headquarters, Clark AB, Philippines

Commander
Maj. Gen. Donald Snyder

3d Tactical Fighter Wing
Clark AB, Philippines
(F-4E/G, F-16)

headquarters were moved to Hickham AFB. It had 89,679 personnel and a total of 959 aircraft. Over the next seven years its forces were slowly reduced. By the start of the Vietnam War PACAF had been reduced to a total of 65,155 personnel and 582 aircraft. This was quickly changed and by the peak of the conflict in 1968 it had a total of almost 170,000 men and women and 2,100 aircraft. The Seventh Air Force was brought back into service for the duration and then again disbanded. PACAF reached a low point in 1976 when it could only muster 34,111 personnel and 255 aircraft. Today it has 24,000 personnel but now has 300 plus fighter/attack aircraft. It also has nearly 24,000 personnel belonging to other Air Force units who serve in the region.

General Jack I. Gregory who commands PACAF has his

18th TFW F–15s based at Kadena refuel from a KC–135 operated by the 909th ARS also based at Kadena.

STRATEGIC AIR COMMAND

"Under the guidance and direction of the President's 1981 strategic modernization program, the Air Force has been committed to improving two legs of the (Nuclear) Triad, the land-based ICBM and the manned bomber. While our progress in these areas has not been as rapid as envisioned, we are bringing into the inventory effective weapons systems and improving the efficiency of the ones we have in order to increase our overall strategic capability and survivability. The reliability and effectiveness of our strategic weapon systems are critical to the freedom and well being of the United States. It is therefore imperative that we continue to improve and upgrade existing systems while acquiring new weapons systems in order to maintain our strategic deterrent posture."

Air Force Acquisition Statement for FY 1989

The concept of taking the war to the heart of an enemy country is not new. Attacking both that country's power sources and resources coupled with the ability to undermine the enemy's will to fight was developed during World War II by USAF and Britain's RAF. The Army Air Force created three separate air forces dedicated to this vital role: The Eighth and Fifteenth operating over Europe and the Twentieth which operated in the Pacific Theater.

Since that time the concept has only been used on a few occasions. It was used in a limited way during the Korean War. During the Vietnam War the Joint Chiefs of Staff drew up a plan for a 16-day bombing which was designed to take out all strategic targets. The plan was rejected by the Government for political reasons. This was to have a major effect later on in the war when the war was taken to North Vietnam. By the time the

headquarters at Hickham AFB, Hawaii and most of the Command's support units operate from the island. The Fifth Air Force is based at Yokota AB in Japan and its teeth are supplied by the 18th Tactical Fighter Wing who fly their F-15s from Kadena AB and the F-16s of the 432nd Tactical Fighter Wing at Misawa AB. Regular "Cope North" exercises are run jointly with the Japanese Air Force from Misawa AB. These are designed to test the area's air defense capabilities. The Seventh Air Force reformed in September 1986 and has its headquarters at Kunsan AB in South Korea. It took over all the 5th Air Force assets in the region, including the A-10s of the 25th Tactical Fighter Squadron, and the F-4Es of the 36th and 497th TFS which make up the 51st Tactical Fighter Wing. It also includes the F-16s of the 8th TFW and the OV-10s of the 5th Tactical Air Control Group based at Osan AB.

The highlight of the Seventh Air Force Year is the annual Team Spirit exercise which involves more than 200,000 US and Republic of Korea forces. This is an all-services exercise and is a visible demonstration of America's support for the region. In the Philippines the Thirteenth Air Force has its headquarters at Clark Air Base, the oldest and largest American Air Base outside of CONUS. The Thirteenth has only a single fighter wing; the 3rd TFW has a mix of F4E/Gs operated by the 3rd and 90th TFSs and the F-16s aggressors of the 26th Tactical Fighter Training Squadron. Seven times a year the Thirteenth Air Force holds a "Cope Thunder" exercise. This is PACAF's answer to TAC's "Red Flat" exercise. It is held on the Crow Valley Gunnery Range situated close to Clark AFB, and is used by all the American forces as well as other friendly forces in the region.

The roll-out of the Northrop B–2 "stealth bomber". Gen. Larry D. Welch, USAF Chief of Staff, stated that the B–2 "combines all the best attributes of a penetrating bomber – long range, efficient cruise, heavy payload, all-altitude penetration capability, accurate delivery and reliability and maintainability."

bombers crossed the border the North Vietnamese had, with the help of the Russians, created a vast air defense network which was to prove costly for American attacks.

As the war approached its climax President Nixon at last allowed unrestricted air operations over the north. Linebacker was released and thousands of tons of explosives rained down on targets all over the north. The effect was magnetic. The North Vietnamese, who had for months stayed away from the Paris Peace Talks, agreed to return and so the Linebacker Campaign was suspended. Strategic bombing had proved its worth. The problem was that with the cessation of the bombing the North refused yet again to talk constructively. This was too much for the Americans and Linebacker II was launched on 18 December. The B-52s of Strategic Air Command's (SAC's) Eighth Air Force supported by PACAF and Seventeenth Fleet fighter bomber hit targets all over the country both by day and night. Except for Christmas Day, Linebacker II ran for 11 solid days. Targets were hit time after time, the north losing its power to respond to the attacks as its runways were destroyed and its SAM sites ran out of missiles or were taken out by the attacking aircraft. The North returned to the Talks and a ceasefire was quickly agreed to. The war in Vietnam was drawn to a close by the concept of strategic air warfare.

Strategic warfare also played a part in the Falklands War during 1982. With the invasion of the islands by Argentinian forces, Britain was faced with attacking an enemy entrenched and well supplied 1,300 km (8,000 miles) away. On 1 May a lone Vulcan bomber flying at 3,050 m (10,000 ft) dropped twenty-one 450Kg (1000 lb)

bombs across the runway at Port Stanley. Although only one bomb hit the center of the runway, almost all the others produced considerable damage to aircraft and equipment around the airfield. The effect this raid had on the Argentinian forces should not be underestimated. They were forced to keep their Mirage Fighters for the defense of mainland Argentina and the airfield at Stanley was denied to jet aircraft for the duration of the war.

Today the Strategic Air Command controls a vast arsenal dedicated to the strategic warfare concept. With two-thirds of the US nuclear triad under its control it is responsible for providing the United States with the capability to launch a nuclear response strong enough to deter an attack on both America and its allies. It is also responsible for maintaining a large long-range bomber force which can operate in a conventional role

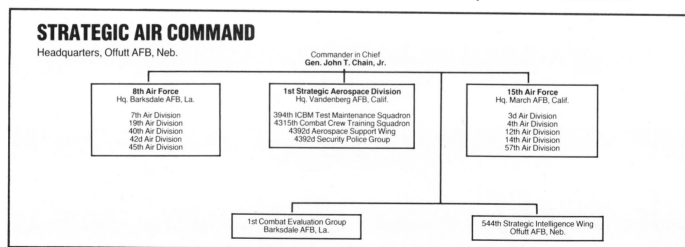

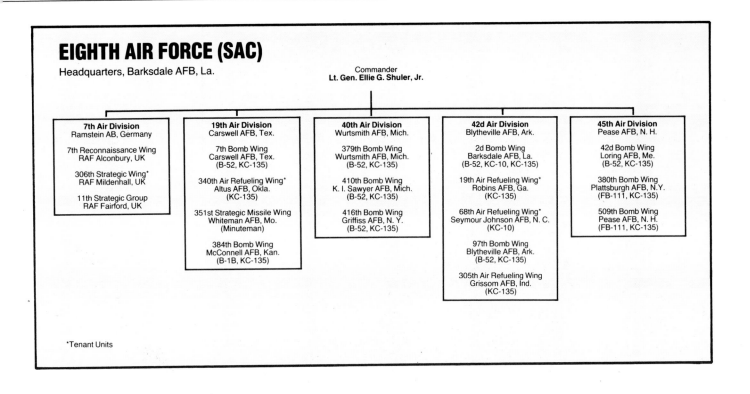

EIGHTH AIR FORCE (SAC)

Headquarters, Barksdale AFB, La.

Commander
Lt. Gen. Ellie G. Shuler, Jr.

7th Air Division
Ramstein AB, Germany

7th Reconnaissance Wing
RAF Alconbury, UK

306th Strategic Wing*
RAF Mildenhall, UK

11th Strategic Group
RAF Fairford, UK

19th Air Division
Carswell AFB, Tex.

7th Bomb Wing
Carswell AFB, Tex.
(B-52, KC-135)

340th Air Refueling Wing*
Altus AFB, Okla.
(KC-135)

351st Strategic Missile Wing
Whiteman AFB, Mo.
(Minuteman)

384th Bomb Wing
McConnell AFB, Kan.
(B-1B, KC-135)

40th Air Division
Wurtsmith AFB, Mich.

379th Bomb Wing
Wurtsmith AFB, Mich.
(B-52, KC-135)

410th Bomb Wing
K. I. Sawyer AFB, Mich.
(B-52, KC-135)

416th Bomb Wing
Griffiss AFB, N. Y.
(B-52, KC-135)

42d Air Division
Blytheville AFB, Ark.

2d Bomb Wing
Barksdale AFB, La.
(B-52, KC-10, KC-135)

19th Air Refueling Wing*
Robins AFB, Ga.
(KC-135)

68th Air Refueling Wing*
Seymour Johnson AFB, N. C.
(KC-10)

97th Bomb Wing
Blytheville AFB, Ark.
(B-52, KC-135)

305th Air Refueling Wing
Grissom AFB, Ind.
(KC-135)

45th Air Division
Pease AFB, N. H.

42d Bomb Wing
Loring AFB, Me.
(B-52, KC-135)

380th Bomb Wing
Plattsburgh AFB, N. Y.
(FB-111, KC-135)

509th Bomb Wing
Pease AFB, N. H.
(FB-111, KC-135)

*Tenant Units

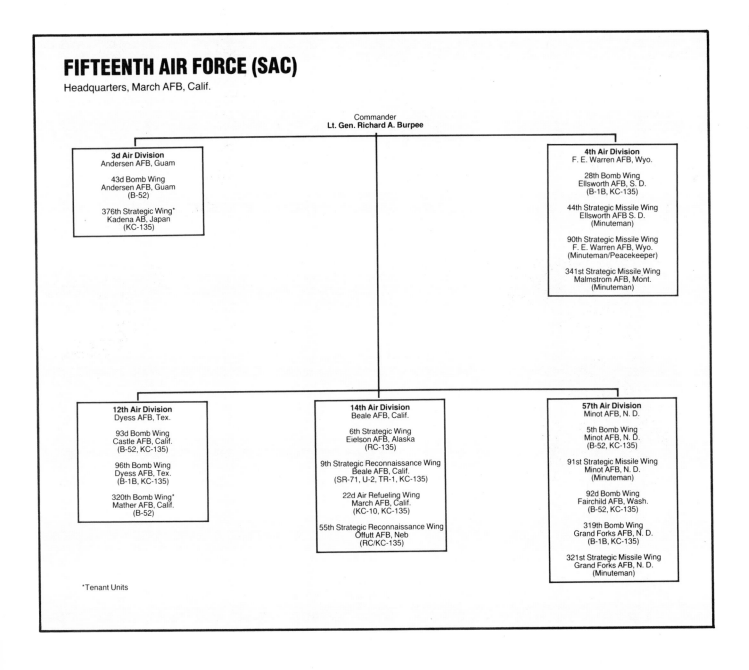

FIFTEENTH AIR FORCE (SAC)

Headquarters, March AFB, Calif.

Commander
Lt. Gen. Richard A. Burpee

3d Air Division
Andersen AFB, Guam

43d Bomb Wing
Andersen AFB, Guam
(B-52)

376th Strategic Wing*
Kadena AB, Japan
(KC-135)

4th Air Division
F. E. Warren AFB, Wyo.

28th Bomb Wing
Ellsworth AFB, S. D.
(B-1B, KC-135)

44th Strategic Missile Wing
Ellsworth AFB S. D.
(Minuteman)

90th Strategic Missile Wing
F. E. Warren AFB, Wyo.
(Minuteman/Peacekeeper)

341st Strategic Missile Wing
Malmstrom AFB, Mont.
(Minuteman)

12th Air Division
Dyess AFB, Tex.

93d Bomb Wing
Castle AFB, Calif.
(B-52, KC-135)

96th Bomb Wing
Dyess AFB, Tex.
(B-1B, KC-135)

320th Bomb Wing*
Mather AFB, Calif.
(B-52)

14th Air Division
Beale AFB, Calif.

6th Strategic Wing
Eielson AFB, Alaska
(RC-135)

9th Strategic Reconnaissance Wing
Beale AFB, Calif.
(SR-71, U-2, TR-1, KC-135)

22d Air Refueling Wing
March AFB, Calif.
(KC-10, KC-135)

55th Strategic Reconnaissance Wing
Offutt AFB, Neb
(RC/KC-135)

57th Air Division
Minot AFB, N. D.

5th Bomb Wing
Minot AFB, N. D.
(B-52, KC-135)

91st Strategic Missile Wing
Minot AFB, N. D.
(Minuteman)

92d Bomb Wing
Fairchild AFB, Wash.
(B-52, KC-135)

319th Bomb Wing
Grand Forks AFB, N. D.
(B-1B, KC-135)

321st Strategic Missile Wing
Grand Forks AFB, N. D.
(Minuteman)

*Tenant Units

The Rail Garrison when it enters service will be based at F.E. Warren AFB, Wyoming. The missiles will be removed from their silos and repositioned on special rail cars which could then be moved around the rail network.

Like the Rail Garrison the fate of the Small Intercontinental Ballistic Missile will be decided by President Bush in 1989. The Small ICBM will weigh about 13,608kg (30,000 lb), have a diameter of less than 1.22m (4ft) and be 14m (46ft) long. It will be able to carry a 1,000-lb payload over 9,656km (6,000 miles).

anywhere in the world in response to any conflict or event. SAC forces operate from more than a hundred bases around the globe and its 119,000 officers, enlisted members and civilian staff, supported by 14,000 members of SAC reserve dedicated units, operate a wide and diverse range of equipment and aircraft.

At the spearhead of SAC are the mighty Minuteman and Peacekeeper Inter-Continental-Ballistic-Missiles, and the B-1Bs, B-52s (both G and H models) backed by FB-111 medium-range strategic bombers.

KC-135 and KC-10 tankers act as force-multipliers by providing a vital extended range capability to SAC's bomber forces. The U-2, TR-1, SR-71 and RC-135 reconnaissance aircraft act as SAC's eyes and ears. For command and control SAC operates EC-135 aircraft and the E-4B, National Emergency Airborne Command Post.

In the 1990's the Northrop B-2 bomber, with its low-observable stealth characteristics, combined with future systems like the Short-Range Attack Missile (SRAM) II and the Advanced Cruise Missile, will farther enhance SAC's ability to penetrate deep into Soviet Territory.

Battles in Congress have forced reappraisals with regard to basing and numbers of Peacekeeper missiles and to the development of the Small ICBM (SICBM). Secretary of Defense, Dick Cheney in his first defense budget is to ask Congress for funds to redeploy the 50 Peacekeeper missiles currently in silos on to mobile rail garrisons. The Midgetman project will be kept with limited development funds. This mix of missiles would provide President Bush with a strong hand in the joint American/Soviet Strategic Arms Reduction Talks.

The Atlas ICBM was the first strategic missile to enter service in February 1958 and was retired from service in April 1965. The LGM-30 Minuteman entered service in 1962 and, following a series of major

upgrades, is still the major element of the SAC ICBM force with a total of 450 Minuteman IIs and 500 Minuteman IIIs. The Minuteman missiles are operated by the 44th Strategic Missile Wing at Ellsworth AFB, 90th SMW based at F.E. Warren, 91st SMW at Minot AFB, 314th SMW at Malmstrom AFB, 321st SMW at Grand Forks AFB and the 351st Strategic Missile Wing based at Whiteman AFB.

Over the years various upgrades to the Minuteman fleet have included the introduction of the LGM-30F Minuteman II to replace the Minuteman I in 1965 with an increased range, accuracy and payload, and five years later the introduction of Minuteman IIIs to support the LGM-30Fs. The silo complexes were upgraded during the Upgrade Silo program which was completed in January 1980. Other upgrades include the fitting of a Command Data Buffer System which provides for remote targeting capability, a Guidance Improvement Program, and the deployment of the 12A re-entry vehicle.

The Titan LGM-25, which was almost twice the size of the later Minuteman ICBMs, followed on in 1963 and was only retired from service in 1987, when the last five missiles of the 308th Strategic Missile Wing at Little Rock, Ark were decommissioned.

The newest member of the ICBM family is the LGM-118A Peacekeeper which started to be deployed at F.E. Warren AFB during 1986. Following a number of problems with some missiles' Inertial Measurement Units the program is now back on schedule for its full operational capability (FOC) in December 1988. The Peacekeeper research and development flight test program, consisting of 20 launches, was initiated at Vandenberg AFB, California, in June 1983. The 18th test firing on 19 March 1989 may well be the last firing in the series because according to the Air Force all the test objectives have now been achieved. The test firing was the first time that a launch had been controlled from an airborne launch control center. The proposal to remove the Peacekeepers from their silos will mean that the Air Force will only get a total of 50 missiles instead of the original 100.

The SICBM designed to be deployed in a hardened mobile launcher will

provide a high degree of flexibility, accuracy and endurance as part of SAC's contribution to the Nuclear Triad. The decision to carry on with reduced funding for Midgetman in the FY 90 budget allows President Bush to use the possibility of deployment of the missile as a major bargaining counter with the Soviets as the GLCM was in the Intermediate Nuclear Forces Treaty.

The second leg of SAC's nuclear forces is provided by its fleet of manned bombers. The B-52 has been the backbone of the strategic bomber force for over a quarter of a century. SAC has a total of 234 B-52s in 11 Bombardment Wings in mainland America plus the 43rd Bomb Wing stationed at Andersen AFB Guam. The B-52G and H bombers have been continually upgraded with the

incorporation of state-of-the-art avionics systems. Continuing modernization programs include improvements in electronic countermeasures, upgrading the airborne radar.

The B-52 will still have a major role in the 1990's when the B-2 enters service. The 96 B-52Hs are being refitted to provide the capability of carrying 20 cruise missiles, 12 externally and 8 internally. They are being fitted with the Common Strategic Rotary Launcher (CSRL). This is a multipurpose internal launcher, which can accommodate gravity weapons, short-range attack missiles, cruise missiles and future conventional standoff munitions. The CSRLs will be transferred at a later date to the B-1B fleet. The B-52H CSRL initial

operational capability is scheduled for the second quarter of FY 1990. Strategic Air Command has 61 B-52Gs which provide the bulk of its conventional warfare needs. The modernization of 30 B-52s to carry the AGM-84 Harpoon anti-ship missile was completed in June 1985. The Strategic Conventional Standoff Capability program is designed to "provide conventional improvements to put high value targets in the low end of the conflict spectrum at risk regardless of the target environment." Its contribution in nuclear, conventional and maritime roles is still large. It provides a world-wide capability not found in any other aircraft. The mighty B-52s have still got a lot of miles left to fly before they are finished.

The Rockwell B-1B entered service

A B–1B pulling a tight climb during an acceptance flight. The B–1B operates very close to the ground and must have the ability to maneuver while hugging the ground below.

Left: A B–52 with rotary launch AGM–69A SRAM dispenser. SRAM will be replaced by the supersonic SRAM II starting in 1992.

Below: ALCMs under the wing of a 2nd Bomb Wing B–52G at Barksdale.

Left: A B–52 is readied for take-off with a full load of ALCMs under its wings. Even after the Northrop B–2 has entered service, the B–52 will still have an important role in SAC well into the next century.

Below: A B–52 is scrambled at Barksdale AFB.

Bottom left: Maintenance work on an AGM–86B ALCM. The Air Launched Cruise Missiles were not covered by the INF Treaty.

in September 1986 with the 96th Bomb Wing at Dyess AFB, Texas. On 1 October 1986 SAC placed its first B-1B on continuous alert. During 1987 B-1Bs were delivered to the 28th Bomb Wing at Ellsworth AFB, South Dakota and the 319th Bomb Wing at Grand Forks, South Dakota. The last wing became operational in July 1988 when the 384th Bomb Wing was activated. The B-1B provides SAC with improved range and payload capability for strategic nuclear bombing and, in the future, cruise missile launch missions. The B-1B, with its high-speed, low-altitude flight, advanced electronic countermeasures and reduced radar cross section, would prove a hard target for the Soviet Air Defense

Forces. In addition the B-1B will be able to perform tactical and strategic conventional bombing missions. As the B-1B is further developed from its present penetration role it will be able to fly cruise missile shoot-then-penetrate missions.

The Northrop B-2 Advanced Technology Bomber is scheduled to enter service in the mid 1990's. Its low observable technology (stealth) will enable it to operate in the densest air defense environments that the Soviets can develop. Its first operational base has been announced as Whiteman AFB, Missouri and construction work at the base has started.

The last bomber in SAC's inventory is the General Dynamics FB-111

which provides a medium-range strategic bombing capability. Its radar is being modified under the Avionics Modernization Program to provide enhanced navigation, bombing and terrain following capabilities. It is planned that the FB-111s of the 380th Bomb Wing at Plattsburgh AFB and 509th Bomb Wing at Pease AFB will be transferred to the Tactical Air Forces in the early 1990's.

To enhance the effect of the bomber force SAC has its own tanker fleets which have been undergoing major modernization. A total of 640 KC-135s Stratotankers support SAC as well as the other commands. Thirteen Air National Guard units plus three Air Force Reserve units operate 128 of

Designed to detect low-flying aircraft and cruise missiles, the AN/FPS–118 Over the Horizon, Backscatter radar has a vastly superior range over conventional radars.

Insert: This diagram shows how the coverage of the AN/FPS–118 fits into the air defense coverage of the United States.

them. It is planned that the entire fleet will be modernized to provide service well into the next century. The first SAC unit to have its KC-135s updated was the 384th Air Refueling Wing at McConnell AFB, in June 1985. Since then the 28th Bomb Wing at Ellsworth AFB, South Dakota; the 19th Air Refueling Wing at Robins AFB, Georgia and the 340th Air Refueling Wing at Altus AFB have been upgraded to KC-135R standard. All KC-135s are to be brought up to this standard. The KC-135R modernization program provides a 50 per cent increase in fuel available for transfer when compared to the basic KC-135A load. This has largely been achieved by the fitting of the new CFM56 high by-pass turbofan engine. They provide increased thrust, decreased fuel consumption and decreased noise and air pollution. Operational sorties overseas which formerly required the support of two KC-135As are now routinely supported by a single KC-135R.

Three SAC air wings fly the McDonnell Douglas KC-10 based on the DC-10 Series 30CF. The KC-10 Extender provides SAC with an operational tanker which dispenses with the need for forward bases, each KC-10 providing three times the offload capability of a KC-135A. The Extender first entered service with SAC in March 1981. SAC units which operate the KC-10 include the 2nd Bomb Wing at Barksdale AFB, Louisiana; 22nd Air Refueling Wing at March AFB, California and the 68th Air Refueling Wing at Seymour-Johnson AFB, North Carolina.

SAC is also responsible for operating a wide range of reconnaissance aircraft both on its own behalf and of other theater commanders. Its U-2, TR-1, SR-71 and RC-135 aircraft provide the vital eyes and ears of the Air Force. The Lockheed U-2 entered service in the 1950's to monitor Soviet ICBMs. Over the years the U-2 has grown both in size and capability, culminating in the 103ft wing span TR-1 which entered service in 1981. Both the U-2 and the more advanced TR-1 are designed to operate at extremely high altitudes, equipped with cameras, and radars operate both day and night providing all weather reconnaissance. The U-2, TR-1 and SR-71 are operated by the 9th Strategic Reconnaissance Wing based at Beale AFB, California. The Lockheed SR-71 Blackbird, powered by two 15,400 kg (34,000 lb) thrust Pratt & Whitney turbojets, operates at the edge of space at speeds in excess of Mach 3. It holds the absolute world speed record of Mach 3.3 (3,530 km/h (2,193.67 mph)). Its sensor suite can monitor 260,000 sq. km (100,000 sq. miles) in 60 minutes. SAC also operates the EC-135 and E-4B aircraft. The EC-135 Airborne Command Post provides an airborne operations center for survivable command and control of SAC's nuclear forces. The E-4B National Emergency Airborne Command Post plus the EC-135s form the basis of the Worldwide Airborne Command Post system. Each system is undergoing modernization to provide communications upgrades. And on-the ground a new command center is being built to provide CINCSAC with a system that will allow him to direct his forces in the minimum time with the maximum effect.

An SR–71 of the 9th Strategic Reconnaissance Wing is refueled by a KC–10. The SR–71 still holds the world height and speed records, but it will be withdrawn from service during the 1990's.

TACTICAL AIR COMMAND

◆

"The Air Force must capitalize on advantages in technology, tactics and dedicated, well trained people to maintain combat-ready, flexible, tactical air forces. Because of the growth in Soviet military power and the steady improvement in Soviet combat capabilities, we must continue to modernize our tactical air forces while maintaining current levels of readiness."

The United States Air Force Report to the 100th Congress of the United States of America. Fiscal Year 1989

With its roots going back to World War I, Tactical Air Command (TAC) has grown into the Air Force's largest tactical command in personnel and has more aircraft than any other command. With its assigned Air National Guard and Air Force Reserve units it has under its control more than 4,000 aircraft and 192,000 personnel made up of 23,000 officers, 152,000 enlisted men and women, and 17,000 civilians.

Its task is to provide the organization, training and equipment needed to maintain combat-ready forces that are capable of rapid deployment anywhere in the world as required. It is also responsible for the air defense of the United States mainland. It provides the air

component of the United States Readiness Command (USREDCOM), US Central Command (USCC), US Atlantic Command (LANTCOM), and the US Southern Command (SOUTHCOM). General Robert D. Ross commander of the Tactical Air Command wears three hats, those of MAJCOM, CINCAFRED and CINCAFLANT.

To fulfill these tasks TAC is divided into three numbered air forces, the First Air Force with its HQ at Langley AFB, the Ninth whose headquarters is at Shaw AFB and the 12th controlled from Bergstrom AFB. It also has the 28th Air Division responsible for airborne warning and control and the Tactical Fighter Weapons and Tactical Air Warfare Centers. To provide realistic training TAC operates a number of specialist exercises. These "Flag" exercises include:

Black Flag
This is designed to train aircraft maintenance crews to operate under wartime conditions and still keep their aircraft flying.

Blue Flag
These exercises are dedicated to real-time Command, Control and Communications training. They are designed to cover all areas of the world where USAF operates. And are used not only by TAC personnel but by other branches of USAF, US Army and Navy personnel and other allied air forces.

Checkered Flag
This is designed to enable TAC fighter squadrons and tactical air control units to prepare for operations from their assigned overseas bases. Units and personnel are regularly deployed to these bases so that they can operate efficiently in times of crisis.

Copper Flag
Based at Tyndall AFB, Copper Flag exercises are used to increase the readiness of air defense forces using simulated enemy attacks.

Left: A Westinghouse APG–66 radar installed in an F–16.

A beautiful shot of TAC's latest fighter, the F–15E.

Green Flag

Operated by USAFTAWC and USAFTFWC these exercises are designed to test and train aircrew in how to operate and survive in a hostile electronic warfare environment.

Red Flag

The most famous of the Flag programs, Red Flag exercises are a regular part of life at Nellis AFB. They provide tactical fighter training against simulated enemy air and ground forces. Up to 300 aircraft can be involved in a Red Flag exercise; the pilots and aircraft come from all commands of the Air Force, US Navy and Marine Corps, NATO and other allied air forces. The one aspect of the exercise that never changes is the 4440th Tactical Fighter Training Group who fly their Soviet-colored F-5s. Once a year a Green Flag exercise is held in conjunction with Red Flag.

Silver Flag

This is designed for combat support units to operate in a hostile environment. They are set a variety of combat problems with which they might be tasked in a combat or emergency situation.

Langley AFB, became TAC's headquarters in May 1946 and is also home to TAC's First Air Force. Its commander is also head of the CONUS North American Aerospace Defense Region of NORAD. The First AF is made up of four air divisions in CONUS, plus Air Forces Iceland, the USAF Air Defense Weapons Center at Tyndall AFB, the 4700th Air Defense Squadron, the 4702nd Computer Services Squadron and the 4722nd Support Squadron in Canada.

The 24th Air Division was the last regular unit to fly the F-106 and these were retired during 1987. Other aircraft in the First include F-4C/Ds, F-15s and F-16s. The First Air Force maintains the Air Forces Iceland at Keflavik Naval Station. Its F-15s fly valuable interceptor missions along the Arctic Circle. As one of its

Above: F-15s of the 58th TFS/33rd TFW on deployment to West Germany. TAC units regularly deploy to areas that they would be called upon to defend during a war.

Above right: Air Force combat support force troops are taught to survive in combat environments during Silver Flag exercises.

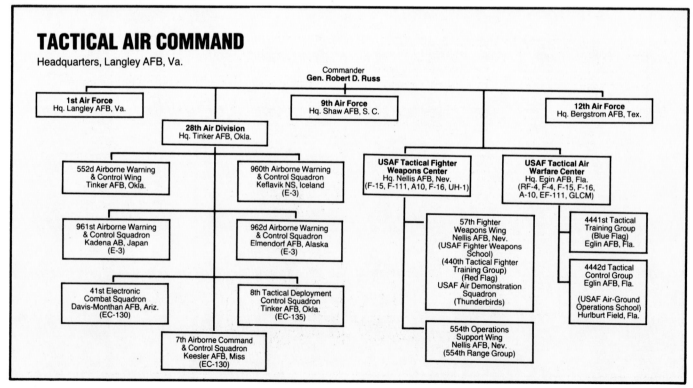

TACTICAL AIR COMMAND

Headquarters, Langley AFB, Va.

Commander
Gen. Robert D. Russ

1st Air Force
Hq. Langley AFB, Va.

9th Air Force
Hq. Shaw AFB, S. C.

12th Air Force
Hq. Bergstrom AFB, Tex.

28th Air Division
Hq. Tinker AFB, Okla.

USAF Tactical Fighter Weapons Center
Hq. Nellis AFB, Nev.
(F-15, F-111, A10, F-16, UH-1)

USAF Tactical Air Warfare Center
Hq. Egin AFB, Fla.
(RF-4, F-4, F-15, F-16, A-10, EF-111, GLCM)

552d Airborne Warning & Control Wing
Tinker AFB, Okla.

960th Airborne Warning & Control Squadron
Keflavik NS, Iceland
(E-3)

57th Fighter Weapons Wing
Nellis AFB, Nev.
(USAF Fighter Weapons School)
(440th Tactical Fighter Training Group)
(Red Flag)
USAF Air Demonstration Squadron
(Thunderbirds)

4441st Tactical Training Group
(Blue Flag)
Eglin AFB, Fla.

961st Airborne Warning & Control Squadron
Kadena AB, Japan
(E-3)

962d Airborne Warning & Control Squadron
Elmendorf AFB, Alaska
(E-3)

4442d Tactical Control Group
Eglin AFB, Fla.

(USAF Air-Ground Operations School)
Hurlburt Field, Fla.

41st Electronic Combat Squadron
Davis-Monthan AFB, Ariz.
(EC-130)

8th Tactical Deployment Control Squadron
Tinker AFB, Okla.
(EC-135)

554th Operations Support Wing
Nellis AFB, Nev.
(554th Range Group)

7th Airborne Command & Control Squadron
Keesler AFB, Miss.
(EC-130)

FIRST AIR FORCE (TAC)

Headquarters, Langley AFB, Va.

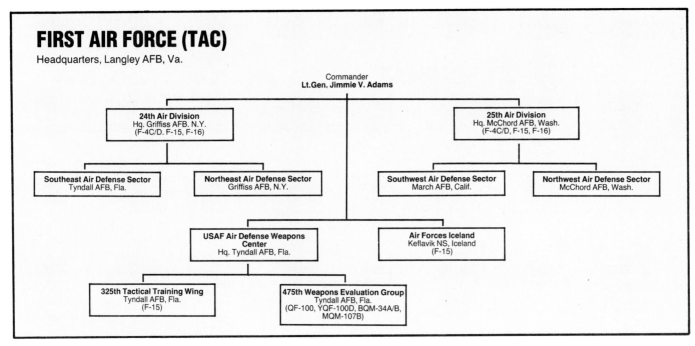

Commander
Lt.Gen. Jimmie V. Adams

24th Air Division
Hq. Griffiss AFB. N.Y.
(F-4C/D. F-15, F-16)

25th Air Division
Hq. McChord AFB, Wash.
(F-4C/D, F-15, F-16)

Southeast Air Defense Sector
Tyndall AFB, Fla.

Northeast Air Defense Sector
Griffiss AFB, N.Y.

Southwest Air Defense Sector
March AFB, Calif.

Northwest Air Defense Sector
McChord AFB, Wash.

USAF Air Defense Weapons Center
Hq. Tyndall AFB, Fla.

Air Forces Iceland
Keflavik NS, Iceland
(F-15)

325th Tactical Training Wing
Tyndall AFB, Fla.
(F-15)

475th Weapons Evaluation Group
Tyndall AFB, Fla.
(QF-100, YQF-100D, BQM-34A/B, MQM-107B)

NINTH AIR FORCE (TAC)

Headquarters, Shaw AFB, S.C.

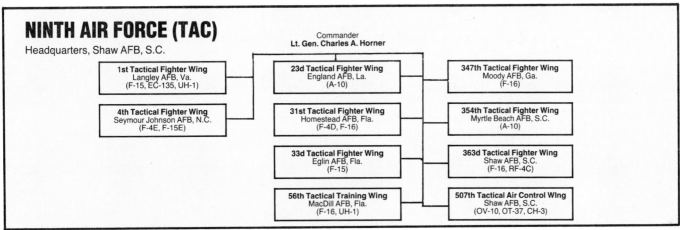

Commander
Lt. Gen. Charles A. Horner

1st Tactical Fighter Wing
Langley AFB, Va.
(F-15, EC-135, UH-1)

23d Tactical Fighter Wing
England AFB, La.
(A-10)

347th Tactical Fighter Wing
Moody AFB, Ga.
(F-16)

4th Tactical Fighter Wing
Seymour Johnson AFB, N.C.
(F-4E, F-15E)

31st Tactical Fighter Wing
Homestead AFB, Fla.
(F-4D, F-16)

354th Tactical Fighter Wing
Myrtle Beach AFB, S.C.
(A-10)

33d Tactical Fighter Wing
Eglin AFB, Fla.
(F-15)

363d Tactical Fighter Wing
Shaw AFB, S.C.
(F-16, RF-4C)

56th Tactical Training Wing
MacDill AFB, Fla.
(F-16, UH-1)

507th Tactical Air Control Wing
Shaw AFB, S.C.
(OV-10, OT-37, CH-3)

TWELFTH AIR FORCE (TAC)

Headquarters, Bergstrom AFB, Tex.

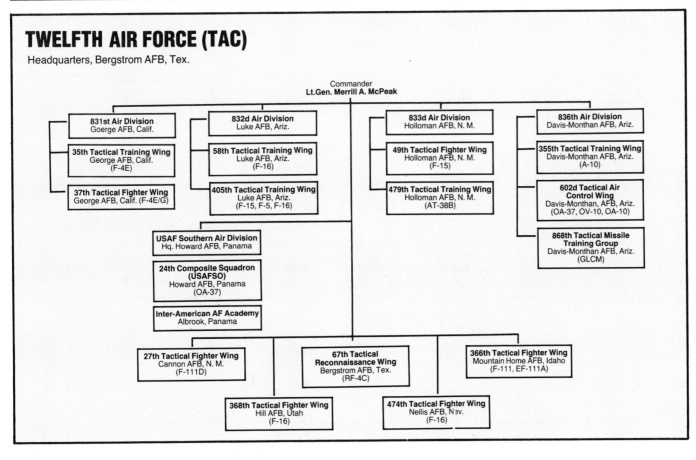

Commander
Lt.Gen. Merrill A. McPeak

831st Air Division
Goerge AFB, Calif.

832d Air Division
Luke AFB, Ariz.

833d Air Division
Holloman AFB, N. M.

836th Air Division
Davis-Monthan AFB, Ariz.

35th Tactical Training Wing
George AFB, Calif.
(F-4E)

58th Tactical Training Wing
Luke AFB, Ariz.
(F-16)

49th Tactical Fighter Wing
Holloman AFB, N. M.
(F-15)

355th Tactical Training Wing
Davis-Monthan AFB, Ariz.
(A-10)

37th Tactical Fighter Wing
George AFB, Calif. (F-4E/G)

405th Tactical Training Wing
Luke AFB, Ariz.
(F-15, F-5, F-16)

479th Tactical Training Wing
Holloman AFB, N. M.
(AT-38B)

602d Tactical Air Control Wing
Davis-Monthan, AFB, Ariz.
(OA-37, OV-10, OA-10)

USAF Southern Air Division
Hq. Howard AFB, Panama

868th Tactical Missile Training Group
Davis-Monthan AFB, Ariz.
(GLCM)

24th Composite Squadron (USAFSO)
Howard AFB, Panama
(OA-37)

Inter-American AF Academy
Albrook, Panama

27th Tactical Fighter Wing
Cannon AFB, N. M.
(F-111D)

67th Tactical Reconnaissance Wing
Bergstrom AFB, Tex.
(RF-4C)

366th Tactical Fighter Wing
Mountain Home AFB, Idaho
(F-111, EF-111A)

368th Tactical Fighter Wing
Hill AFB, Utah
(F-16)

474th Tactical Fighter Wing
Nellis AFB, Nev.
(F-16)

An F–15 of the 48th Fighter Interceptor Squadron at Langley AFB, Virginia. Langley is also Headquarters, Tactical Air Command.

command and control and as a jamming platform against enemy C3 networks. It also supervises the EC-135s operated by the 8th Tactical Deployment Squadron. These aircraft are using as flying command posts and are used to provide assistance for overseas deployments of tactical fighters.

The Ninth Air Force with its headquarters at Shaw AFB operates a variety of fighter and attack aircraft. These include: A-10s, flown by the 23rd and 354th Tactical Fighter Wings; F-4s, flown by the 4th, 31st and 347th TFWs; F-15s, flown by the 1st and 33rd TFWs; and F-16s, flown by the 31st, 347th and 363rd TFWs. The 363rd also operates the RF-4C reconnaissance aircraft. The largest of TAC's Air Forces is the Twelfth which has its HQ at Bergstrom AFB. It has training wings dedicated to each of USAF's front-line fighters and attack aircraft, plus the 868th Tactical Missile Training Group at Davis-Monthan which trains GLCM crews. The USAF Southern Air Division (USAFSO) based at Howard AFB in

contributions to NORAD, the 4700th Air Defense Squadron operates the DEW Line radar sites. Also contained in the First AF is the USAF Air Defense Weapons Center (USAFADWC) located at Tyndall AFB, Florida. Its role is to train aircrews and weapons controllers, develop air defense tactics and it also

manages all CONUS USAF drone aerial target operations.

The 28th Air Division oversees TAC's fleet of E-3 AWACS which operate over mainland America, Alaska, Iceland and Japan. It also has a detachment in Saudi Arabia in support of Saudi E-3s, and it operates EC-130s for airborne battlefield

An Aggressor pilot reviews the last combat mission flown with ACMI equipment. The ACMI range allows pilots to get a clear and accurate account of an air-to-air combat. A sensor on each of the aircraft transmits all relevant information on aircraft status to ground receivers.

Insert: A computer-generated image produced by the ACMI at Nellis AFB.

Panama provides air defense for the Panama Canal. The Division also provides training facilities for South American air forces.

TAC also has two Weapons Centers. The USAF Tactical Fighter Weapons Center (USAFTFWC) at Nellis AFB is concerned with advanced training and developing new tactical air combat concepts, the doctrine of air warfare and the testing of new weapons systems. It is host unit for Red Flag exercises and is also home of the USAF Air Demonstration Squadron (The Thunderbirds). The USAF Tactical Air Warfare Center (USAFTAWC) at Eglin AFB works on similar lines to USAFTWC but is concerned with the electronic battlefield. It also organizes the Green Flag program of exercises.

UNITED STATES AIR FORCE ACADEMY

"We will not lie, steal, or cheat, nor tolerate among us anyone who does."

The Cadet Honor Code

Entry to the Air Force Academy is restricted to men and women who fulfill five specific eligibility requirements. They

1. must be a citizen of the United States
2. must be of good moral character
3. must have attained the age of 17 years and must not have passed the age of 22 years as of 1 July of the year admitted to the academy
4. must be unmarried and have no dependent children. Any Air Force Cadet who marries will be discharged from the academy
5. must be in good physical condition.

Created by Act of Congress and signed into law by President Dwight D. Eisenhower on 1 April 1954, the United States Air Force Academy is required "to provide instruction and experience to all cadets so they graduate with the knowledge and character essential to leadership and the motivation to become career officers in the US Air Force."

The first 306 cadets started their course in July 1955 in temporary quarters at Lowry AFB, Denver. Just

Cadets of the Air Force Academy pass in Review Order at the annual passing-out parade.

The magnificent chapel at the Academy.

over three years later in August 1958 they were able to move into the new purpose-built Academy at Colorado Springs. The Academy, which is situated at the foot of the Rampart Range of the Rockies, covers 7,326 hectares (18,000 acres) and is considered by many to be the most beautiful of all the Air Force installations. The first class of the Academy graduated in May 1959 with 207 cadets having completed the course.

It soon became clear that there was a need to raise the number of students from 2,500 and in 1964 President Johnson authorized an increase in student numbers to 4,417. In October 1975 President Ford signed legislation allowing women to enter America's military academies, and the following

June the first female cadets entered the Academy.

Cadets undertake a four-year course which is divided into academics, military training and moral and spiritual areas. On completion they will leave the Academy with a Bachelor of Science degree and they have to commit themselves to serving in the Air Force for at least five years.

Students are expected to take part in a wide range of physical activities. To take part in any intercollegiate competition, cadets have to keep up their academic work and have to score at least seventy per cent in each of their academic studies. The work is long and hard but the rewards are large for those men and women who complete the course in the Air Force.

USAF HISTORICAL RESEARCH CENTER

■

Located at Maxwell AFB, Alabama, the Center was formed during World War II as the repository for all historical documents relating to the AAF and then the USAF. It was originally formed in Washington but was moved to Maxwell in 1949 as storage became a major problem. In 1984 the collection contained some 45,000,000 pages of Air Force-related material, and by 1988 this figure had risen to some 60,000,000 pages so that it is by far the largest collection of Air Force artefacts in the world.

It is divided into four branches. The Reference Division deals with documents and microfilm, produces bibliographies, collects and collates personnel records and papers. It also has the responsibility for declassification of Air Force records. The Research Division issues books and papers relating to Air Force history. It is also responsible for maintaining the lineage and honors of all Air Force units and their predecessors. It maintains all records relating to seals emblems and flags of the Air Force. It has the final say in determining aerial victory credits. The Department of Oral History has built up a unique collection of oral recordings of historical interviews. The Technical Services has the mammoth task of keeping track of the collection and microfilming it. It uses the Inferential Retrieval Index System (IRIS) for automated data processing. It started to place material in computer files in 1983 and that year the system became operational, becoming fully accessible in 1987.

Today more than 85 per cent of the pre 1955 material has been declassified and is available for study at the Center, the National Archives and Record Administration, Washington, DC and across the river at Bolling AFB at the Office of Air Force History. The work still goes on to bring the collection up to date, but as long as there is an Air Force its work will never be finished.

Two F–16s of the 401st TFW based at Torrejon AB fly high over the bullring in Madrid. The 401st is due to leave Spain by 1991 and will take up residence in Italy.

UNITED STATES AIR FORCES IN EUROPE

▲

"The Tip of the Sword"
Organized as a Major Command since the formation of the Air Force in 1947, the United States Air Forces in Europe is an integrated part of NATO's Allied Air Forces Central Europe (AAFCE). Their aircraft operate from England in the west to their outpost behind the Iron Curtain at Berlin's Tempelhof Central Airport, and from the Arctic Circle down to the Mediterranean.

USAFE with its HQ at Ramstein AB, West Germany, has a total of 31 combat squadrons, and is divided into three separate Air Forces, the Third, Sixteenth and Seventeenth plus the 7455th Tactical Intelligence Wing and the 7350th Air Base Group at Tempelhof Airport in Berlin. It has a total of 63,000 military personnel and 11,000 civilians. This would be increased greatly in time of conflict. It is the second largest tactical

Command, beaten only by TAC. And in wartime this figure would change as TAC would supply large numbers of men and aircraft who are assigned to Europe. They would take up their places at NATO bases designated as Collocated Operating Bases (COBs).

The 3rd Air Force, with its HQ at Mildenhall, England, provides most of USAFE's support activities. Mildenhall is also the dedicated gateway to the United Kingdom. The 3rd Air Force underwent a major change around during 1988. RAF Alconbury lost the 527th Aggressor Squadron and their F-5s and gained two A-10 squadrons, the 509th and 511th TFS. The 527th moved to RAF Bentwaters and traded in their F-5s for

A C–130 makes a tactical landing on a German autobahn at Alhorn. The C–130's ability to land in short distances provides a valuable asset in carrying out resupply missions on the central front.

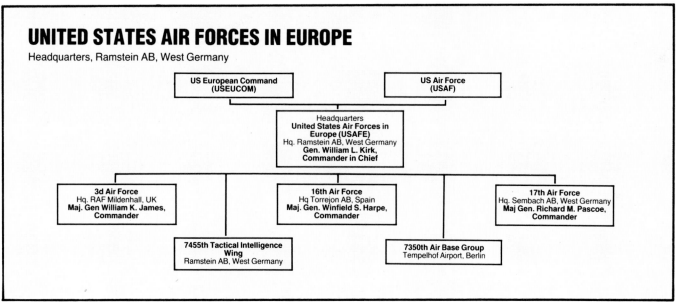

UNITED STATES AIR FORCES IN EUROPE
Headquarters, Ramstein AB, West Germany

US European Command (USEUCOM)

US Air Force (USAF)

Headquarters
United States Air Forces in Europe (USAFE)
Hq. Ramstein AB, West Germany
Gen. William L. Kirk, Commander in Chief

3d Air Force
Hq. RAF Mildenhall, UK
Maj. Gen William K. James, Commander

16th Air Force
Hq Torrejon AB, Spain
Maj. Gen. Winfield S. Harpe, Commander

17th Air Force
Hq. Sembach AB, West Germany
Maj Gen. Richard M. Pascoe, Commander

7455th Tactical Intelligence Wing
Ramstein AB, West Germany

7350th Air Base Group
Tempelhof Airport, Berlin

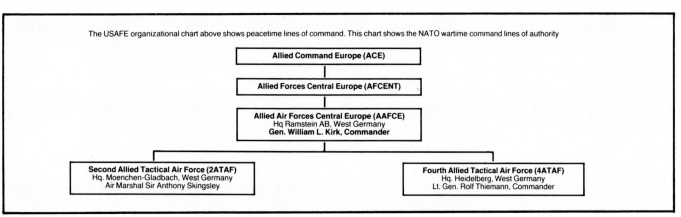

The USAFE organizational chart above shows peacetime lines of command. This chart shows the NATO wartime command lines of authority

Allied Command Europe (ACE)

Allied Forces Central Europe (AFCENT)

Allied Air Forces Central Europe (AAFCE)
Hq Ramstein AB, West Germany
Gen. William L. Kirk, Commander

Second Allied Tactical Air Force (2ATAF)
Hq. Moenchen-Gladbach, West Germany
Air Marshal Sir Anthony Skingsley

Fourth Allied Tactical Air Force (4ATAF)
Hq. Heidelberg, West Germany
Lt. Gen. Rolf Thiemann, Commander

The Hunter-Killer team of F–4G and F–16C operated by the 52nd Tactical Fighter Wing based at Spangdahlem.

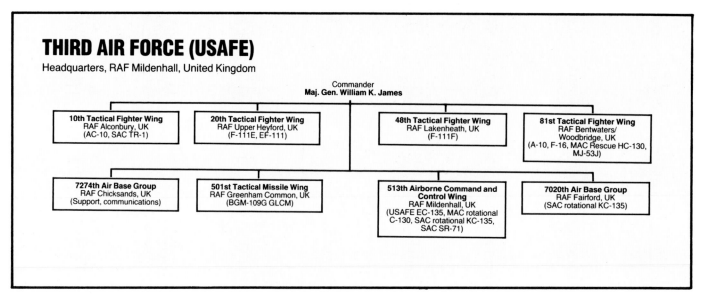

THIRD AIR FORCE (USAFE)

Headquarters, RAF Mildenhall, United Kingdom

Commander
Maj. Gen. William K. James

10th Tactical Fighter Wing
RAF Alconbury, UK
(AC-10, SAC TR-1)

20th Tactical Fighter Wing
RAF Upper Heyford, UK
(F-111E, EF-111)

48th Tactical Fighter Wing
RAF Lakenheath, UK
(F-111F)

81st Tactical Fighter Wing
RAF Bentwaters/
Woodbridge, UK
(A-10, F-16, MAC Rescue HC-130,
MJ-53J)

7274th Air Base Group
RAF Chicksands, UK
(Support, communications)

501st Tactical Missile Wing
RAF Greenham Common, UK
(BGM-109G GLCM)

**513th Airborne Command and
Control Wing**
RAF Mildenhall, UK
(USAFE EC-135, MAC rotational
C-130, SAC rotational KC-135,
SAC SR-71)

7020th Air Base Group
RAF Fairford, UK
(SAC rotational KC-135)

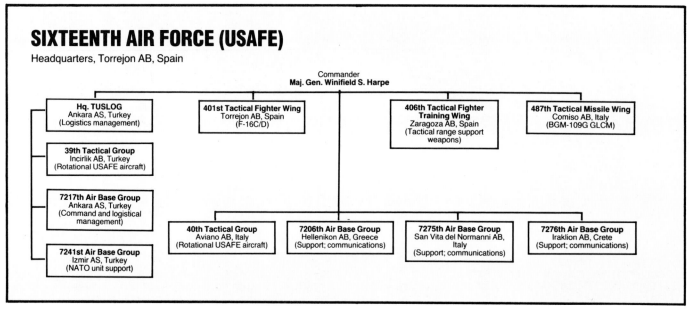

SIXTEENTH AIR FORCE (USAFE)

Headquarters, Torrejon AB, Spain

Commander
Maj. Gen. Winifield S. Harpe

Hq. TUSLOG
Ankara AS, Turkey
(Logistics management)

401st Tactical Fighter Wing
Torrejon AB, Spain
(F-16C/D)

**406th Tactical Fighter
Training Wing**
Zaragoza AB, Spain
(Tactical range support
weapons)

487th Tactical Missile Wing
Comiso AB, Italy
(BGM-109G GLCM)

39th Tactical Group
Incirlik AB, Turkey
(Rotational USAFE aircraft)

7217th Air Base Group
Ankara AS, Turkey
(Command and logistical
management)

7241st Air Base Group
Izmir AS, Turkey
(NATO unit support)

40th Tactical Group
Aviano AB, Italy
(Rotational USAFE aircraft)

7206th Air Base Group
Hellenikon AB, Greece
(Support; communications)

7275th Air Base Group
San Vita del Normanni AB,
Italy
(Support; communications)

7276th Air Base Group
Iraklion AB, Crete
(Support; communications)

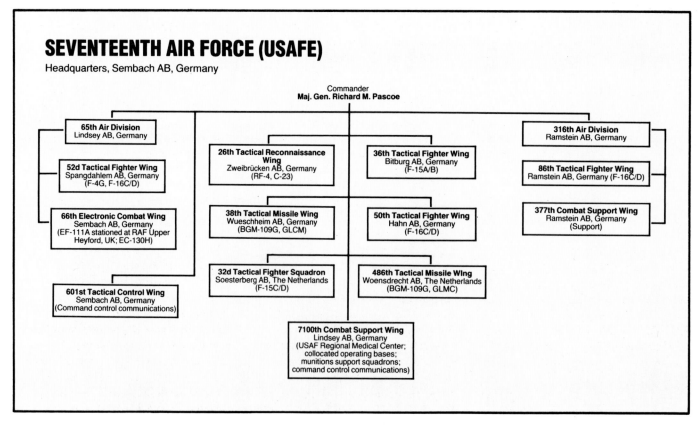

SEVENTEENTH AIR FORCE (USAFE)

Headquarters, Sembach AB, Germany

Commander
Maj. Gen. Richard M. Pascoe

65th Air Division
Lindsey AB, Germany

52d Tactical Fighter Wing
Spangdahlem AB, Germany
(F-4G, F-16C/D)

66th Electronic Combat Wing
Sembach AB, Germany
(EF-111A stationed at RAF Upper
Heyford, UK; EC-130H)

601st Tactical Control Wing
Sembach AB, Germany
(Command control communications)

**26th Tactical Reconnaissance
Wing**
Zweibrücken AB, Germany
(RF-4, C-23)

36th Tactical Fighter Wing
Bitburg AB, Germany
(F-15A/B)

38th Tactical Missile Wing
Wueschheim AB, Germany
(BGM-109G, GLCM)

50th Tactical Fighter Wing
Hahn AB, Germany
(F-16C/D)

32d Tactical Fighter Squadron
Soesterberg AB, The Netherlands
(F-15C/D)

486th Tactical Missile Wing
Woensdrecht AB, The Netherlands
(BGM-109G, GLMC)

316th Air Division
Ramstein AB, Germany

86th Tactical Fighter Wing
Ramstein AB, Germany (F-16C/D)

377th Combat Support Wing
Ramstein AB, Germany
(Support)

7100th Combat Support Wing
Lindsey AB, Germany
(USAF Regional Medical Center;
collocated operating bases;
munitions support squadrons;
command control communications)

F-16s. The unit regularly tours NATO Air Bases conducting dissimilar air combat exercises. SAC's 17th RW TR-1s are based at RAF Alconbury. These aircraft are not under USAFE command but do support USAFE requirements.

The 3rd Air Force also operates two wings of F-111s: the F-111Es of the 20th Tactical Fighter Wing at RAF Upper Heyford and the F-111Fs of the 48th TFW at RAF Lakenheath. It is possible that USAFE may receive more F-111s from SAC during the early 1990's and that they will be based in the United Kingdom.

The 21st Special Operations Squadron was formed at RAF Woodbridge in the summer of 1988. The EF-111s based at Upper Heyford are tasked with electronic warfare missions in support of USAFE's F-111s and are in fact part of the Seventeenth Air Forces, 66th Electronic Combat Wing. It was felt that it was sensible to have these complex aircraft based in England so that maintenance could be run side by side with the other F-111s. With funding supplied by NATO and USAFE, two avionics maintenance facilities have been installed at RAF Lakenheath, Suffolk and RAF Upper Heyford, Oxfordshire.

These hardened facilities have been built to withstand bomb blast and chemical warfare agents. USAFE air bases in England are protected by Rapier point air defense missiles operated by the RAF Regiment. The 303rd and 501st Tactical Missile Wings operate the GLCM and will be disbanned after the cruise missiles are destroyed following the INF agreement.

USAFE will lose its six BGM-109G ground-launched cruise missile units over the next three years following the signing of the Intermediate Nuclear Forces treaty. The installation of these missiles has had a profound effect on the Soviets, and it is this which brought them to the conference table, and the Russians have started to remove their SS-20s even before the Treaty has been ratified. The loss of the GLCMs has increased the need of NATO's, including USAFE's, nuclear-capable, tactical aircraft to provide an increased deterrent capability.

The Sixteenth Air Force, with its HQ at Torrejon AB, Spain, is tasked with the defense of NATO's southern flank and also operates support, surveillance and communications bases. The 487th Tactical Missile Wing will be disbanded as their GLCM's are scrapped. The Spanish Government decided in 1987 that USAFE could no longer operate its 401st Tactical Fighter Wing from Torrejon Air Base and the wing will move to a new and as yet undecided base by 1989. It was felt that Italy was the most likely country to take the 401st TFWs F-16s. There is also doubt over bases in both Turkey and Greece.

The strongest of the three Air Forces in Europe is the Seventeenth AF, which has its HQ at Sembach AB, West Germany. Over the last few years, USAFE's fighters have been going through a major upgrading program. The Command's last F16A/Bs operated by the 50th Tactical Fighter Wing will be replaced by the F-16C/D during FY 1988. During 1987 the F-15s of the 36th Tactical Fighter Wing and the 32nd TFS began to undergo the Multinational Staged Improvement Program (MSIP). The retrofit will provide improved avionics. The 52nd Tactical Fighter Wing at Spangdahlem has converted from the F-4E to the F-16C/D to support its Wild Weasel F-4Gs.

An aircraft unique to USAFE is the Shorts C-23 which is operated by the MAC's 10th Military Airlift Squadron based at Zweibrucken AB. They are part of the European Distribution System Aircraft program and have meant that urgently needed supplies can be quickly moved around the Command. The West Germans man and operate US-owned Patriot and Roland air defense missile units to protect USAFE bases in Germany.

BASES

Preceding pages: KC–10As of the 32nd ARS, in the pre-dawn light at Barksdale AFB.

Right: Belching a mass of smoke, a KC–135 of the 43rd Bombardment Wing takes off from Anderson AFB, Guam.

ADMIRAL BYRD

Admiral Richard E. Byrd International Airport
Richmond
Virginia 23150
USA

Phone:
(804) 222-8884

Autovon:
274-8210

Command:
Air National Guard

Named after:
Admiral Byrd, a famous Arctic and Antarctic explorer

Acreage:
ANG area 143

Personnel:
1,085 military personnel, 226 civilians

Units:
192nd Tactical Fighter Gp; 149th Tactical Fighter Sqdn (ANG)

Operational Aircraft:
A-7D/K   (VA)

ALLEN C. THOMPSON

Allen C. Thompson Field
Jackson
Mississippi 39208–0810
USA

Phone:
(601) 939-3633

Autovon:
731-9310

Command:
Air National Guard

Acreage:
ANG Area 84

Personnel:
1,193 military personnel, 213 civilians

Units:
172nd Tactical Airlift Gp (ANG);
183rd Military Airlift Sqdn (ANG)

Operational Aircraft:
C-141B

ALTUS

Altus AFB
Oklahoma 73523-5000
USA

Phone:
(405) 482-8100

Autovon:
866-1110

Command:
Military Airlift Command

Date est:
January 1943, inactivated May 1945, reactivated Jan. 1953

Acreage:
3,582 plus 818 acres leased

Personnel:
3,552 military personnel, 957 civilians

Units:
443rd Military Airlift Wing (Training); 340th Air Refueling Wing (SAC) 2002nd Communications Sqdn (AFCC); Field Training Det. 403; 71st Flying Training Wing OLK ACE Det (ATC); Det 4, 17th Weather Sqdn; Det 3, 1600th Management Engineering Sqdn; Det 4, 1365th Audiovisual Sqdn

Operational Aircraft:
443rd Military Airlift Wing
C5A/B   56th MATS
C141B   57th MATS

340th Air Refueling Wing
KC-135A   11th ARS
             340th ARS

Notes:
Approx. 400–500 TDY students in training each month

ANDERSEN

Andersen AFB
Guam
APO San Francisco 96334–500

Phone:
(671) 366-2921

Autovon:
322-1110

Command:
Strategic Air Command

Named after:
Brigadier General James Roy Andersen who was lost at sea when his plane crashed after a flight from Guam in 1945

Units:
HQ 3rd Air Div; 43rd Bombardment Wing; 54th Weather Reconnaissance Sqdn (MAC); 605th Military Airlift Support Sqdn (MAC); 27th Communications Sqdn (AFCC); Det 11, 2nd Aircraft Delivery Gp (TAC)

Operational Aircraft:
B-52G   60th BS

54th Weather Reconnaissance Sqdn
WC-130E/H

Notes:
The 3rd Air Div, 15th Air Force (SAC), is responsible for SAC operations in the Pacific area to the west of the International Date Line

ANDREWS

Andrews AFB
Maryland 20331-5000
USA

Phone:
(301) 981-9111

Autovon:
858-1110

Command:
Military Airlift Command

Date est:
1942

Named after:
Lt. Gen. Frank M. Andrews who was killed in an air crash during 1943 in Iceland

Acreage:
4,982

Personnel:
8,958 military personnel, 2,620 civilians

Units:
HQ Air Force Systems Command; 1776th Air Base Wing; 89th Military Airlift Wing; 113th Tactical Fighter Wing (ANG); 459th Military Airlift Wing (AFRES); 2045th Communications Group (AFCC); Det 11, 1361st Audiovisual Sqdn

Operational Aircraft:
756th Military Airlift Sqdn (AFRES) C-141B

121st Tactical Fighter Sqdn (ANG) F-4D   (DC)

HQ Air National Guard Bureau (Eastern Division)
C-22B
T-33A
CT-39A

89th Military Airlift Wing (MAC)
C-9C	C-137B/C VC-25A
C-12A	C-140B
C-20A/B	UH-1N
C-135B/C	CH-3E

1402nd Military Airlift Sqdn (MAC)
C-12F, C-21A Det 1 Langley AFB
C-21A Det 3 Maxwell AFB, Det 4

ARNOLD

Arnold AFB
Tennessee 37389
USA

Phone:
(615) 455-2611

Autovon:
882-1520

Command:
Air Force Systems Command

Date est:
Jan. 1950

Named after:
General H.H. "Hap" Arnold who was Chief of the AAF during WWII

Acreage:
40,118

Personnel:
186 military personnel, 220 civilians plus 3,600 contractors personnel

Units:
Arnold Engineering Development Center (AEDC)

Operational Aircraft:
Various

Notes:
The home of the Western world's largest collection of wind tunnels, simulation systems plus jet and rocket test beds. It supports USAF's and other government agencies' research into new aerospace technologies.

ATLANTIC CITY

Atlantic City Municipal Airport
New Jersey 0 8405-5199
USA

Phone:
(609) 645-6000

Autovon:
445-6000

Command:
Air National Guard

Acreage:
ANG area 286

Personnel:
926 military personnel, 316 civilians

Units:
177th Fighter Interceptor Gp (ANG);
119th Fighter Interceptor Sqdn (ANG)

Operational Aircraft:
F-16A/B

Left: The Department of Defense conducting a Farewell Review and Awards Ceremony in honor of President and Mrs. Ronald Reagan in the new hanger at Andrews AFB on 12 January 1989.

Below: Atlantic City AB, home for many years of the F–106s operated by the 177th Interceptor Group.

Bottom: The old and the new take off from Atlantic City. The unit has replaced its F–106s for F–16s. All F–106s were finally withdrawn from service in 1988.

AVIANO

Aviano AB
Italy
APO New York 09292-5000

Phone:
(434) 651141

Autovon:
632-1110

Command:
United States Air Forces in Europe

Units:
40th Tactical Group, USAFE; 2387th
Communications Group, AFCC

BAER

Baer Field
Fort Wayne Municipal Airport
Indiana 46809-5000
USA

Phone:
(219) 478-3210

A technician studies a plot from the AN/FPS–118, Over the Horizon, Backscatter radar at Bangor ANGB. The radar is divided into three components with the transmitter situated near Moscow, Maine, the receiver near Columbia Falls, Maine and the control center at Bangor. The radar can detect aircraft at ranges up to ten times that of conventional radars.

Autovon:
786-1210

Command:
Air National Guard

Acreage:
ANG area 87

Personnel:
1,381 military personnel, 269 civilians

Units:
122nd Tactical Fighter Wing (ANG);
163rd Tactical Fighter Sqdn (ANG)

Operational Aircraft:
F-4E   163rd TFS   (FW)
C-131D

BANGOR

Bangor International Airport
Maine 04401-3099
USA

Phone:
(207) 947-0571

Autovon:
476-6210

Command:
Air National Guard

Acreage:
ANG area 299

Personnel:
1,024 military personnel, 273 civilians

Units:
101st Air Refueling Wing (ANG);
132nd Air Refueling Sqdn (ANG);
776th Radar Sqdn (TAC)

Operational Aircraft:
KC-135E 132nd AFS

BARKSDALE

Barksdale AFB
Louisiana 71110-5000
USA

Phone:
(318) 456-2252

Autovon:
781-1110

Command:
Strategic Air Command

Date est:
Feb. 1933

Named after:
Lt. Eugene H. Barksdale a WWI flyer,
who was killed in an air crash in
August 1926

Acreage:
22,000

Personnel:
7,000 military personnel, 1,207
civilians

Units:
HQ 8th Air Force; 2nd BW; 1st
Combat Evaluation Gp; 46th
Communications Gp RED HORSE
(AFCC); Det 1, 307th Civil
Engineering Sqdn (AFRES); Det 1,
14th FTW (ATC); 26th Weather Sqdn
(MAC); Det 3, 1401st Military Airlift
Sqdn (MAC); 49th Test Sqdn; 3097th
Aviation Depot Sqdn (AFLC); Det 2,
4200th Test Sqdn; Det 5, 3904th
Management Engineering Sqdn;
3903rd School Sqdn (SAC NCO
Academy); 745th Air Force Band
Sqdn; 78th Air Refueling Sqdn
(AFRES); 917th TF Gp (AFRES); 8th
Air Force Museum

Covered by protective plastic bags, the crew of a B–52 prepare to board their aircraft at Barksdale.

Above: The 2nd Bomb Wing's command post at Barksdale AB.

Above right: The 2nd Bomb Wing's B–52s at their dispersal sites.

Right: In full NBC equipment maintenance crews prepare the Wing's bombers for take-off.

Below: B–52s taxi out during a base readiness inspection.

Operational Aircraft:
2nd Bombardment Wing (SAC)

B-52G	62nd BS
	596th BS
KC-10A	32nd ARS
KC-135A	71st ARS

47th Tactical Fighter Sqdn (AFRES)

A-10A	(BD)

46th Tactical Fighter Sqdn (AFRES)

A-10A	(BD)

BARNES

Barnes Municipal Airport
Westfield
Massachusetts 01085
USA

Phone:
(413) 568-9151

Autovon:
636-1210/11

Command:
Air National Guard

Acreage:
133

Personnel:
1,028 military personnel, 199 civilians

Units:
131st Tactical Fighter Sqdn (ANG)

Operational Aircraft:

A-10A	(MA)

BEALE

Beale AFB
California 95903-5000
USA

Phone:
(916) 634-3000

Autovon:
368-1110

Command:
Strategic Air Command

Date est:
Apr. 1948

The crew of an SR–71 walk from their aircraft at Beale AFB following a training flight which will have taken them to the upper limits of the atmosphere.

Right: The pilot and Reconnaissance Systems Officer talk about the flight over coffee at Beale.

Below: In the early morning light an SR–71 Blackbird is prepared for a mission from Beale AFB, near Sacramento, California. Beale is home to the 9th Strategic Reconnaissance Wing. The Wing operates the world's most complex reconnaissance aircraft.

Named after:
General Edward Fizgerald Beale who prior to the American Civil War had been an Indian Agent in California. His main claim to fame was trying to introduce camels in the south west as pack animals. The experiment failed.

Acreage:
22,944

Personnel:
4,442 military personnel, 528 civilians

Units:
14th Air Division; 9th Strategic Reconnaissance Wing; 7th Missile Warning Sqdn (AFSPACECOM); 1883rd Communications Sqdn (AFCC)

Operational Aircraft:
9th Strategic Reconnaissance Wing (SAC)
SR-71A/B/C TR-1A T-38A U-2CT/R
KC-135Q   349th ARS
             350th ARS

BERGSTROM

Bergstrom AFB
Texas 78743-5000
USA

Phone:
(512) 479-4100

Autovon:
685-1100

Command:
Tactical Air Command

Date est:
Sep. 1942

Named after:
Capt. John A.E. Bergstrom who was
killed at Clark Field, Phillippines on 8
Dec. 1941

Acreage:
3,998

Personnel:
5,188 military personnel, 1,007
civilians

Units:
67th TRW; HQ 12th Air Force; HQ
10th Air Force (AFRES); 924th TFG
(AFRES); TAC NCO Academy West;
Det 8, 602nd TACW; Det 1, 4400th
Management Engineering Sqdn; Det
12, Tactical Commiunications Divn

Operational Aircraft:
67th Tactical Reconnaissance Wing
(TAC)
RF-4C	12th TRS	
	45th TRTS	
	62nd TRTS	
	91st TRS	(BA)

704th Tactical Fighter Sqdn (AFRES)
| F-4D | (TX) |

BITBURG

Bitburg AB
West Germany
APO New York 09132–5000

Phone:
6561-61113

Autovon:
453-1110

Three F–15s of the 36th Tactical
Fighter Wing based at Bitburg
AB, West Germany.

Command:
United States Air Forces in Europe

Date est:
1952

Units:
36th Tactical Fighter Wing (USAFE);
22nd Tactical Fighter Sqdn (USAFE);
53rd Tactical Fighter Sqdn (USAFE);
525th Tactical Fighter Sqdn (USAFE)

Operational Aircraft:
| F-15C/D | (BT) |

BLYTHEVILLE

Blytheville AFB
Arkansas 72315-5000
USA

Phone:
(501) 762-7000

Autovon:
721-1110

Command:
Strategic Air Command

Date est:
June 1942; inactivated Feb. 1947;
reactivated Aug. 1955

Acreage:
3,092

Active Personnel:
3,143 military personnel, 345 civilians

Units:
42nd Air Divn; 97th BW

Operational Aircraft:
97th Bombardment Wing (SAC)
| B-52G | 340th BS |
| KC-135A | 97th ARS |

BOLLING

Bolling AFB
Washington, DC. 20332-5000
USA

Phone:
(202) 545-6700

Autovon:
721-1110

Command:
Air Force District of Washington

Date est:
Oct. 1917

Named after:
Col. Raynal C. Bolling was killed
during WWI

Acreage:
604

Personnel:
2,800 military personnel, 1,000
civilians

Units:
AF District of Washington; 1100th Air
Base Group; USAF Honor Guard;
USAF Band; AFO of Scientific
Research (AFSC); AF Chief of
Chaplains; AF Surgeon General; AFO
of History; HQ AFO of Special
Investigations

Operational Aircraft:
None

BRADLEY

Bradley ANG Base
Bradley International Airport
Connecticut 06026-5000
USA

Phone:
(203) 623-8291

Autovon:
636-8310

Command:
Air National Guard

Named after:
Lt. Eugene M. Bradley who died in a
P-40 crash in Aug. 1941

Acreage:
ANG area 125

Personnel:
989 military personnel, 208 civilians

Units:
103rd Tactical Fighter Gp (ANG);
118th Tactical Fighter Sqdn (ANG)

Operational Aircraft:
A-10A
C-12F   (CT)

BROOKS

Brooks AFB
Texas 78235
USA

Phone:
(512) 536-1110

Autovon:
240-1110

Command:
Air Force Systems Command

Date est:
Dec. 1917

Named after:
Cadet Sidney J. Brooks, killed in 1917
on his final solo flight before he was
commissioned

Acreage:
1,310

Personnel:
1,576 military personnel, 1,063
civilians

Units:
Human Systems Divn; USAF School of
Aerospace Medicine; USAF
Occupational and Environmental Lab;
USAF Drug Testing Lab; USAF
Human Resource Lab; 6570th Air
Base Gp

BUCKLEY

Buckley ANGB
Colorado 880011-5000
USA

Phone:
(303) 366-5563

Autovon:
877-9011

Command:
Air National Guard

Date est:
1959 when ANG took over base from
US Navy

Named after:
Lt. John H. Buckley, a WWI pilot
killed in action in 1918

Acreage:
3,897

Personnel:
1,493 military personnel, 278 civilians

Units:
HQ Colorado Air National Guard;
140th Fighter Wing; 154th Tactical
Control Gp

Operational Aircraft:
120th Tactical Fighter Sqdn (ANG)
A-7D/K

HQ Air National Guard Bureau
(Western Divn)
T-34A

BURLINGTON

Burlington International Airport
Vermont 05401
USA

Phone:
(802) 658-0770

Autovon:
689-4310

Command:
Air National Guard

Acreage:
ANG area 241

Personnel:
1,095 military personnel, 238 civilians

Units:
158th Tactical Fighter Gp (ANG)
134th Tactical Fighter Sqdn (ANG)

Operational Aircraft:
F16A/B

CANNON

Cannon AFB,
New Mexico 88103-5000
USA

Phone:
(505) 784-3311

Autovon:
681-1110

Command:
Tactical Air Command

Date est:
Aug. 1942

Named After:
General John K. Cannon, one of
America's leaders in the development of
air power. He served as Commander of
Allied Air Forces in the Mediterranean
during the later stages of WWII

Acreage:
25,663

Personnel:
3,650 military personnel, 782 civilians

Units:
27th Tactical Fighter Wing

Operational Aircraft:
27th Tactical Fighter Wing (TAC)
F-111D   522nd TFS
              523rd TFS
              524th TFS

CAPITAL

Capital Airport
Springfield
Illinois 62707
USA

Phone:
(217) 753-8850

Autovon:
892-8210

Command:
Air National Guard

Acreage:
ANG area 91

Personnel:
1,117 military personnel, 264 civilians

Units:
138th Tactical Fighter Gp (ANG);
170th Tactical Fighter Sqdn (ANG);
219th Electronic Installation Sqdn

Operational Aircraft:
F-4D   170th TFS (SI)

CARSWELL

Carswell AFB
Texas 76127-5000
USA

Phone:
(817) 782-5000

Autovon:
739-1110

Command:
Strategic Air Command

Date est:
Aug. 1942

Named after:
Maj. Horace S. Carswell, a WWII B-24 pilot and posthumous recipient of the Medal of Honor

Acreage:
3,274

Personnel:
5,050 military personnel, 1,060 civilians

Units:
19th Air Divn; 7th BW (SAC); 301st Tactical Fighter Wing (AFRES)

Operational Aircraft:
7th Bombardment Wing (SAC)
B-52H   9th BS
               20th BS
KC-135A   7th ARS

457th Tactical Fighter Sqdn (AFRES)
F4D   (TH)

CASTLE

Castle AFB
California 95342-5000
USA

Phone:
(209) 726-2011

Autovon:
347-1110

Command:
Strategic Air Command

Date est:
Sep. 1941

Named after:
Brig. Gen. Frederick Castle, WWII Medal of Honor recipient

Acreage:
2,700

Personnel:
5,419 military personnel, 671 civilians

Units:
93rd BW; 84th FIT Squadron (TAC);
Det 1, 318th Fighter Interceptor Sqdn

Operational Aircraft:
93rd Bombardment Wing (SAC)
B-52G   328th BS
KC-135A   93rd ARS
               924th ARS

CHANUTE

Chanute AFB
Illinois 61868-5000
USA

Phone:
(217) 495-1110

Autovon:
862-1110

Command:
Air Training Command

Date est:
1 May 1917

Named after:
Octave Chanute, an early aviation engineer and glider pilot, who died in 1910

Acreage:
2,125

Personnel:
7,433 military personnel, 1,072 civilians

Units:
Chanute Technical Training Center

Operational Aircraft:
Chanute Technical Training Center (ATC) various

Notes:
The Center specializes in training missile and aircraft mechanics, and aerospace ground systems, life support, metallurgy and all aspects of weather-forecasting and equipment. It also provides training in fire protection and rescue.

BASE REALIGNMENTS AND CLOSURES
Report of the Defense Secretary's Commission December 1988

The Commission recommends Chanute Air Force Base for closure primarily due to reduced mission effectiveness caused by lower quality and limited availability of facilities, and because of excess capacity within the category. The net cost of closure and relocation will be paid back within three years. The Commission expects annual savings to be $68.7 million.

Chanute AFB is lower in military value than other technical-training centers because the facilities significantly detract from its mission effectiveness.

Chanute AFB is one of five Air Training Command Technical Training Centers providing specialized training for officers, airmen, and civilians of the Air Force, and for other Department of Defense agencies. Major training courses include fire fighting, aircraft and missile maintenance, and fuel contamination and inspection training. The base also prepares extension and career-development courses, specialty-training standards, and training manuals. In addition, Chanute provides on-the-job training advisory services and reviews field training courses.

Chanute AFB can be closed without degrading the overall capability of the Air Force to provide technical training. Shortcomings of this installation include a shortage of buildings for training and administration purposes, maintenance, and warehousing. The quality of life for assigned personnel is affected by a shortage of family housing units, bachelor housing, recreational amenities, and medical and dental facilities.

This closure will have no negative impact on the environment. The cleanup of hazardous materials and waste contamination at Chanute AFB is covered by the Defense Environmental Restoration Program.

Cleanup is independent of the closure. The movement of the units currently assigned to Chanute will not significantly alter the environmental situation at the gaining bases, since comparable training is presently conducted at those locations.

This closure will have moderate impact on local employment.

The Commission recommends the following relocations of major units and related support activities of the 3330th Technical Training Wing to existing technical training wings at Sheppard, Keesler, Lowry, and Goodfellow AFBs. Some examples of the types of training to be relocated are:

Sheppard AFB, Texas will absorb 52 courses including aircraft engine, propulsion, maintenance, and aircrew life-support training.

Keesler AFB, Mississippi will absorb 22 courses including avionics and weather-equipment maintenance, weather-satellite system, and photo-interpretation training.

Lowry AFB, Colorado will absorb 45 courses including missile support-equipment maintenance, intercontinental ballistic missile maintenance-officer, and cryogenic-operations training.

Goodfellow AFB, Texas will absorb 25 courses including fire fighting, fire truck operation and maintenance, and fuel inspection training.

These relocations will consolidate similar courses and improve training.

CHARLESTON

Charleston AFB
South Carolina 29404-5000
USA

Phone:
(803) 554-0230

Autovon:
583-0111

Command:
Military Airlift Command

Date est:
1941 inactivated Feb. 1946;
reactivated 1952

Acreage:
6,314

Personnel:
7,790 military personnel including AFRES, 1,378 civilians

Units:
437th Military Airlift Wing; 315th Military Airlift Wing (AFRES Assoc.); 1968th Communications Sqdn; Det 1 107th Fighter Interceptor Sqdn (TAC); Det 7, 1361st Audiovisual Sqdn

Operational Aircraft:
437th Military Airlift Wing (MAC)
C-141B   3rd MAS
         4th MAS
         76th MAS

CHEYENNE MOUNTAIN

Cheyenne Mountain Complex
Colorado 80914-5515
USA

Phone:
(719) 554-7321

Autovon:
692-7011

Command:
Air Force Space Command

Date est:
1966

Acreage:
4.5; most of the area is within the mountain itself

Personnel:
1,400 plus, including USAF, ARMY, NAVY, Canadian Armed Forces and civilians

Units:
3rd Space Support Wing (AFSPACECOM); Cheyenne Mountain Support Gp; North American Aerospace Defense Command (NORAD) Command Post; US Space Command operations centres

Top right: Captain Gaetno Degiola briefs members of the 60th Bomber Squadron while the squadron visited Clark AB.

Right: A 44th TFS pilot shows a maneuver with his hands during a discussion with members of the 60th Bomber Squadron.

CHEYENNE MUNICIPAL

Cheyenne Municipal Airport
Wyoming 82001
USA

Phone:
(719) 554-7321

Autovon:
692-7011

Command:
Air National Guard

Acreage:
ANG area 67

Personnel:
1,017 military personnel, 179 civilians

Units:
153rd Tactical Airlift Gp; 187th Tactical Airlift Sqdn

Operational Aircraft:
C-130B,   187th TAS

CHICAGO O'HARE

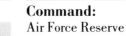

Chicago O'Hare International Airport
O'Hare Air Reserve Forces Facility
Chicago
Illinois 60666
USA

Phone:
(312) 694-6000

Autovon:
930-1110

Command:
Air Force Reserve

Date Est:
Apr. 1946

Named after:
Lt. Commander Edward H. "Butch" O'Hare who was killed in action 26 Nov. 1943, during the battle for the Gilbert Islands

Acreage:
391

Personnel:
1,500 military personnel, 1,440 civilians

Units:
928th Tactical Airlift Gp (AFRES); 64th Tactical Airlift Sqdn (AFRES); 126th Air Refueling Wing (ANG); 108th Air Refueling Sqdn (ANG)

Operational Aircraft:
 C-130A   64th TAS
 KC-135E   108th ARS

Left: Cheyenne Mountain Complex has staff from both America and Canada who operate the North American Aerospace Defense Command.

CLARK

Clark AB
Philippines
APO San Francisco 96274–5000

Phone:
6345350

Autovon:
860-1110

Command:
Pacific Air Forces

Date est:
1903

Acreage:
131,000

Left: A joint TAC and SAC air crew briefing at Clark AB.

Personnel:
4,000 military personnel, 2,000 civilians

Units:
HQ 13th Air Force (PACAF); 3rd Tactical Fighter Wing (PACAF); 374th Tactical Airlift Wing (MAC); 1961st Communications Gp (AFCC); 6200th Tactical Fighter Training Gp (PACAF); 6922nd Electronic Security Sqdn (ESC); 1st Special Operations Sqdn (MAC); 9th Aeromedical Evacuation Sqdn (MAC); 31st Aerospace Rescue and Recovery Sqdn (MAC); 600th Air Force Band (PACAF)

Operational Aircraft:

3rd Tactical Fighter Wing
F-4E	3rd TFS
F-4E/G	90th TFS
F-5E	26th TFTAS (PN)

31st Aerospace Rescue & Recovery Sqdn
CH/HH-3E

374th Tactical Airlift Wing
C-9A	20th AAS
C-130E/H	21st TAS

1st Special Operations Sqdn (MAC)
MC-130E

Above: Crew briefing at Clark.
Right: Ground crew work on a C–141 at Clark AFB during an NBC exercise.
Below right: Pre-flight checks on a Lockheed C–141 based at Charleston while operating from Clark AFB.
Below: NBC masked ground crew work on a C–141 at Clark.

CLEAR

Clear AFS
Alaska 98704-5000
USA

Phone:
(907) 585–6113

Autovon:
317-585-6409

Command:
Air Force Space Command

Personnel:
116 military personnel, 68 civilians

Notes:
Provides missile warning and space surveillance for NORAD, USSPACECOM, AFSPACECOM

COLUMBUS

Columbus AFB
Mississippi 39701-5000
USA

Phone:
(601) 434-7322

Autovon:
742-110

Command:
Air Training Command

Date Est:
1941

Named after:
The city of Columbus

Acreage:
6,013

Personnel:
2,000 military personnel, 1,040 civilians

Units:
14th FTW

Operational Aircraft:
14th Flying Training Wing (ATC)
T-37B   37th FTS
T-38A   38th FTS

Notes:
Its major role is the training of undergraduate pilots

COMISO

Comiso AB
Italy
APO New York 09694-5000

Phone:
932–965418

Autovon:
628-8110

Command:
United States Air Forces in Europe

Units:
487th Tactical Missile Wing, USAFE

DALLAS NAS

Dallas Naval Air Station
Texas 75211
USA

Phone:
(214) 266-6111

Autovon:
874-6111

Command:
Air National Guard

Acreage:
ANG area 49

Personnel:
975 military personnel, 185 civilians

Units:
136th Tactical Airlift Wing (ANG);
181st Tactical Airlift Sqdn (ANG)

Operational Aircraft:
C-130H

DANNELLY

Dannelly Field
Montgomery
Alabama 36196
USA

Phone:
(205) 284-7210

Autovon:
742-9210

Command:
Air National Guard

Named after:
Ensign Clarence Dannelly, killed in a crash at Pensacola during WWII

Acreage:
ANG area 42

Personnel:
1,203 military personnel, 281 civilians

Units:
187th Tactical Fighter Wing; 160th Tactical Fighter Sqdn; 232nd Combat Communications Sqdn

Operational Aircraft:
F16A/Bs   160th TFS (AL)

DAVIS-MONTHAN

Davis-Monthan AFB
Arizona 85707-5000
USA

Phone:
(602) 750-3900

Autovon:
361-1110

Command:
Tactical Air Command

GLCM launchers at Davis Monthan AFB wait to be destroyed.

Davis Monthan is the end of the line for all GLCMs. The INF treaty requires all missiles to be destroyed, and observers from the Soviet Union will regularly monitor progress.

Date est:
1927

Named after:
1st Lt. Samuel H. Davis and 2nd Lt. Oscar Monthan, both killed in flying accidents during the early 1920's

Acreage:
11,000

Personnel:
5,503 military personnel, 1,372 civilians

Units:
836th Air Divn; 355th TTW; 602nd TACW; 868th Tac Missile Training Wing;* 41st ECS; Det 1, 318th FIGP (ANG); Military Aerospace Maintenance and Regeneration Center (AFLC)

Operational Aircraft:
23rd Tactical Air Support Sqdn (TAC)
OA-37B

41st Electronic Countermeasures Sqdn (TAC)
EC-130H   (DM)

355th Tactical Training Wing (TAC)
A-10A   333rd TFTS
            357th TFTS
            358th TFTS   (DM)

Notes:
* Training for Ground Launched Cruise Missiles

DES MOINES

Des Moines Municipal Airport
Iowa 50321
USA

Phone:
(515) 285-7182

Autovon:
939-8210

Command:
Air National Guard

Acreage:
ANG area 112

Personnel:
1,142 military personnel, 252 civilians

Units:
132nd Tactical Fighter Wing (ANG); 124th Tactical Fighter Sqdn (ANG)

Operational Aircraft:
A-7D/K   124th TFS
C-131B
The C-131B will be changed for a C-12J

DOBBINS

Dobbins AFB
Georgia 30069-5000
USA

Phone:
(404) 421-5000

Autovon:
925-1110

Command:
Air Force Reserve

Date est:
1943

Named after:
Capt. Charles Dobbins, a WWII pilot killed in action over Sicily

Acreage:
1,800

Personnel:
AFRES: 3,148 military personnel, 985 civilians; ANG: 1,202 military personnel, 211 civilians

Units:
HQ 14th Air Force (AFRES); 94th Tactical Airlift Wing (AFRES); 700th Tactical Airlift Sqdn (AFRES); 116th Tactical Fighter Wing (ANG); 128th Tactical Fighter Sqdn (ANG)

Operational Aircraft:
C-130H   700th TAS
F-15A/B   128th TFS

DOUGLAS

Douglas Municipal Airport
Charlotte 28208
North Carolina
USA

Phone:
(704) 399-6363

Autovon:
583-9210

Command:
Air National Guard

Acreage:
ANG area 69

Personnel:
1,256 military personnel, 233 civilians

Units:
145th Tactical Airlift Gp (ANG); 156th Tactical Airlift Sqdn (ANG)

Operational Aircraft:
C-130B   156th TAS

DOVER

Dover AFB
Delaware 19902-5000
USA

Phone:
(302) 678-7011

Autovon:
455-1110

Command:
Military Airlift Command

Date est:
Dec. 1941; inactivated 1946; reactivated Feb. 1951

Left: A wet day on the flightline at Dobbins AFB, Georgia. It is home to the F–15A/Bs of the 116th TFW.

Below: A 3rd MAS/ 436th MAW C–5 pilot from Dover AFB.

Opposite: A head-on view of a B–1B based at Dyess AFB.

Named after:
The city of Dover

Acreage:
3,734

Personnel:
4,574 military personnel, 1,358 civilians

Units:
436th Military Airlift Wing; 512th Military Airlift Wing (AFRES)

Operational Aircraft:
436th Military Airlift Wing (MAC)
C-5A/B   9th MAS
                 20th MAS

Date est:
Apr. 1942; deactivated Dec. 1945; reactivated Sept. 1955

Named after:
Lt. Col. William E. Dyess, a WWII fighter pilot who escaped from the Bataan Death march. He was later killed in a P-38 crash in 1943

Acreage:
6,405

Personnel:
5,760 military personnel, 448 civilians

Units:
12th Air Division; 96th BW; Det 1, 4201st Test Sqdn (SAC); 463rd Tactical Airlift Wing; Det 4, 1722nd Combat Control Sqdn; 1993rd

Communications Sqdn (AFCC); 417th Field Training Det; Det 1, 47th Flying Training Wing (ATC); 12th Flying Training Wing ACE Det OLC; B-1B Site Activation Task Force (AFSC); B-1B FOT&E Test Team (AFOTEC)

Operational Aircraft:
96th Bombardment Wing
B-1B   337th BS
KC-135A   917th ARS

463rd Tactical Airlift Wing (MAC)
C-130H   772nd TAS
                 773rd TAS
                 774th TAS

Notes:
Dyess AFB was the first Air Force base to receive an operational B-1B Wing

DULUTH

Duluth International Airport
Minnesota 55811-5000
USA

Phone:
(218) 727-6886

Autovon:
825-7210

Command:
Air National Guard

Acreage:
ANG area 152

Personnel:
1,058 military personnel, 275 civilians

Units:
148th Fighter Interceptor Gp (ANG); 179th Fighter Interceptor Sqdn (ANG)

Operational Aircraft:
F-4D

DYESS

Dyess AFB
Texas 79607-5000
USA

Phone:
(915) 696-0212

Autovon:
461-1110

Command:
Strategic Air Command

Center right: A B–1B crew reacts to an alert klaxon at Dyess AFB.

Right: Take-off for a B–1B of the 337th Bomb Squadron at Dyess.

The interior of a B–1B cockpit.

EBING

Ebing ANGB
Fort Smith Municipal Airport
Arkansas 72906
USA

Phone:
(501) 646-1601

Autovon:
962-8210

Command:
Air National Guard

Acreage:
ANG area 98

Personnel:
961 military personnel, 226 civilians

Units:
188th Tactical Fighter Gp (ANG);
184th Tactical Fighter Sqdn (ANG)

Operational Aircraft:
F-4C   184th TFS

EDWARDS

Edwards AFB
California 93523-5000
USA

Phone:
(805) 277-1110

Autovon:
527-1110

Command:
Air Force Systems Command

Date est:
Sep. 1933

Named after:
Capt. Glen W. Edwards who was killed while test flying a YB-49 Flying Wing at Muroc Field in 1948

Acreage:
301,000

Personnel:
5,369 military personnel, 8,447 civilians (this figure includes contractors)

Units:
Air Force Flight Test Center (AFFTC); USAF Test Pilot School; USAF Rocket Propulsion Laboratory; US Army

Aviation Engineering Flight Activity; NASA Dryden Flight Research Facility; Jet Propulsion Laboratory Test Facility

Operational Aircraft:
6512th Test Squadron/Air Force Flight Test Center
various   (ED)

Notes:
The Test Pilot School trains flight-test pilots, engineers and navigators. Edwards AFB has been the primary landing site for all the Space Shuttle missions

EGLIN

Eglin AFB
Florida 32542-5000
USA

Phone:
(904) 881-6668

Autovon:
872-1110

Command:
Air Force Systems Command

Date est:
1935

Named after:
Lt. Col. Frederick I. Eglin, a WWI flyer killed in an air crash in 1937

Acreage:
464,980

Personnel:
11,007 military personnel, 3,991 civilians plus 894 contractor staff

Units:
Air Force Armament Divn; Air Force Armament Test Lab; 33rd Tactical Fighter Wing; 39th Aerospace Rescue & Recovery Wing; 55th Aerospace Rescue & Recovery Sqdn; Tactical Air Warfare Center; 1972nd Communications Sqdn 919th Special Operations Group (AFRES); 20th Missile Warning Sqdn; 728th Tactical Control Sqdn; plus a US Navy Explosive Ordnance Disposal School and the US Army Florida Ranger School

Operational Aircraft:
3246th Test Wing/Armament Divn (AFSC)
various

39th Aerospace Rescue & Recovery Sqdn (MAC)
CH-3E Det 5 Tyndall AFB FL
HH-3E Det 11 Myrtle AFB SC
CH-3E Det 12 Patrick AFB Fl

55th Aerospace Rescue & Recovery Sqdn (MAC)
HC-130 N/P
UH-60A

33rd Tactical Fighter Wing (TAC)
F15C/D   58th TFS
          59th TFS
          60th TFS   (EG)

4485th Test Sqdn (TAC)
various   (OT)

Notes:
Eglin AFB is the largest air force base in the Western world

EIELSON

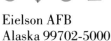

Eielson AFB
Alaska 99702-5000
USA

Phone:
(907) 377-1178

Autovon:
(317) 377-1110

Command:
Alaskan Air Command

Date est:
Oct. 1944

Named after:
Carl Ben Eielson who in 1924 became the first airmail pilot to operate in Alaska

Acreage:
23,500

Personnel:
3,365 military personnel, 618 civilians

Units:
343rd Tactical Fighter Wing; 343rd Combat Support Gp; 18th Tactical Fighter Sqdn; 25th Tactical Air Support Sqdn; 6th Strategic Wing (SAC); 1995th Communications Sqdn (AFCC); Arctic Survival School; 168th AREFS (ANG)

Operational Aircraft:
6th Strategic Wing
RC/TC-135   24th SRS

343rd Tactical Fighter Wing (AAC)
A-10A   18th TFS
0-2A   25th TASS

The 0-2As are due for retirement

Notes:
The base is regularly visited by tankers from the 6th Strategic Wing

Left: Two armorers at Eglin AFB carry out final pre-flight checks on an Advanced Medium Range Air-to-Air Missile during missile testing. Eglin, home of the Air Force Test Center, is the Western world's largest air force base.

Below: A–10 pilots from the 18th TFS based at Eielson AFB are welcomed to South Korea with flower garlands on their arrival for Team Spirit 88.

Bottom left: The shoulder badge of an A–10 pilot based at Eielson AFB.

Bottom: An armorer loads the GAU–8/A 30mm seven-barreled gun of an A–10 at Eielson.

An EC–135 of the 4th ACCS based at Ellsworth overflies Mt. Rushmore.

ELLINGTON

Ellington ANGB
Texas 77034-5586
USA

Phone:
(713) 929-2221

Autovon:
954-2110

Command:
Air National Guard

Named after:
Lt. Eric L. Ellington, an early army pilot killed in a crash Nov. 1913

Acreage:
ANG area 213

Personnel:
1,062 military personnel, 287 civilians

Units:
147th Fighter Interceptor Gp (ANG); 111th Fighter Interceptor Sqdn (ANG); NASA Flight Operations; US Coast Guard; Army National Guard; FAA

Operational Aircraft:
F-4C/D   111th FIS
C-131B

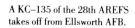
A KC–135 of the 28th AREFS takes off from Ellsworth AFB.

ELLSWORTH

Ellsworth AFB
South Dakota 57706-5000
USA

Phone:
(605) 385-1000

Autovon:
675-1000

Command:
Strategic Air Command

Date est:
July 1942

Named after:
Brig. Gen. Richard E. Ellsworth a WWII pilot. He flew 400 missions in the China-Burma-India Theater. He died in 1953 flying an RB-36

Acreage:
4,906

Personnel:
6,700 military personnel, 800 civilians

Units:
44th Strategic Missile Wing; 28th Bomb Wing; Det 2, 37th ARRS; OL A, 84th Flying Training Wing (ATC); Det

17, 9th Weather Sqdn; 2148th Communications Sqdn (AFCC)

Operational Aircraft:
28th Bombardment Wing
B-1B/B-52H   37th BS
EC-135A/C/G   4th ACCS
KC-135R   28th ARS

Notes:
Ellsworth is SAC's largest air base. The 44th SMW operates MMII missiles

ELMENDORF

Elmendorf AFB
Alaska 99506-5000
USA

Phone:
(907) 552-1110

Autovon:
(317) 552-1110

Command:
Alaskan Air Command

Date est:
July 1940

Named after:
Capt. Hugh M. Elmendorf, a pioneer pursuit pilot who was killed near Patterson Field, Ohio while testing a new aircraft

Acreage:
13,130

Personnel:
7,333 military personnel, 1,721 civilians

Units:
HQ Alaskan Air Command; 21st Tactical Fighter Wing; NORAD Region Operations Control Center; Rescue Coordination Center; 11th Tactical Control Gp; 43rd Tactical Fighter Sqdn; 5021st Tactical Operational Sqdn; 962nd AWACS (TAC); 1931st Communications Wing (AFCC); 6981st Electronic Security Sqdn (ESC)

Operational Aircraft:
21st Tactical Fighter Wing (AAC)
F-15A/B   43rd TFS (AK)

616th Military Airlift Gp (AAC)
C-12F
C-130E   17th TAS

FAIRCHILD

High above Alaska's mountains three F–15s from the 21st TFW based at Elmendorf AFB.

Fairchild AFB
Washington 99011-5000
USA

Phone:
(509) 247-1212

Autovon:
352-1110

Command:
Strategic Air Command

Date est:
Jan. 1942

Named after:
USAF Vice Chief of Staff, Gen. Muir S. Fairchild, who died in 1950

Acreage:
6,127

Personnel:
4,859 military personnel, 610 civilians

Units:
47th Air Divn; 92nd Bomb Wing (SAC); 3636th Combat Crew Training Wing (ATC); 141st Air Refueling Wing (ANG); 116th ARS (ANG); Det 24, 40th ARRS (MAC); 2039th Communications Sqdn (AFCC); 1000th Satellite Operations Gp (AFSPACECOM)

Operational Aircraft:
92nd Bombardment Wing (SAC)
B52G/H
KC-135A

116th Air Refueling Sqdn (ANG)
KC-135E
C-131D
The C-131D will be replaced by a Beechcraft C-12J

A mighty B–52G of the 92nd Bomb Wing based at Fairchild AFB.

ENGLAND

England AFB
Louisiana 71311-5004
USA

Phone:
(318) 448-2100

Autovon:
683-1110

Command:
Tactical Air Command

Date est:
Oct. 1942

Named after:
Lt. Col. John B. England a WWII P-51 ace who was killed in an F-86 crash while serving in France in 1954

Acreage:
2,282

Personnel:
3,057 military personnel, 667 civilians

Units:
23rd Tactical Fighter Wing

Operational Aircraft:
23rd Tactical Fighter Wing (TAC)
A-10A   74th TFS
          75th TFS
          76th TFS

The old control tower at Falcon AFB. The base is used in support of Cheyenne Mountain AFB operations.

FALCON

Falcon AFB
Colorado 80912-5000
USA

Phone:
(719) 550-4113

Autovon:
560-1110

Command:
Air Force Space Command

Date est:
July 1985

Acreage:
640

Personnel:
1,200 military personnel, 170 civilians plus 1,434 contractors

Units:
2nd Space Wing; 3rd Space Support Wing; Strategic Defense Initiative Test Facility

FLORENNES

Florennes AB
Belgium
APO New York 098188-5000

Phone:
(71) 694111

Autovon:
791-3255

Command:
United States Air Forces in Europe

Units:
487th Tactical Missile Wing, USAFE, disbanded in December 1988

Notes:
The 487th TMW was the first GLCM Wing to be disbanded under the INF Treaty

FRANCIS E. WARREN

Francis E. Warren AFB
Wyoming 802005-5000
USA

Phone:
(307) 775-1110

Autovon:
481-1110

Command:
Strategic Air Command

Date est:
1947; the base was originally activated 4 July 1867 as Fort D. A. Russel

Named after:
Francis Emory Warren, the first senator for Wyoming

Acreage:
5,866, plus 200 Minuteman III silos scattered over 12,600 sq. miles in Wyoming, Colorado and Nebraska

Personnel:
3,940 military personnel, 602 civilians

Units:
4th Air Divn; 90th SMW (SAC); 90th Combat Support Gp; 37th ARRS (MAC)

Operational Aircraft:
37th Aerospace Rescue & Recovery Sqdn (MAC)
TH-1F, UH-1H Det. 2 Ellsworth AFB SD
HH-1H Det 3 Grand Forks AFB ND
HH-1H Det 4 Little Rock AFB AR
TH-1F Det 5 Malmstrom AFB MT
HH-1H Det 6 McConnell AFB KS
HH-1H Det 7 Minot AFB ND
UH-1N Det 8 Vandenberg AFB CA
HH-1H Det 9 Whiteman AFB MO
TH-1F, UH-1F Det 10 F.E. Warren AFB WY

Notes:
Home for the first 50 Peacekeeper missiles. It is also the oldest continually used base in the USAF

FORBES

Forbes Field ANGB
Kansas 66619-5000
USA

Phone:
(913) 862-1234

Autovon:
720-1234

Command:
Air National Guard

Acreage:
ANG area 200

Personnel:
960 military personnel, 259 civilians

Units:
190th Air Refueling Gp (ANG); 117th Air Refueling Sqdn (ANG)

Operational Aircraft:
KC-135E   (ANG)
C-131B
The C-131B will be replaced by a C-12J

FRESNO

Fresno Air Terminal
California 93727-2199
USA

Phone:
(209) 454-5155

Autovon:
949-9210

Command:
Air National Guard

Acreage:
ANG area 139

Personnel:
1,046 military personnel, 291 civilians

Units:
144th Fighter Interceptor Wing (ANG); 194th Fighter Interceptor Sqdn (ANG); 26th NORAD Region; 25th Air Division (TAC)

Operational Aircraft:
F-4D   194th FIS

GEN. B. MITCHELL

General Billy Mitchell Field
Milwaukee
Wisconsin 53207
USA

Phone:
ANG (414) 747-4410
AFRES (414) 481-6400

Autovon:
ANG 580-8410
AFRES 786-9110

Command:
Air Force Reserve

Named after:
General Mitchell who conducted tests
to show that Army Air Service bombers
could sink a battleship. This his unit
did but the War and Navy Departments
took no notice of him. Following the
crash of the airship *Shenandoah* he
accused the authorities of "Criminal
negligence." This was too much and he
was court-martialed, convicted and
suspended for five years from duty.
The General resigned his commission
and carried on the fight for the concept
of modern air power. He died in 1936

Acreage:
AFRES 100
ANG 111

Personnel:
ANG: 1,094 military personnel, 209
civilians; AFRES: 991 military
personnel, 373 civilians

Units:
128th Air Refueling Gp (ANG); 126th
Air Refueling Sqdn (ANG); 440th
Tactical Airlift Wing (AFRES); 95th
Tactical Airlift Sqdn (AFRES)

Operational Aircraft:
KC-135E	126th AFS
C-130A	95th TAS

GEORGE

George AFB
California 92394-5000
USA

Phone:
(619) 269-1110

Autovon:
353-1110

A snowy welcome to the George
AFB guard house.

Command:
Tactical Air Command

Date est:
1941

Named after:
Brig. Gen. Harold H. George, a WWI
fighter ace, who died in a flying
accident over Australia in 1942

Acreage:
5,347

Personnel:
5,527 military personnel, 516 civilians

Units:
831st Air Division; 37th Tactical
Fighter Wing; 35th Tactical Training
Wing; OLAD, 144th FIW (TAC); 27th
Tactical Air Support Sqdn; 207th
Communications Sqdn (AFCC)

Operational Aircraft:
37th Tactical Fighter Wing (TAC)
F-4E&G	561st TFS	
	562nd TFS	
	563rd TFS	(WW)

35th Tactical Training Wing (TAC)
F-4E	20th TFTS	
	21st TFTS	
UH-1F		(GA)

27th Tactical Air Support Sqdn (TAC)
OV-10A	(VV)

Notes:
The 35th TTW provides training on the
F-4 for German Air Force and F-4
transitional and upgrade training for
the USAF

BASE REALIGNMENTS AND CLOSURES
Report of the Defense Secretary's Commission December 1988

The Commission recommends George
Air Force Base for closure primarily
due to degrading training
effectiveness, air traffic congestion and
because of excess capacity within the
category. The net cost of closure and
relocation will be paid back
immediately. The Commission expects
annual savings to be $70.2 million.

The military value of George AFB is

An OV-10A of the 27th Tactical
Air Support Squadron overflies
George AFB.

Line maintenance on an engine at George AFB.

lower than other tactical-fighter installations due to its distance to specialized training ranges and the increasing air-traffic congestion in the vicinity of the base.

Training for George's defense suppression units is hampered by a distance of over 150 nautical miles to an electronic-combat training range. This results in a considerable waste of time and money flying to and from the range. All flight operations are constrained by increasing air traffic congestion in the greater Los Angeles area.

Other short-comings of the installation include a shortage of facilities for operation and maintenance purposes. The water supply system is presently inadequate, and is scheduled for replacement in FY 1991. There are other deficiencies at George in the area of quality of life, the most prominent being a severe shortage of bachelor housing. The installation also has difficulty hiring civilian workers due to the demand for technically qualified workers in other industries within the civilian community.

George AFB is one of 11 Tactical Air Command tactical-fighter bases. The wings assigned there have the

The crew of an F–4 belonging to the 37th Tactical Fighter Wing wait for the signal to take off.

wartime mission of providing conventional tactical air support primarily in the defense-suppression role as well as close air support, air interdiction, and counterair. The early retirement of the F-4 fighter aircraft from George, caused by a recent Air Force budget reduction, enabled the Commission to consolidate similar units. There is sufficient capacity within the tactical-fighter category to absorb the remaining units at other locations.

This closure will have no negative impact on the local environment. Cleanup of hazardous materials and waste contamination at George is covered by the Defense Environmental Restoration Program. Cleanup is independent of the closure. The movement of units currently assigned to George should not significantly alter the environmental situation at the gaining bases. There will, however, be a requirement for increased storage of hazardous waste at Mountain Home AFB, Idaho, and Cannon AFB, New Mexico. The Commission has been advised that these bases will have no difficulty providing the appropriate, conforming storage facilities required for the relocations.

This closure will have minimal impact on local employment.

The Commission recommends the following relocations of major units and related support activities:

The 35th Tactical Training Wing and the 37th Tactical Fighter Wing (F-4E/G aircraft) to Mountain Home AFB. This move will enhance command and control by consolidating functions with EF-111 air defense suppression aircraft. The recent expansion of the electronic-combat and weapons ranges in the Mountain Home area provides the capability to relocate operational and training assets, which will increase efficiency and enhance mission effectiveness. To accommodate the move of the F-4E/G into Mountain Home, it will be necessary to move part of the 366th Tactical Fighter Wing (F-111E and F111A aircraft) from Mountain Home to Cannon AFB. This will collocate all U.S.-based F-111 aircraft with a similar mission at a single base, improving command and control while enhancing mission effectiveness at a reduced cost.

The 27th Tactical Air Support Squadron (OV-10 aircraft) will relocate to Davis-Monthan AFB, Arizona. OV-10 aircraft are already stationed at Davis-Monthan, and consolidation of the OV-10 aircraft there will improve command and control, and provide increased efficiency while enhancing mission effectiveness. To accommodate the additional OV-10 aircraft at Davis-Monthan, it will be necessary to move the 41st Electronic Combat Squadron (EC-130H aircraft) from Davis-Monthan to Bergstrom AFB, Texas. This relocation will absorb excess capacity and enhance the implementation of the tactical ground-surveillance mission of the EC-130H at Bergstrom, AFB, provide increased efficiency, improve command and control and reduce operating costs.

GILA BEND

Gila Bend Air Force Auxiliary Field
Arizona 85337-5000
USA

Phone:
see Luke AFB

Autovon:
853-5220

Command:
Tactical Air Command

Date est:
1941

Acreage:
2,700,000

Personnel:
177 military personnel, 80 civilians

Units:
832nd Combat Support Sqdn

Notes:
The Field is used by Luke AFB as a bombing and gunnery range. The 832nd are responsible for construction and maintenance of the various target complexes

GLENN L. MARTIN

Glenn L. Martin State Airport
Baltimore
Maryland 21220-2899
USA

Phone:
(301) 687-6270

Autovon:
235-9210

Command:
Air National Guard

Acreage:
ANG area 78

Personnel:
1,873 military personnel, 310 civilians

Units:
175th Tactical Fighter Gp (ANG);
104th Tactical Fighter Sqdn (ANG);
135th Tactical Airlift Gp (ANG); 135th
Tactical Airlift Sqdn (ANG)

Operational Aircraft:
| A-10A | 104th TFS | (MD) |
| C-130B | 135th TAS | |

GOODFELLOW

Goodfellow AFB
Texas 76908-5000
USA

Phone:
(915) 657-3231

Autovon:
477-3231

Command:
Air Training Command

Date est:
Jan. 1941

Named after:
Lt. John J. Goodfellow, a WWI fighter pilot who was killed in action 14 Sept. 1918

Acreage:
1,127

Personnel:
3,415 military personnel, 414 civilians

Units:
Goodfellow Technical Training Center; 3480th Technical Training Wing; 3480th Training Gp; 3480th Air Base Gp (ATC); 3480th Student Gp; 3490th Technical Training Gp; 8th Missile Warning Sqdn (AFSPACECOM) (at nearby Eldorado AFS, the Southwest Pave Paws side); Det 6, USAF Occupational Measurement Center (USAFOMC); 2081st Communications Sqdn (AFCC); Det 12, 3314th Management Engineering Sqdn (ATC); NCO Professional Military Education Center (ESC); US Army Intelligence Training Battalion; Naval Technical

Training Center Det; Marine Corps Administrative Det

Notes
All Air Force intelligence training will be operated from the GTTC by 1989 as part of the Intelligence Training Consolidation program

GOWEN

Gowen Field
Boise Municipal Airport
Idaho 83707
USA

Phone:
(208) 389-5011

Autovon:
694-2260

Command:
Air National Guard

Named after:
Lt. Paul Gowen who died in a B-10 crash in July 1938

Acreage:
ANG area 1,994

Personnel
1,388 military personnel, 272 civilians

Units:
124th Tactical Reconnaissance Gp (ANG); 189th Tactical Reconnaissance Sqdn (ANG); plus an ARNG Army Field Training Site

Operational Aircraft:
C-131D
RF-4C
The aircraft are shared with the 189th TRTF

GRAND FORKS

Grand Forks AFB
North Dakota 58205-5000
USA

Phone:
(701) 747-3000

Autovon:
362-1110

Command:
Strategic Air Command

Date est:
1956

Acreage:
6,912, plus an additional 7,500 sq. miles which contain the missile silos

Personnel:
5,325 military personnel, 571 civilians

Units:
319th BW; 321st Strategic Missile Wing

Operational Aircraft:
319th Bombardment Wing (SAC)
B-52G   46th BS
KC-135A   905th ARS

Notes:
The 321st operate Minuteman IIIs

GREAT FALLS

Great Falls International Airport
Montana 59401-5000
USA

Phone:
(406) 727-4650

Autovon:
279-2301

Command:
Air National Guard

Named after:
The city of Great Falls whose citizens paid for the base

Acreage:
ANG area 139

Personnel:
1,009 military personnel, 281 civilians

Units:
25th NORAD Region; 25th Air Divn; 120th Fighter Interceptor Gp (ANG); 186th Fighter Interceptor Sqdn (ANG)

Operational Aircraft:
C-130A
F-16A/B
The unit went through a major change in 1987: Their old C-131 and F-106s were exchanged for a C-130A and F16A/Bs, and like many other units they lost their T-33s

GTR. PEORIA

Greater Peoria Airport
Illinois 61607
USA

Phone:
(309) 633-3000

Autovon:
724-9210

Command:
Air National Guard

Acreage:
ANG area 385

Personnel:
1,012 military personnel, 173 civilians

Units:
182nd Tactical Air Support Gp (ANG); 169th Tactical Air Support Sqdn (ANG)

Operational Aircraft:
OA-37B   169th TASS
C-131D   (IL)

GTR. PITTSBURGH

Greater Pittsburgh International Airport
Pennsylvania 15231
USA

Phone:
171st ARW ANG (412) 268-8402
112th TFG ANG (412) 269-8441
AFRES   (412) 269-8000

Autovon:
171st ARW ANG 277-8402
112th TFG ANG 277-8441
AFRES   277-8000

Command:
Air Force Reserve

Acreage:
AFRES 165; ANG 90

Personnel:
AFRES: 1,071 military personnel, 239 civilians; ANG: 1,860 military personnel, 362 civilians

Units:
911th Tactical Airlift Gp (AFRES); 758th Tactical Airlift Sqdn (AFRES); 146th Tactical Fighter Sqdn (ANG); 147th Air Refueling Sqdn (ANG); 1998th Communications Installation Gp (AFCC)

Operational Aircraft:
A-7D/K   146th TFS (PT)
KC-135E   147th ARS(ANG)

GTR. WILMINGTON

Greater Wilmington Airport
Delaware 19720
USA

Phone:
(302) 322-3361

Autovon:
455-3000

Command:
Air National Guard

Acreage:
ANG area 57

Personnel:
1,064 military personnel, 170 civilians

Units:
166th Tactical Airlift Gp (ANG);
142nd Tactical Airlift Sqdn (ANG);
plus an Army National Guard aviation
company

Operational Aircraft:
C-130H

GRIFFISS

Griffiss AFB
New York 13441-5000
USA

Phone:
(315) 330-1110

Autovon:
587-1110

Command:
Strategic Air Command

Date est:
Feb. 1942

Named after:
Lt. Col. Townsend E. Griffiss, killed
in an air accident 15 Feb. 1942. He
was the first US airman to die in
Europe during WWII in the line of
duty

Acreage:
3,896

Personnel:
4,523 military personnel, 3,204
civilians

Units:
416th BW; Rome Air Development

Center (AFSC); 485th Engineering
Installation Gp (AFCC); HQ 24th Air
Div (TAC); Northeast Air Defense
sector (TAC); 933rd Civil Engineering
Sqdn (AFRES)

Operational Aircraft:
416th Bombardment Wing (SAC)
B-52G   668th BS
KC-135A   41st ARS

24th Air Div
F-4C/D
F-15
F-16

GRISSOM

Grissom AFB
Indiana 46971-5000
USA

Phone:
(317) 689-5211

Autovon:
928-1110

Command:
Strategic Air Command

Date est:
1947 as a Navy flying base; it was
taken over by the Air Force in June
1954 and named Bunker Hill AFB

Named after:
Lt. Col. Virgil I. Grissom who was
killed along with two other pilots in the
Apollo capsule fire on 27 Jan. 1967

Acreage:
3,000

Personnel:
2,350 military personnel, 1,056
civilians

Units:
305th Air Refueling Wing; 930th
Tactical Fighter Gp (AFRES); 434th
Air Refueling Wing (AFRES)

Operational Aircraft:
305th Air Refueling Wing (SAC)
EC-135G/L   70th & 305th ARS
KC-135A/D

72nd Air Refueling Sqdn (AFRES)
KC-135E

45th Tactical Fighter Sqdn (AFRES)
A-10A   (IN)

A B-52G of the 416th Bomb
wing from Griffiss AFB. It is
carrying a full load of ALCMs as
it formates on a KC-135, also
from Griffiss.

Far right: The squadron crest of the 496th TFS based at Hahn.

GULFPORT-BILOXI

Gulfport-Biloxi Regional Airport
Mississippi 39501
USA

Phone:
(601) 868-6200

Autovon:
363-8200

Command:
Air National Guard

Acreage:
ANG area 206

Personnel:
496 military personnel, 20 civilians

Units:
255th Combat Communications Sqdn

GUNTER

Gunter AFB
Alabama 36114-5000
USA

Phone:
(205) 279-1110

Autovon:
446-1110

Command:
Air University

Date est:
27 Aug. 1940

Named after:
William A. Gunter, an airpower supporter and mayor of Montgomery

Acreage:
368

Personnel:
1,619 military personnel, 968 civilians

Units:
HQ Standard Systems Center (AFCC);
Air Force Logistics Management
Center (AFLC); USAF Extention
Course Institute; USAF Senior NCO
Academy

Notes:
The Commander at Maxwell Air Force
Base is also in command at Gunter
AFB

Right: An F–16 of the 496th TFS on a visit to RAF Mildenhall.

HAHN

Hahn AB
West Germany
APO New York 09122-5000

Phone:
(65) 4351113

Autovon:
450-1110

Command:
United States Air Forces in Europe

Date est:
1953

Units
50th Tactical Fighter Wing (USAFE)

Operational Aircraft:
50th Tactical Fighter Wing
F-16C/D   10th TFS
             313th TFS
             496th TFS (HR)

Notes:
The French originally started
construction of the air base in 1951

Right: High above the European clouds two F–16s of the 50th TFW based at Hahn AB, West Germany on patrol.

HANCOCK

Hancock Field
Syracuse
New York 13211-7099
USA

Phone:
(315) 470-6100

Autovon:
587-9100

Command:
Air National Guard

Acreage:
764

Personnel:
1,355 military personnel, 359 civilians

Units:
174th Tactical Fighter Wing (ANG);
138th Tactical Fighter Sqdn (ANG);
Base operations for Hancock ANG
Base; 152nd Tactical Control Gp;
108th Tactical Control Flight; 113rd
Tactical Control Flight

Operational Aircraft:
A-10A   138th TFS   (NY)

HANSCOM

Hanscom AFB
Massachusetts 01730-5000
USA

Phone:
(617) 861-4441

Autovon:
478-5980

Command:
Air Force Systems Command

Named after:
Laurence G. Hanscom, a great
supporter of private flying

Acreage:
846

Personnel:
2,300 military personnel, 3,000
civilians

Units:
HQ Electronic Systems Divn (AFSC);
Air Force Geophysics Lab

HECTOR

Hector Field
Fargo
North Dakota 58105-5536
USA

Phone:
(701) 237-6030

Autovon:
362-8100

Command:
Air National Guard

Acreage:
ANG area 133

Personnel:
1,108 military personnel, 276 civilians

Units:
119th Fighter Interceptor Gp (ANG);
178th Fighter Interceptor Sqdn

Operational Aircraft:
F-4D   178 FIS
        C/130A

HELLENIKON

Hellenikon AB
Greece
APO New York 09223-5000

Phone:
(81) 761196

Autovon:
662-1110

Command:
United States Air Forces in Europe

Units:
7206th Air Base Gp, USAFE; 2140th
Communications Gp, AFCC

Far left: Lt. Col. Carl Scheibegg
from the Electronic Systems
Division based at Hanscom AB
has a present wrapped up for
him while taking a little time off
during Team Spirit 88.

Left: Hickham AFB is the home
for the headquarters of the
Pacific Air Forces.

HICKAM

Hickam AFB
Hawaii 96853-5000
USA

Phone:
(808) 422-0531

Autovon:
449-0111

Command:
PACAF

Date est:
Sep. 1938

Named after:
Lt. Col. Horace M. Hickam, an air pioneer who died in a crash in Nov. 1934

Acreage:
2,694

Personnel:
3,612 military personnel, 1,1961 civilians

Units:
HQ Pacific Air Forces; 15th Air Base Wing; 9th Airborne Command & Control Sqdn; 834th Airlift Divn (MAC); HQ Pacific Communications Divn (AFCC); 1st Weather Wing (MAC); 154th Composite Gp (ANG); 619th Military Airlift Support Sqdn (MAC); Det 1, 89th Military Airlift Wing (MAC)

Operational Aircraft:
199th Fighter Interceptor Sqdn (ANG)
F-15A/B
C-130A
9th Air Command & Control Sqdn (PACAF)
EC-135J
Comes under control of the 15th ABW

HILL

Hill AFB
Utah 84056-5990
USA

Phone:
(801) 777-7221

Autovon:
458-1110

Command:
Air Force Logistics Command

Date est:
Nov. 1940

Named after:
Major Ployer P. Hill who was killed test-flying the first B-17 in 1935

Acreage:
6,666 plus 961,102 it manages

Personnel:
5,100 military personnel, 15,300 civilians

Units:
HQ Ogden Air Logistics Center; 388th Tactical Fighter Wing; 419th Tactical Fighter Wing (AFRES); 40th ARRS; 729th TCS; 6545th Test Gp

Operational Aircraft:
388th Tactical Fighter Wing (TAC)
F16A/B   4th TFS
             34th TFS
             421st TFS   (HL)

466th Tactical Fighter Sqdn (AFRES)
F16A/B   (HI)

6514th Test Sqdn (AFSC)
Various

40th Aerospace Rescue & Recovery Sqdn (MAC) UH-1N, Det 5 Edwards AFB CA, Det 6 Holloman AFB NM, Det 18 Plattsburgh AFB NY, Det 22 Mountain Home AFB ID, Det 24 Fairchild AFB WA

Notes:
The logistics center provides support for Peacekeeper, Minuteman and Titan II strategic missiles, Maverick AGM, laser and electro-optical bombs. The unit is systems manager for the F-4 and F-16; it also handles air munitions, aircraft landing gears, wheels, brakes and struts, tires and tubes,

F–15As of the 49th TFW based at Holloman AFB fly over the New Mexico landscape.

photographic and aerospace training equipment.

HOLLOMAN

Holloman AFB
New Mexico 88330-5000
USA

Phone:
(505) 479-6511

Autovon:
867-11100

Command:
Tactical Air Command

Date est:
1942

Named after:
Col. George Holloman, a guided missile pioneer killed in a B-17 on Formosa in 1946

Acreage:
50,697

Personnel:
6,352 military personnel, 1,756 civilians

Units:
833rd Air Divn; 49th Tactical Fighter Wing; 479th TTW; 4449th Mobility Support Sqdn; 82nd and 83rd Tactical Control Flights; 6585th Test Gp (AFSC) conducts test and evaluation of aircraft and missile systems. There are 21 other tenant units on base including 1877th Information Systems Sqdn, 4th Satellite Communications Sqdn (AFPSACECOM), 1984th Communications Sqdn, 40th ARRS and an Air Force Geophysical Lab Det

Operational Aircraft:
49th Tactical Fighter Wing (TAC)
F15A/B	7th TFS	
	8th TFS	
	9th TFS	(HO)

475th Tactical Training Wing (TAC)
T-38A/AT/38B	433rd TFTS	
	434th TFTS	
	435th TFTS	
	436th TFTS	(HM)

93rd Tactical Fighter Sqdn (AFRES)
HC-130H/N

HOMESTEAD

Homestead AFB
Florida 33039-5000
USA

Phone:
(305) 257-8011

Autovon:
791-0111

Command:
Tactical Air Command

Date est:
Apr. 1955

Acreage:
3,345

Personnel:
7,200 military personnel, 10,200 civilians

Units:
31st Tactical Fighter Wing; ATC Sea-Survival School; 726th Tactical Control Sqdn (TAC); Naval Security Gp; 482nd Tactical Fighter Wing (AFRES); 125th Fighter Interceptor Gp (TAC)

Operational Aircraft:
27th Tactical Fighter Wing
F-16A/B	307th TFS
	308th TFS
	309th TFS

301st Aerospace Rescue & Recovery Sqdn (AFRES)
HC-130H/N

HOWARD

Howard AFB
Panama
APO Miami 34001-5000

Phone:
845554

Autovon:
284-110

Command:
Military Airlift Command

Date est:
1948

Units:
HQ USAF Southern Air Divn; 310th Military Airlift Sqdn

Operational Aircraft:
C-22A
C-130E

HULMAN FIELD

Hulman Field
Hulman Regional Airport
Terre Haute
Indiana 47803
USA

Phone:
(812) 877-5210

Autovon:
724-1210

Command:
Air National Guard

Acreage:
ANG area 279

Personnel:
1,217 military personnel, 234 civilians

Units:
181st Tactical Fighter Gp (ANG); 113th Tactical Fighter Sqdn (ANG)

Operational Aircraft:
| F-4C | 113TFS | (HF) |

HURLBURT FIELD

Hurlburt Field
Florida 32544-5000
USA

Phone:
(904) 881-6668

Autovon:
579-1110

Command:
Military Airlift Command

Date est:
1943

Named after:
Lt. Donald W. Hurlburt, A WWII pilot killed in a crash on the Elgin reservation on 2 Oct. 1943

The colorful artwork on the nose of an AC–130 of the 16th SOS based at Hurlburt Field, seen during Team Spirit 88.

Personnel:
4,200 military personnel, 400 civilians

Units:
HQ 23rd Air Force; 1st Special Operations Wing; 20th Special Operations Sqdn (MAC); the USAF Special Operations School; 1723rd Combat Control Sqdn; Special Operations Weather Team; 6th Weather Sqdn; 7th Weather Wing; Special Missions Operational Test and Evaluation Center; 4442nd Tactical Control Gp which includes the US Air Force Air-Ground Operations School and the 727th Tactical Control Sqdn; 823rd Civil Engineering Sqdn RED HORSE; Det 8, 1361st Audiovisual Sqdn

Operational Aircraft:
20th Special Operations Sqdn (MAC)
HH-53H
MH-53H
MC-130J

8th Special Operations Sqdn (MAC)
MC-130E/H

16th Special Operations Sqdn (MAC)
AC-130H

Notes:
The Field is located within Eglin AFB

INCIRLIK

Incirlik AB
Turkey
APO New York 09289-5000

Phone:
(711) 14228

Autovon:
676-1110

Command:
United States Air Forces in Europe

Units:
39th Tactical Group, USAFE; 628th Military Airlift Support Sqdn, MAC; USAF Hospital Incirlik

INDIAN SPRINGS

Indian Springs Air Force Auxiliary Field
Nevada 89108-5000
USA

Phone:
see Nellis AFB

Autovon:
682-6201

Command:
Tactical Air Command

Date Est:
1942

Acreage:
1,652

Personnel:
289 military personnel, 19 civilians

Units:
554th Combat Support Sqdn; 4460th Helicopter Sqdn

Notes:
The field supplies bombing and gunnery range support for units operating out of Nellis AFB. The 554th are responsible for construction of realistic targets, both vehicles and defense works

IRAKLION

Iraklion AB
Crete
APO New York 09291

Phone:
817–61196

Autovon:
668–1110

Command:
United States Air Forces in Europe

Units:
7266th Air Base Gp, USAFE

JACKSONVILLE

Jacksonville International Airport
Florida 32229
USA

Phone:
(904) 757-1360

Autovon:
460-7210

Command:
Air National Guard

Acreage:
ANG area 332

Personnel:
1,003 military personnel, 255 civilians

Units:
125th Fighter Interceptor Gp (ANG); 159th Fighter Interceptor Sqdn (ANG)

Operational Aircraft:
C-131D
F-16A/B

JOE FOSS

Joe Foss Field
Sioux Falls
South Dakota 57104
USA

Phone:
(605) 336-0670

Autovon:
939-7210

Command:
Air National Guard

Named after:
Brg. Gen. Joseph J. Foss, a WWII ace and former Governor of South Dakota; he was also a National President of the Air Force Association and founded the South Dakota ANG

Acreage:
ANG area 145

Personnel:
1,075 military personnel, 210 civilians

Units:
114th Tactical Fighter Gp (ANG);
175th Tactical Fighter Sqdn (ANG)

Operational Aircraft:
A-7D/K
C-12F   (SD)

KADENA

Kadena AFB
Okinawa
Japan
APO San Franciso 96239-5000

Phone:
Not available

Autovon:
630-1110

Date est:
1945

Acreage:
11,000

Units:
313rd Air Divn (PACAF); 18th
Tactical Fighter Wing (PACAF); 376th
Strategic Wing (SAC); 1962nd
Communications Gp (AFCC); 6990th
Electronic Security Gp (ESC); 961st
Airborne Warning and Control Sqdn
(TAC); 400th Munitions Maintenance
Sqdn (Theater) (PACAF); 18th Combat
Support Wing

Operational Aircraft:
18th Tactical Fighter Wing
RF-4C   15th TRS
F-15C/D   12th TRS
                  44th TRS
                  67th TRS   (ZZ)

33rd Aerospace Rescue & Recovery
Sqdn
Hc-130H/N/P
HH-3E

376th Strategic Wing
KC-135A/Q   909th ARS

KEESLER

Keesler AFB
Mississippi 39534-5000
USA

Phone:
(601) 377-1110

Autovon:
868-1110

Command:
Air Training Command

Date est:
June 1941

Named after:
2nd Lt. Samuel R. Keesler, a WWI
aerial observer killed in action near
Verdun on 9 Oct. 1918

Acreage:
3,600

Personnel:
13,300 military personnel, 3,312
civilians

Units:
Keesler Technical Training Center;
Keesler Medical Center; AFCC
Engineering Installation Gp; AFCC
NCO Academy/Leadership School;
USAF First Sergeant's Academy

Operational Aircraft:
815th Weather Reconnaissance Sqdn
(AFRES)
WC-130H

53rd Weather Reconnaissance (MAC)
WC-130E/H

7th Airborne Command & Control
Sqdn (TAC)
EC-130E   (KS)

Notes:
The training center handles
communications, electronics,
avionics, radar systems, computer and
command and control systems,
personnel and administration courses

KEFLAVIK

Keflavik NAS
Iceland

Phone:
2 43 24

Autovon:
(314) 228-0127

Command:
Tactical Air Command

Units:
57th Fighter Interceptor Sqdn (TAC)
96th Airborne Warning and Control
Sqdn

Operational Aircraft:
F-15C/D   57th FIS (IS)
E-3B/C   96th AW&CS

Notes:
The E-3s are supplied on a rotational
basis from the 552nd AW&CW at
Tinker AFB, Oklahoma

Two F–15s from the 57th
Fighter Interceptor Squadron
based at Keflavik NAS formate
on a Soviet Bear over the Arctic
Circle. The F–15 pilots of the
57th FIS probably eyeball more
Soviet aircraft than any other
USAF flying unit.

KELLY

Kelly AFB
Texas 78245-5000
USA

Phone:
(512) 925-1110

Autovon:
945-1110

Command:
Air Force Logistics Command

Date est:
21 Nov. 1916

Named after:
Lt. George E. M. Kelly, the first army pilot to be killed in a flying accident on 10 May 1911

Acreage:
4,660

Personnel:
4,988 military personnel, 18,970 civilians

Units:
HQ San Antonio Air Logistics Center; HQ Electronic Security Command; Air Force Electronic Warfare Center; Air Force Cryptologic Support Center; Joint Electronic Warfare Center; USAF Service Information and News Center; HQ Air Force Commissary Service; 433rd Military Airlift Wing (AFRES); 149th Tactical Fighter Gp (ANG); 1923rd Communications Gp; 1827th Electronics Installation Sqdn; Defense Reutilization and Marketing Office; Air Force Audit Agency Office

Operational Aircraft:
68th Military Airlift Sqdn (AFRES)
C-5A

182nd Tactical Fighter Squadron (ANG)
F-16A/B   (SA)

Notes:
The SA-ALC is responsible for modernization and heavy depot maintenance for all USAF C-5S and a large number of Strategic Air Command B-52s. It is also responsible for MAC C-130s and various engines, including TF39s, TF56s and F100s. In total the center is charged with managing half the Air Force's engine inventory, plus all fuel lubricants in use with the USAF and NASA. The center also provides logistics management, procurement and distribution support for the C5B, C-17, C-9, F-5, O-2, OV-10, T-38 and T-46A. The base is the oldest continuously active air base in America

KEY FIELD

Key Field
Meridian
Mississippi 39302-1825
USA

Phone:
(601) 693-5031

Autovon:
694-9210

Command:
Air National Guard

Acreage:
ANG area 64

Personnel:
1,291 military personnel, 254 civilians

Units:
186th Tactical Reconnaissance Gp (ANG); 153rd Tactical Reconnaissance Sqdn (ANG); 238th Combat Communications Sqdn (ANG)

Operational Aircraft:
RF-4C   (KE)

ANG F–16s of the 182nd Tactical Fighter Squadron on the flightline at Kelly AFB.

KINGSLEY

Kingsley Field
Oregon 97603-0400
USA

Phone:
(503) 883-6350

Autovon:
830-6350

Command:
Air National Guard

Named after:
Lt. David Kingsley from Oregon, who
was killed in the Pacific during WWII

Acreage:
ANG area 405

Personnel:
214 military personnel, 50 civilians

Units:
114th Tactical Fighter Training Sqdn
(ANG); 142nd OLAD (ANG)

Operational Aircraft:
F-4C

KIRTLAND

Kirtland AFB
New Mexico 87117-5000
USA

Phone:
(505) 844-0011

Autovon:
244-0011

Command:
Military Airlift Command

Date est:
Jan. 1941

Named after:
Col. Roy S. Kirtland, an air pioneer
and commandant of Langley Field
during the 1930s

Acreage:
52,450

Personnel:
4,984 military personnel, 14,223
civilians

Units:
Air Force Contract Management Divn
(AFSC); Air Force Operational Test
and Evaluation Center; Air Force
Space Technology Center; Air Force
Weapons Lab (AFSC); Air Force Office
of Security Police; New Mexico ANG;
1550th Combat Crew Training Wing
(MAC); Defence Nuclear Agency Field
Command; Naval Weapons Evaluation
Facility; Sandia National Lab;
Lovelace Biomedical and
Environmental Research Institute;
AFSC NCO Academy; Air Force
Directorate of Nuclear Surety; 150th
Tactical Fighter Gp (ANG); 1960th
Communications Sqdn (AFCC); 3098th
Aviation Depot Sqdn; Det 1, 1369th
Audiovisual Sqdn; a number of other
agencies situated on the base are
involved in nuclear and laser research

Operational aircraft:
1550th Combat Crew Training Wing
(MAC)
TH-1F/UH-1N   1550th FTS
HC-130H/P   1551st FTS
CH-HH-3E
HH-53B & CH-53C

188th Tactical Fighter Sqdn (ANG)
A-7D/K
C-131B
The C-131 will be changed for a C-
130A

K.I. SAWYER

K. I. Sawyer AFB
Michigan 49843-5000
USA

Phone:
(906) 346-6511

Autovon:
472-1110

Command:
Strategic Air Command

Date est:
1959

Named after:
Kenneth I. Sawyer who proposed the
site for a county airport

Acreage:
5,278

Personnel:
3,637 military personnel, 610 civilians

Units:
410th Bomb Wing; 2001st
Communications Sqdn (AFCC)

Operational Aircraft:
410th Bombardment Wing (SAC)
B-52H   644th BS
KC-135A   46th ARS
            307th ARS

KULIS

Kulis ANGB
Anchorage International Airport
Alaska 99502
USA

Phone:
(907) 243-1145

Autovon:
(317) 626-1444

Command:
Air National Guard

Named after:
Lt. Albert Kulis who was killed during
a training flight in 1954

Acreage:
ANG area 129

Personnel:
848 military personnel, 165 civilians

Units:
176th Tactical Airlift Gp (ANG); 144th
Tactical Airlift Sqdn (ANG)

Operational Aircraft:
C-130H

KUNSAN

Kunsan AB
Kunsan
South Korea
APO San Francisco 96218-5000

Phone:
(654) 73596

Autovon:
272-2345

Command:
Pacific Air Command

Units:
8th Tactical Fighter Wing

Operational Aircraft:
8th Tactical Fighter Wing
F16A/B   35th TFS
            80th TFS   WP

Members of the 3700th SPS based at Lackland AFB taking part in Team Spirit 86.

LACKLAND

Lackland AFB
Texas 78236-5000
USA

Phone:
(512) 671-1110

Autovon:
473-1110

Command:
Air Training Command

Date est:
1941

Named after:
Brig. Gen. Frank D. Lackland, an early commandant of Kelly Field flying school

Acreage:
6,783

Personnel:
19,522 military personnel; 6,671 civilians

Units:
Officer Training School; Defense Language Institute – English Language Center; Wilford Hall USAF Medical Center; ATC NCO Academy; 539th Airforce Band; 3504th Recruiting Gp; Det 40, Air Logistics Center

Notes:
The base provides basic military training for regular, Air Guard and Air Reserve airmen. It also provides technical training of security police and law enforcement personnel.

Above right: Langley is home to the 1st Tactical Fighter Wing. The memorial aircraft commemorate a long and distinguished line of jet aviation connected with the base.

Right: Sign at Langley.

Courses are run for dog handlers. The Medical Center is the Air Force's largest medical establishment

LAJES

Lajes Field
Azores
APO New York 09406

Phone:
95-52101

Autovon:
723-1410

Command:
Military Airlift Command

Units:
1605th Military Airlift Support Wing, MAC

LAMBERT

Lambert Field
St Louis International Airport
Minnesota 63145
USA

Phone:
(314) 263-6356

Autovon:
693-6356

Command:
Air National Guard

Acreage:
ANG area 50

Personnel:
1,594 military personnel, 306 civilians

Units:
131st Tactical Fighter Wing (ANG);
110th Tactical Fighter Sqdn (ANG)

Operational Aircraft:
F-4E   (SL)
C-12F

LANGLEY

Langley AFB
Texas 78236-5000
USA

Phone:
(804) 764-9990

Autovon:
574-1110

Command:
Tactical Air Command

Date est:
30 Dec. 1916

Named after:
Samuel Pierpont Langley, an early air pioneer and scientist, who died in 1906

Acreage:
3,439

Personnel:
9,581 military personnel, 3,000 civilians

Units:
HQ Tactical Air Command; 1st Tactical Fighter Wing; HQ 1st Air Force (TAC); HQ CONUS NORAD; 2nd Aircraft Delivery Gp (TAC); 1913th Communications Gp (AFCC); 1912th Computer Systems Gp (AFCC); 564th Air Force Band (TAC); Det 7, 3rd Weather Sqdn (MAC); 48th Fighter Interceptor Sqdn; 6th Airborne Command and Control Sqdn (TAC); Low Intensity Conflict Center; NASA Langley Research Center; plus 20 other units

Operational Aircraft:
1st Tactical Fighter Wing (TAC)
F-15C/D   27th TFS
              71st TFS
              94th TFS   (FF)

6th Airborne Command & Control Sqdn (TAC)
EC-135H
EC-135P

48th Fighter Interceptor Sqdn (TAC)
F15A/B

Above left: The command post at Langley during a CPX.

Above: An F-15 pilot navigates his aircraft through the densely packed area of the Langley flightline.

Left: A member of the ground crew guides an F-15 pilot at Langley AFB.

LAUGHLIN

Laughlin AFB
Texas 78843-5000
USA

Phone:
(512) 298-3511

Autovon:
732-1110

Command:
Air Training Command

Date est:
Oct. 1942

Named after:
1st Lt. Jack T. Laughlin, a B-17 pilot killed over Java in 1942

Acreage:
4,008

Personnel:
2,738 military personnel, 790 civilians

Units:
47th Flying Training Wing

Operational Aircraft:
47th Flying Training Wing (ATC)
T-37B   85th FTS
T-39A   86th FTS

Notes:
The base provides undergraduate pilot training

Far right: Little Rock plays host to the regular Volant Scorpion exercises.

LINCOLN

Lincoln Municipal Airport
Nebraska 68524-1897
USA

Phone:
(402) 473-1326

Autovon:
720-1210

Command:
Air National Guard

Acreage:
ANG area 163

Far right: A B–52 of the 42nd Bomb Wing at Loring AFB. The B–52 is loaded with McDonnell Douglas AGM–84A Harpoon anti-ship missiles.

Personnel:
1,124 military personnel, 239 civilians

Units:
155th Tactical Reconnaissance Gp;
173rd Tactical Reconnaissance Sqdn;
plus an Army National Guard Unit

Operational Aircraft:
C-12F
RF-4C

LINDSEY

Lindsey AB
West Germany
APO New York 09634-5000

Phone:
6121-827283

Autovon:
339-1110

Command:
United States Air Forces in Europe

Units:
HQ 65th Air Divn, USAFE; 7100th Combat Support Wing, USAFE; USAF Regional Medical Center (Wiesbaden); 1st Combat Communications Gp, AFCC

LITTLE ROCK

Little Rock AFB
Arkansas 72099-5000
USA

Phone:
(501) 988-3131

Autovon:
731-1110

Command:
Military Airlift Command

Date est:
1955

Acreage:
6,898

Personnel:
6,000 military personnel, 748 civilians

Units:
314th Tactical Airlift Wing; 2151st Communications Sqdn; 22nd Air Force NCO Leadership School

Operational Aircraft:
314th Tactical Airlift Wing (MAC)
C-130E   16th TATS
             48th TAS
             61st TAS
             62nd TAS

154th Air Refueling Sqdn (ANG)
KC-135E

Notes:
Little Rock was the home of the 308th Strategic Missile Wing, the last Titan II wing. The missiles were taken out of service in 1987. It is DoD's only C-130 training center

LORING

Loring AFB
Maine, 04751-5000
USA

Phone:
(207) 999-1110

Autovon:
920-1110

Command:
Strategic Air Command

Date est:
1953

Named after:
Major Charles Loring Jr, an F-80 pilot killed in action over North Korea in 1952. He was posthumously awarded the Medal of Honor

Acreage:
9,000

Personnel:
3,763 military personnel, 582 civilians

Units:
42nd Bomb Wing

Operational Aircraft:
42nd Bombardment Wing (SAC)
B-52G   69thBS
KC-135A   42nd ARS
               407th ARS

LOS ANGELES

Los Angeles AFB
California 80230-5000
USA

Phone:
(213) 643-1000

Autovon:
833-1110

Command:
Air Force Systems Command

Date est:
Dec. 1960

Named after:
The city of Los Angeles

Acreage:
96 plus 96 at Fort MacArthur Annex

Personnel:
2,109 military personnel, 2,278 civilians

Units:
HQ 1st Space Divn, 6592nd Air Base Gp

Notes:
The Space Division manages the majority of America's military space systems. The base is at the heart of a large complex of space contractors

LOWRY

Lowry AFB
Colorado 80230-5000
USA

Phone:
(303) 370-1110

Autovon:
926-1110

Command:
Air Training Command

Date est:
Feb. 1938

Named after:
1st Lt. Francis B. Lowry, killed on a photographic reconnaissance over Crepion, France in 1918

Acreage:
1,863 plus a 3,511 acre training annex 25 miles east of Lowry

Personnel:
12,693 military personnel (3,592 in 1987) 4,395 civilians

Units:
Lowry Technical Training Center; Air Force Training Center; Air Force Accounting and Finance Center; Air Reserve Personnel Center; 3320th Correction and Rehabilitation Sqdn

Five F-16s from the 58th Tactical Training Wing at Luke AFB.

Operational Aircraft:
Lowry Technical Training Center
(ATC)
various

Notes:
The Lowry Technical Training Center
is responsible for training in avionics,
space operations, munitions, logistics
and audiovisual equipment

LUKE

Luke AFB
Arizona 85309
USA

Phone:
(602) 856-7411

Autovon:
853-1110

Command:
Tactical Air Command

Date est:
1941

Named after:
2nd Lt. Frank Luke, Jr. a WWI
observation-balloon-busting ace,
killed in action near Murvaux, France
in 1918. He was the first aviator to be
awarded the Medal of Honor

Acreage:
4,197*

Personnel:
5,543 military personnel, 1,450
civilians

Units:
832nd Air Divn; 405th Tactical
Training Wing; 58th Tactical Training
Wing; 302nd Special Operations Sqdn
(AFRES)

Operational Aircraft:
58th Tactical Training Wing (TAC)
F16A/B   310th TFTS 311th TFTS
F16C/D   312th TFTS 314th TFTS

405th Tactical Training Wing (TAC)
F-5E/F   425th TFS Williams AFB
F-16A   426th TFTS
F15A/Bs   461st TFTS
550th TFTS 555th TFTS   (LA)

302nd Special Operations Sqdn
(AFRES)
HC-130H/N (LH)

Notes:
The largest fighter training base in the
Western world. It trains both USAF

and foreign pilots on the F-5, F-15 and
F-16.
* Plus a 2,700,000 acre range at Gila
Bend.

MACDILL

MacDill AFB
Florida 33608-5000
USA

Phone:
(813) 830-1110

Autovon:
968-1110

Command:
Tactical Air Command

Date est:
Apr. 1941

Named after:
Col. Leslie MacDill, killed in an
aircraft accident near Washington, DC
in 1938

Acreage:
5,631

Personnel:
7,031 military personnel, 1,777
civilians

Units:
56th Tactical Training Wing; HQ
Special Operations Command; HQ US
Central Command; Joint
Communication Support Element

Operational Aircraft:
56th Tactical Training Wing (TAC)
F16A/B   61st TFTS
          62nd TFTS
          63rd TFTS
          72nd TFTS
The wing will lose one squadron with
the transfer of aircraft to the 161st
TFTS (ANG) during 1988

Notes:
The 56th TTW is responsible for
replacement training on the F-16

MALMSTROM

Malmstrom AFB
Montana 59402-5000
USA

Phone:
(406) 731-9990

Autovon:
632-1110

Command:
Strategic Air Command

Date est:
Dec. 1942

Named after:
Col. Einar A. Malmstrom, a WWII
fighter commander, killed in a flying
accident in 1954

Acreage:
3,573 plus approx. 23,000 sq. miles of
missile complex

Personnel:
3,768 military personnel (6,824 in
1987), 530 civilians

Units:
341st Strategic Missile Wing

Notes:
The site of the first SAC Minuteman
Wing

MANSFIELD LAHM

Mansfield Lahm Airport
Ohio 44901-5000
USA

Phone:
(419) 522-9355

Autovon:
696-6210

Command:
Air National Guard

Named after:
The nearby city and Brig. Gen. Frank
P. Lahm, an early aviation pioneer

Acreage:
45

Personnel:
930 military personnel, 167 civilians

Units:
179th Tactical Airlift Gp; 164th
Tactical Airlift Sqdn

Operational Aircraft:
C-130B

Opposite: F–16s of the 56th Tactical Training Wing based at MacDill AFB.

MARCH

March AFB
California 9518-5000
USA

Phone:
(714) 655-1110

Autovon:
947-1110

Command:
Strategic Air Command

Date est:
Mar. 1918

Named after:
2nd Lt. Peyton C. March, Jr who died as a result of injuries sustained from an aircraft crash in 1918

Acreage:
7,703

Personnel:
4,034 military personnel, 2,171 civilians (949 in 1987)

Units:
HQ 15th Air Force; 22nd Air Refueling Wing Southwest Air Defense Sector (TAC); 22nd Strategic Hospital; 452nd Air Refueling Wing (AFRES); 943rd Tactical Airlift Gp; 163rd Tactical Fighter Gp (ANG)

Operational Aircraft:
22nd Air Refueling Wing (SAC)
KC-10A   9th ARS
KC-135A   22nd ARS

336th Air Refueling Sqdn (AFRES)
KC-135A/E

303rd Tactical Airlift Sqdn (AFRES)
C-130B

196th Tactical Fighter Sqdn (ANG)
F-4C/E

MARTINSBURG

Martinsburg Municipal Airport
(Shepherd Field)
West Virginia 25401
USA

Phone:
(304) 267-5100

Autovon:
696-6210

Command:
Air National Guard

Acreage:
ANG area 346

Personnel:
930 military personnel, 167 civilians

Units:
167th Tactical Airlift Gp (ANG); 167th Tactical Airlift Sqdn

Operational Aircraft:
C-130B

MATHER

Mather AFB
California 95655-5000
USA

Phone:
(916) 364-1110

Autovon:
828-1110

Command:
Air Training Command

Date est:
1918

Named after:
2nd Lt. Carl S. Mather, who was killed in a midair crash over Texas in 1918

Acreage:
5,800

Personnel:
5,410 military personnel, 2,079 civilians

Units:
323rd Flying Training Wing (ATC); 320th Bomb Wing (SAC); 940th Air Refueling Gp (AFRES); 3506th Recruiting Gp; 323rd Air Base Gp (ATC); 2034th Communications Sqdn (AFCC)

Operational Aircraft:
320th Bombardment Wing (SAC)
B-52G   441st BS
KC-135A   904th ARS

314th Air Refueling Sqdn (AFRES)
KC-135A/E

323rd Flying Training Wing (ATC)
T-37B   454th FTS
T-38A   455th FTS

Notes:
The base is the centre for all DoD navigation training. It also trains navigators from the 2nd German Air Force and 90 other countries and trains USAF electronic warfare officers

BASE REALIGNMENTS AND CLOSURES
Report of the Defense Secretary's Commission December 1988

The Commission recommends Mather AFB for closure primarily due to its deficiencies in the quality and availability of facilities and excess capacity within the category. The net cost of closure and relocation will be paid back within one year.
The Commission expects annual savings to be $78.7 million.

The military value of Mather AFB is lower than other flying-training installations. Mather has a shortage of buildings for operational and training purposes, and a shortage of maintenance and administrative facilities. Additionally, the availability of vehicle pavements is less than required. The installation has also had difficulty in hiring civilian workers in the area, due to the demand for technically qualified workers by other industries within the civilian community.

While Mather AFB has a hospital, the base requires additional medical and dental facilities. The closure of Mather will save construction costs for these facilities.

Mather AFB is one of eight Air Training Command flying-training bases. Mather conducts undergraduate navigator training for the Air Force, Navy, and Marine Corps, as well as foreign countries. The base also conducts advanced and tactical navigation, electronic-warfare, instructor, and other training. The B-52 bombers at Mather are programmed to retire, which will leave only the navigator training mission and an Air Force Reserve KC-135 unit. These missions can be relocated within the immediate vicinity to provide improved multi-Service training capability in a more cost-effective manner.

This closure will have no negative impact on the local environment. Cleanup of hazardous materials and waste contamination at Mather is covered by the Defense Environmental Restoration Program. Cleanup is independent of the closure.
The relocation of the units currently assigned to Mather will not significantly alter the environmental situation at the gaining bases because comparable operations are presently

underway at those bases.

This closure will have minimal impact on local employment.

The Commission recommends the following relocations of major units and related support activities:

The 323rd Flying Training Wing to Beale AFB, California. This move will take advantage of force-structure drawdown at Beale and improve multi-Service training.

The 940th Air Refueling Group (Air Force Reserve) to McClellan AFB, California if local authorities do not elect to operate the Mather facility as an airport. McClellan is only 10 miles from Mather and has the capacity to absorb the unit. Additional savings could be realized if this reserve unit could remain at the Mather facility.

MAXWELL

Maxwell AFB
Alabama 36112
USA

Phone:
(205) 293-1110

Autovon:
875-1110

Command:
Air University

Date est:
1918

Named after:
2nd Lt. William C. Maxwell, killed in an air accident in 1920, while serving with the 3rd Aero Sqdn in the Philippines

Acreage:
2,535

Personnel:
4,326 military personnel, 1,632 civilians

Units:
HQ Air University; 3800th Air Base Wing; Air War College; Air Command and Staff College; Center for Aerospace Doctrine, Research and Education; Center for Professional Development; Squadron Officer School; Air Force Historical Research Center; HQ Air Force ROTC (ATC); HQ Civil Air Patrol-USAF; Community College of the Air Force (ATC); 908th Tactical Airlift Gp (AFRES)

Operational Aircraft:
357th Tactical Airlift Sqdn (AFRES)
C-130H

Notes:
In 1910 Orville Wright chose the site to establish a Flying School, which became the army's Wright Field in 1918. The Commander of Maxwell AFB is also Commander of Gunter Air Force Station which is on the other side of the city of Montgomery

MAY

May ANGB
Reno-Cannon International Airport
Nevada 89502
USA

Phone:
(702) 788-4500

Autovon:
830-4500

Command:
Air National Guard

Named after:
Maj. Gen. James A. May, a state Adjutant General

Acreage:
ANG area 123

Personnel:
1,090 military personnel, 222 civilians

Units:
152nd Tactical Reconnaissance Gp (ANG); 192nd Tactical Reconnaissance Sqdn (ANG)

Operational Aircraft:
RF-4C
C-131D
The C-131D is due to be replaced by a C-12J

McCHORD

McChord AFB
Washington 98438-5000
USA

Phone:
(206) 984-1910

Autovon:
976-1110

Command:
Military Airlift Command

Date est:
May 1938

Named after:
Col. William C. McChord, killed while attempting a forced landing in an A-17 at Maidens, Virginia in 1937

Acreage:
4,609

Personnel:
5,562 military personnel, 1,982 civilians

Units:
62nd Military Airlift Wing; HQ 25th Air Divn (TAC); Northwest Air Defense Sector (TAC); 318th Fighter Interceptor Sqdn (TAC); Region Operations Control Center (NORAD); 446th Military Airlift Wing (AFRES Assoc.)

A Hummer is unloaded from a C–130 of the 36th TAS based at McChord AFB. The squadron has lost a number of its C–130s to the 95th TAS/AFRES.

Above: An AIM–9 Sparrow is launched from an F–15 of the 318th Fighter Interceptor Squadron based at McChord AFB.

Right: A Hummer is directed by ground crew before boarding a C–130 of the 36th TAS based at McChord AFB.

Operational Aircraft:
62nd Military Airlift Wing
C-141B   4th MAS
            8th MAS
C-130E   36th TAS
36th TAS to disband

318th Fighter Interceptor Sqdn (TAC)
F15A/B

Notes:
McChord was established in 1938 as a bomber base

McCLELLAN

McClellan AFB
California 95652
USA

Phone:
(916) 643-2111

Autovon:
633-1110

Command:
Air Force Logistics Command

Date est:
1939

Named after:
Maj. Hezekiah McClellan, an Arctic

aeronautical pioneer who was killed in an aircrash in 1936

Acreage:
2,917

Personnel:
3,859 military personnel, 13,593 civilians

Units:
HQ Sacramento Air Logistics Center; 41st Rescue and Weather Reconnaissance Wing (MAC); 2049th Communication Gp (AFCC); 1849th Electronics Installation Sqdn (AFCC); Technical Operations Divn, Air Force Technical Applications Center (AFSC); Test and Evaluation Center (TAC); HQ 4th Air Force (AFRES); Defense Logistics Agency; US Coast Guard Air Station, Sacramento (DOT)

Operational Aircraft:
55th Weather Reconnaissance Sqdn (MAC)
WC-135B

41st Aerospace Rescue & Recovery Sqdn (MAC)
HC-130
HH-53B/C

Notes:
The Logistics Center provides logistics management, maintenance, procurement and distribution support for the A-10, F-111, FB-111 and EF-111; plus surveillance and warning systems, the Space Transportation System, communication-electronics equipment, radar sites, and generators. They also provide maintenance for the F-4

McCOLLUM

McCollum Airport
Kennesaw
Georgia 30144
USA

Phone:
(404) 422-2500

Autovon:
925-2479

Command:
Air National Guard

Acreage:
13

Personnel:
263 military personnel, 38 civilians

Units:
129th Tactical Control Sqdn

McCONNELL

McConnell AFB
Kansas 67221-5000
USA

Phone:
(316) 652-6100

Autovon:
743-1130

Command:
Strategic Air Command

Date est:
June 1951

Named after:
The "Flying McConnell Brothers,"
three airmen from Wichita who joined
the Army Air Corps during WWII. Two
of the brothers were killed while flying

Acreage:
3,066

Personnel:
3,057 military personnel, 691 civilians

Units:
384th Bomb Wing; 184th Tactical
Fighter Gp (ANG)

Operational Aircraft:
384th Bombardment Wing (SAC)
B-1B
KC-135R   91st ARS
            384th ARS

127th Tactical Fighter Sqdn (ANG)
F-4D

161st Tactical Fighter Training Sqdn
(ANG)
F-16A/B

Notes:
The 384th Bomb Wing was formed
from the 384th Air Refueling Wing in
July 1987. The Wing started to receive
their B-1Bs in Feb. 1988. McConnell
AFB was originally formed to allow
training on the B-47 jet bomber which
was built near the base

McENTIRE

McEntire ANGB
South Carolina 29044
USA

Signs welcoming visitors to the
McEntire ANG Base.

Phone:
(803) 776-5121

Autovon:
583-8201

Command:
Air National Guard

Named after:
ANG Brigadier General B.B. McEntire
who died in an F-104 accident in
1961.

Acreage:
ANG area 2,473

Personnel:
1,386 military personnel, 245 civilians

Units:
169th Tactical Fighter Gp (ANG);
157th Tactical Fighter Sqdn (ANG);
240th Combat Communications Sqdn
(ANG); plus an Army Guard aviation
unit

Operational Aircraft:
F-16A/B   (SC)
C-131D

McGUIRE

McGuire AFB
New Jersey 08641-5000
USA

Phone:
(609) 724-1100

Autovon:
440-0111

Command:
Military Airlift Command

The Air Force operates a large
number of trains at its bases.
This 44–ton 1953 diesel is in
use at McClellan AFB.

Date est:
1949

Named after:
Major Thomas B. McGuire Jr, a P-38 pilot who was the second leading US ace during WWII. He was killed in action over the Philippines in 1945

Acreage:
3,552

Personnel:
5,258 military personnel, 1,592 civilians

Units:
438th Military Airlift Wing; HQ 21st Air Force; New Jersey ANG; New Jersey Civil Air Patrol; 170th Air Refueling Gp (ANG); 108th Tactical Fighter Wing (ANG); 514th Military Airlift Wing (AFRES Assoc.); Military Airlift Command NCO Academy East; Air Force Band of the East; OLB, 1361st Audiovisual Sqdn

Operational Aircraft:
438th Military Airlift Wing (MAC)
C-141B   6th MAS
          18th MAS
          30th MAS

150th Air Refueling Sqdn (ANG)
KC-135E
C-131D
The C-131 will be replaced by a C-130A

141st Tactical Fighter Sqdn (ANG)
F-4E   (NJ)

Notes:
The base is the largest MAC aerial port on the East Coast and is designated as the Gateway to NATO

McGHEE-TYSON

McGhee-Tyson Airport
Knoxville
Tennessee 37901
USA

Phone:
(615) 970-3077

Autovon:
588-8210

Command:
Air National Guard

Acreage:
ANG area 271

Personnel:
1,150 military personnel, 262 civilians

Units:
134th Air Refueling Gp (ANG); 151st Air Refueling Sqdn (ANG); 228th Combat Communications Sqdn (ANG); ANG I.G. Brown Professional Military Education Center

Operational Aircraft:
KC-135E   151st ARS

MEMPHIS

Memphis International Airport
Tennessee 38181-0026
USA

Phone:
(901) 369-4111

Autovon:
966-8210

Command:
Air National Guard

Acreage:
ANG area 85

Personnel:
948 military personnel, 176 civilians

Units:
164th Airlift Gp (ANG); 155th Tactical Airlift Sqdn (ANG)

Operational Aircraft:
C-130A

MINNEAPOLIS ST. PAUL

Minneapolis St. Paul International Airport
Minnesota 55450
USA

Phone:
ANG (612) 725-5011
AFRES (612) 725-5011

Autovon:
ANG 825-5681
AFRES 825-5100

Command:
Air Force Reserve

Acreage:
AFRES 300
ANG 126

Personnel:
AFRES: 1,067 military personnel, 352 civilians; ANG: 1,410 military personnel, 239 civilians

Units:
934th Tactical Airlift Gp (AFRES); 96th Tactical Airlift Sqdn (AFRES); 133rd Tactical Airlift Wing (ANG); 109th Tactical Airlift Sqdn (ANG); 210th Engineering & Installation Sqdn (ANG); 237th Air Traffic Control Flight (ANG); 133rd Field Training Flight (ANG); Navy Readiness Command, Region 16; Naval Air Reserve Center; Marine Wing Support Gp, Det 47; Defense Investigative Service; USAF-CAP/NCLR & CAP MNLO; Det 3, 1974th Teleprocessing Gp (USAF)

Operational Aircraft:
C-130E   109th TAS (ANG)
          96th TAS (AFRES)

MISAWA

Misawa AB
Japan
APO San Francisco 96519-5000

Phone:
(827) 214171

Autovon:
248-1101

Command:
Pacific Air Forces

Date est:
1945

Units:
432nd Tactical Fighter Wing; 6920th Electronic Security Gp (ESC)

Operational Aircraft:
432nd Tactical Fighter Wing
F-16A/B   13th TFS
F-16C/D   14th TFS (MJ)

Notes:
The base was built by the Japanese Naval Air Force in 1942

An F–16 of the 432nd TFW based at Misawa AB, Japan.

MINOT

Minot AFB
North Dakota 58705-5000
USA

Phone:
(701) 723-1110

Autovon:
344-1110

Command:
Strategic Air Command

Date est:
Jan. 1957

Named after:
The city of Minot whose people provided $50,000 towards the cost of the site for the Air Force

Acreage:
5,085*

Personnel:
6,106 military personnel, 980 civilians

Units:
57th Air Divn; 91st Strategic Missile Wing; 5th Bomb Wing; 5th Fighter Interceptor Sqdn; 2150th Communications Sqdn (AFCC); Det 7,

37th ARRS (MAC); 64th Flying Training Wing (ATC); Det 21, 9th Weather Sqdn (AWS); Det 7, Air Force Institute of Technology; AFOSI Det 1312; Det 35, 3904th Management Engineering Sqdn; Det 520, Air Force Audit Agency; 15th Air Force NCO Leadership School

Operational Aircraft:
5th Bombardment Wing (SAC)
B-52H   23rd BS
KC-135A   7th ARS

5th Fighter Interceptor Sqdn (TAC)
F15 A/B
The unit was disbanded in 1988

Notes:
* Plus a farther 19,324 acres which contain the Minuteman III missile silos

MOFFETT

Moffett Field NAS
California 94035
USA

Phone:
(415) 966-4700

Autovon:
462-4600

Command:
Air National Guard

Acreage:
ANG area 12

Personnel:
768 military personnel; 176 civilians

Units:
129th Aerospace Rescue & Recovery Gp (ANG); 129th Aerospace Rescue & Recovery Sqdn (ANG)

Operational Aircraft:
HC-130H/P
HH-3E

MOODY

Moody AFB
Georgia 31699-5000
USA

Phone:
(912) 333-4211

Autovon:
460-1110

Command:
Tactical Air Command

Date est:
June 1941

Named after:
Maj. George P. Moody who was killed in 1941 while test-flying a Beech AT-10

Acreage:
6,050

Personnel:
3,493 military personnel, 664 civilians

Units:
347th Tactical Fighter Wing

Operational Aircraft:
347th Tactical Fighter Wing (TAC)
F-16A/B   68th TFS
           69th TFS
           70th TFS

Far right: Rows of computer banks surround the simulator cockpit of an EF–111 at Mountain AFB.

Below: Two EF–111As of the 366th TFW based at Mountain AFB. All EF–111 crews do their training at Mountain AFB.

MOUNTAIN HOME

Mountain Home AFB
Idaho 83648-5000
USA

Phone:
(208) 828-2111

Autovon:
857-1110

Command:
Tactical Air Command

Date est:
Apr. 1942

Acreage:
9,147

Personnel:
3,929 military personnel, 473 civilians

Units:
366th Tactical Fighter Wing; 2036th Communications Sqdn (AFCC); 513th Field Training Det (ATC); Det. 22, 40th ARRS (MAC); OL AF, 4444th Operations Sqdn; Det 2, USAF Fighter Weapons School; Det 3, Tactical Air Warfare Center; AFOSI Det 2007; Det 454, Air Force Audit Agency; Det 11, 4400th Management Engineering Sqdn; Det 18, 25th Weather Sqdn

MUNIZ

Muniz ANGB
San Juan International Air Port
Puerto Rico 00914
USA

Phone:
(809) 728-5450

Autovon:
860-9210

Command:
Air National Guard

Named after:
Lt. Col. José A. Muniz who was killed
in an aircraft accident in 1960

Personnel:
1,297 military personnel, 209 civilians

Units:
156th Tactical Fighter Gp (ANG);
198th Tactical Fighter Sqdn (ANG)

Operational Aircraft:
A-7D/K

MYRTLE BEACH

Myrtle Beach AFB
South Carolina 29579-5000
USA

Phone:
(803) 238-7211

Autovon:
748-1110

Command:
Tactical Air Command

Date est:
1956

Acreage:
3,793

Personnel:
3,500 military personnel, 760 civilians

Units:
354th Tactical Fighter Wing; 2066th
Communications Sqdn (AFCC); Det
11, 39th ARRW (MAC); 301st Field
Training Det (ATC); 1816th Reserve
Advisor Sqdn; Det 3, 3rd Weather
Sqdn; Det 12, 440th Management
Engineering Sqdn (ATC); Det 2105,
Air Force Office of Special
Investigations; 73rd Tactical Control
Flight (TAC)

Operational Aircraft:
345th Tactical Fighter Wing (TAC)
A-10A   353rd TFS
          355th TFS
          356th TFS (MB)

Notes:
The base shares the runway with
Myrtle Beach Jetport. The 354th
Tactical Fighter Wing's mission is to
provide the capability to deploy world-
wide and to be able to provide close air
support and anti-war support

NASHVILLE

Nashville Metropolitan Airport
Tennessee 37217-0267
USA

Phone:
(615) 361-4600

Autovon:
446-6210

Command:
Air National Guard

Acreage:
ANG area 75

Personnel:
1,419 military personnel, 287 civilians

Units:
118th Tactical Airlift Wing (ANG);
105th Tactical Airlift Sqdn (ANG)

Operational Aircraft:
C-130A   105th TAS

NELLIS

Nellis AFB
Nevada 89191-5000
USA

Phone:
(702) 643-1800

A–10s of the 345th TFW on the
flightline at Myrtle Beach. The
unit shares the runway with the
Myrtle Beach Jetport.

Aggressor pilots study information from their last exercise supplied by the Air Combat Maneuvering Instrumentation (ACMI) computers at Nellis.

Insert: The multi-colored F–5Es from the 57th Fighter Wing at Nellis AFB as they formate over a lake. The Aggressors reckon that theirs is "The only game in town."

Autovon:
682-1800

Command:
Tactical Air Command

Date est:
July 1941

Named after:
1st Lt. William H. Nellis, a P-47 pilot killed over Europe in 1944

Acreage:
11,274*

Personnel:
10,171 military personnel, 1,200 civilians

Units:
Tactical Fighter Weapons Center; 57th

Fighter Weapons Wing; Thunderbirds Air Demonstrations Sqdn; 440th Tactical Fighter Training Gp (Red Flag); 554th Operations Support Wing; 554th Range Gp; 474th Tactical Fighter Wing; 4450th Tactical Training Gp; 820th Civil Engineering Sqdn "Red Horse"; 3096th Aviation Depot Sqdn; 2069th Communications Sqdn

Operational Aircraft:
57th Fighter Weapons Wing (TAC)
A10A
F-5E
F-15C/D
F-16A/B/C F-111D/F   (WA)

F-16A 64th AS
F-5E 65th AS

4450th Tactical Gp (TAC)
A-7D/K   (LV)

Air Demonstration Sqdn (TAC)
(The Thunderbirds)
F-16A/B

Notes:
* Plus ranges totalling 3,012,770 acres. Established as an Army Air Corps gunnery school in 1941, Nellis has become the home of the Tactical Fighter Weapons Center which sets out to provide the nearest thing to real war most fighter jocks will, it is hoped, ever come. See Tonopah Test Range Airfield for details on the F-117 Stealth Fighter, operated by the 4450th Tactical Group.

Two F-15s of the 57th Fighter Weapons Wing based at Nellis AFB.

Left: An A-10, F-15C, F-16 and an F-111 from the 57th Fighter Weapons Wing at Nellis fly over the Hoover Dam.

NEWARK

Newark AFS
Ohio 43057
USA

Phone:
(614) 522-2171

Autovon:
580-2171

Command:
Air Force Logistics Command

Date est:
Nov. 1962

Personnel:
45 military personnel, 2,600 civilians

Units:
Aerospace Guidance and Metrology Center

Notes:
The center repairs inertial guidance and navigation for the majority of the Air Force's aircraft and missiles plus a number of inertial systems for the other armed services. It is also in charge of the AF's world-wide measurement and calibration program. It acts as a bridge between the AF's 130 precision-measurement laboratories which are scattered around the world and the National Bureau of Standards

NEW ORLEANS

New Orleans NAS
Alvin Callender Field
Louisiana
USA

Phone:
ANG (504) 393-3392
AFRES (504) 393-3293

Autovon:
ANG 363-3399
AFRES 363-3293

Command:
AFRES/ANG

Named after:
Alvin A. Callender, who died while flying with the British Royal Flying Corps during WWI

Acreage:
3,245

Personnel:
AFRES: 820 military personnel, 177 civilians; ANG: 1,178 military personnel, 270 civilians

Units:
926th Tactical Fighter Gp (AFRES);
706th Tactical Fighter Sqdn (AFRES);
159th Tactical Fighter Gp (ANG);
122nd Tactical Fighter Sqdn (ANG)

Operational Aircraft:
A-10A   706th TFS (NO)
F-15A/B   122nd TFS
C-12J

Notes:
New Orleans NAS was the first joint Air Reserve Training Facility

NIAGARA FALLS

Niagara Falls International Airport
New York 14304-5000
USA

Phone:
(716) 236-2000

Autovon:
489-3011

Command:
Air Force Reserve

Date est:
Jan. 1952

Acreage:
AFRES area 979

Personnel:
AFRES: 1,045 military personnel, 384 civilians; ANG: 1,023 military personnel, 270 civilians

Units:
914th Tactical Airlift Gp (AFRES);
328th Tactical Airlift Sqdn (AFRES);
107th Fighter Interceptor Gp (ANG);
136th Fighter Interceptor Sqdn

Operational Aircraft:
F-4D   136th FIS
C-130E   328th TAS

NORTON

Norton AFB
California 92409-5000
USA

Phone:
(714) 382-1110

Autovon:
876-1110

Command:
Military Airlift Command

Date est:
Mar. 1942

Named after:
Capt. Leland F. Norton, a WWII A-20 pilot killed in action near Amiens, France in 1944

Acreage:
2,430 acres

Personnel:
8,912 military personnel (includes AFRES), 2,626 civilians

Units:
63rd Military Airlift Wing; HQ Air Force Inspection and Safety Center; HQ Air Force Audit Agency; HQ Aerospace Audiovisual Service (MAC); Ballistic Missile Office (AFSC); 445th Military Airlift Wing (AFRES Assoc.); MAC NCO Academy West; 22nd Air Force NCO Leadership School

Operational Aircraft:
63rd Military Airlift Wing (MAC)
C-141B   14th MAS
            15th MAS
            53rd MAS

1400th Military Airlift Sqdn (MAC)
C-12F Det 3 Nellis AFB
C-21A Det 1 McClellan AFB, Det 2 Randolph, Det 4 Kirkland AFB

Notes:
The base is situated within the city of San Bernadino

Right: A briefing for a C–141 crew from the 63rd Military Airlift Wing based at Norton AFB.

BASE REALIGNMENTS AND CLOSURES
Report of the Defense Secretary's Commission December 1988

The Commission recommends Norton AFB for closure primarily because of air traffic congestion, inadequate facilities, and because of excess capacity within the category. The net cost of closure and relocation will be paid back within two years. The Commission expects annual savings to be $67.9 million.

The military value of Norton AFB is lower than other strategic-airlift installations because of a combination of increasing air-traffic congestion, outdated facilities and increasing competition for skilled personnel.

Norton AFB is currently one of six Military Airlift Command strategic-airlift bases that provide airlift for troops and military cargo. The wing at Norton supports US Army and Marine Corps airlift requirements and participates in other airlift operations. Flight operations at Norton have become constrained because of increasing air trafffic congestion in the Los Angeles area.

Norton AFB has a number of large warehouses of generally poor quality. Only the relatively temperate climate allows their use, but deterioration continues. There is also a shortage of weapons storage facilities. Utilities and most other facilities need a general upgrading to meet today's technological standards. Because of the poor quality of facilities, higher than normal expenditures are required for maintenance, repair, and periodic replacement.

There are also deficiencies at Norton AFB in the area of quality of life. The most prominent include a shortage of family housing units and inadequate medical, dental, and recreational facilities. The installation also has difficulty meeting civilian hiring requirements due to the demand for technically qualified workers by other industries within the civilian sector.

This closure will have no negative impact on the local environment. Cleanup of hazardous materials and waste contamination at Norton is covered by the Defense Environmental Restoration Program. Cleanup is independent of the closure. The movement of the units currently assigned to Norton will not adversely affect the environmental situation at gaining bases since comparable operations are already underway there.

This closure will have minimal impact on local employment.

The Commission recommends the following relocations of major units and related support activities:

Three Squadrons of the 63rd Military Airlift Wing and the 445th Military Airlift Wing (AFRES) (C-141, C-21 and C12 aircraft) to March AFB, California. The remaining squadron (C-141 aircraft) to McChord AFB, Washington. These moves will enhance command and control, and reduce the cost of operations while still providing for three strategic-airlift installations on the West Coast.

The Air Force Inspection and Safety Center to Kirtland AFB, New Mexico, to be consolidated with the Nuclear Safety and Inspection Center.

The Air Force Audit Agency to March AFB. This provides new, modern facilities for this unit within the same local region.

The commission notes the Air Force is exploring other alternatives for accomplishing the Air Force Audio Visual Service Center mission and therefore recommends that the Air Force be given the option of moving this unit to March AFB or retaining it in its present location at Norton. The annual savings reflect the movement to March.

Because of the high cost of relocation and the functional requirement for the Ballistic Missile Office to remain in the local area, the Commission further recommends it remain at Norton AFB. In order to reduce the shortage of family housing in the local area, the Commission further recommends that Norton AFB family housing be retained for use by personnel assigned to March AFB.

Loading a C–141 at Norton AFB in preparation for a mission to Antarctica.

The Headquarters of Strategic Air Command at Offutt Air Force Base, Nebraska.

Aerospace Communications Wing (AFCC); 1000th Satellite Operations Gp (AFSPACECOM); 6949th Electronic Security Sqdn (ESC); 702nd Air Force Band

Operational Aircraft:
55th Strategic Reconnaissance Wing (SAC)
EC-135C   2nd ACCS
C-135, NKC-135, RC-135U/V/W

38th SRS, 343rd SRS
E-4B   1st ACCS

Notes:
* The base was originally activated as the Army's Fort Crook home of the Twenty-Second United States Infantry. It became active as an aviation base in 1921 when the first runway was built

OFFUTT

Offutt AFB
Nebraska 68113-5000
USA

Phone:
(402) 294-1110

Autovon:
271-1110

Command:
Strategic Air Command

Date est:
1896*

Named after:
1st Lt. Jarvis J. Offutt, a WWI pilot who died of injuries received near Valheureux, France in 1918

Acreage:
1,914

Personnel:
12,047 military personnel, 3,490 civilians

Units:
HQ Strategic Air Command; 55th Strategic Reconnaissance Wing; 544th Strategic Intelligence Wing; Air Force Global Weather Center (MAC); 3rd Weather Wing (MAC); 3902nd Air Base Wing; HQ Strategic Communications Divn (AFCC); 1st

OLMSTED

Olmsted Field
Harrisburg International Airport
Pennsylvania 17057
USA

Phone:
(717) 948-2201

Autovon:
454-9201

Command:
Air National Guard

Acreage:
ANG area 70

Personnel:
1,117 military personnel, 269 civilians

Units:
193rd Special Operations Gp (ANG); 193rd Special Operations Sqdn (ANG)

Operational Aircraft:
EC-130E   193rd SOS

ONIZUKA

Onizuka AFB
California 94088-3430
USA

Phone:
(408) 752-3110

Autovon:
359-3100

Command:
Air Force Systems Command

ONTARIO

Ontario International Airport
Ontario
California 91761
USA

Phone:
(714) 984-2705

Autovon:
898-1895

Command:
Air National Guard

Personnel:
176 military personnel, 16 civilians

Acreage:
ANG area 39

Units:
148th Combat Communications Sqdn (ANG)

OSAN

Osan AB
South Korea
APO San Francisco 96461-5000

Phone:
Not available

Autovon:
284-4110

Command:
Pacific Air Forces

Units:
HQ 7th Air Force (PACAF); 51st Tactical Fighter Wing (PACAF); 5th Tactical Air Control Gp (PACAF); 6th Tactical Air Control Gp (PACAF); 2146th Communications Gp (AFCC); 6903rd Electronic Security Gp (ESC)

Operational Aircraft:
51st Tactical Fighter Wing (PACAF)
A-10   25th TFS   (SU) based at Suwon AB
F-4E   36th TFS   (OS) based at OSAN AB
F-4E   497th TFS   (GU) based at Taegu AB

19th Tactical Air Support Sqdn
OV-10A   (OS)
38th Aerospace Rescue & Recovery Sqdn
CH/HH-3E

A beautiful shot of an F–4E of
the 36th TFS based at Osan AB
as it climbs rapidly in the sky
over South Korea.

A technician checks the APG–68 in an F–16.

An ANG F–15A of the 102nd Fighter Interceptor Squadron based at Otis ANGB.

OTIS

Otis ANGB
Massachusetts
USA

Phone:
(617) 968-4003

Autovon:
557-4003

Command:
Air National Guard

Named after:
1st Lt. Frank J. Otis, an ANG flight surgeon and pilot, who was killed in an aircrash in 1937

Acreage:
ANG area 3,858

Personnel:
1,144 military personnel, 598 civilians

Units:
102nd Fighter Interceptor Wing (ANG); 101st Fighter Interceptor Sqdn (ANG); 567th USAF BAND (ANG)

Operational Aircraft:
F-15A/B   101st FIS
C-12F

PATRICK

Patrick AFB
Florida 32925,
USA

Phone:
(305) 494-110

Autovon:
854-1110

Command:
Air Force Systems Command

Date est:
1940

Named after:
Maj. Gen. Mason M. Patrick, head of AEF's Air Service during WWI and Chief of the Army Air Staff between 1921 and 1927

Acreage:
2,341

Personnel:
4,494 military personnel, 1,640 civilians

Units:
USAF Eastern Space and Missile Center; Defense Equal Opportunity Management Institute; Air Force Technical Applications Center; 549th Tactical Air Support Gp; 2nd Combat Communications Gp (AFCC)

Operational Aircraft
549th Tactical Air Support Training Sqdn (TAC)
OV-10A   (FL)

Notes:
The base plays a major role in operations launched from Cape Canaveral. The Eastern Space and Missile Center is responsible for the Eastern Test Range which extends more than 10,000 miles down range from the Cape

PEASE

Pease AFB
New Hampshire 03803-5000
USA

Phone:
(603) 430-0100

Autovon:
852-1110

Command:
Strategic Air Command

Date est:
1956

Named after:
Capt. Harl Pease, a WWII B-17 pilot and holder of the Medal of Honor. He was killed during the attack on Rabaul, New Britain Island in 1942

Acreage:
4,254

Personnel:
3,743 military personnel, 465 civilians

Units:
45th Air Divn; 509th Bomb Wing; 541st Air Force Band; 1916th Communications Sqdn (AFCC); 3519th USAF Recruiting Sqdn (ATC); 157th Air Refueling Gp (ANG)

Operational Aircraft:
509th Bombardment Wing (SAC)
FB-111A   393rd BS
            713th BS
KC-135A   509th ARS

133rd Air Refueling Sqdn (ANG)
KC-135E

BASE REALIGNMENTS AND CLOSURES
Report of the Defense Secretary's Commission December 1988
The Commission recommends Pease Air Force Base for closure primarily due to quality and availability of facilities, and because of excess capacity within the category. The net cost of closure and relocation will be paid back immediately. The Commission expects annual savings to be $95.7 million.

Pease AFB has a shortage of buildings for operational, training and maintenance purposes. In addition, the military family housing is inadequate and requires upgrading. There are also deficiencies in the area of quality of life, the most prominent being lack of recreational facilities.

Pease AFB is currently one of 12 Strategic Air Command bomber bases. An Air National Guard Unit with a peacetime and wartime refueling mission is also assigned to Pease.

Pease's FB-111 bombers are programmed to be transferred to the Tactical Air Forces now that the B-1 bomber aircraft is operational. This will leave the base with only the 509th Air Refueling Squadron. There is sufficient capacity within the strategic-bomber category to absorb the remaining units at other locations at minimum cost.

The military value of Pease AFB is also lower than other strategic-bomber bases because of low pre-launch survivability from submarine-launched ballistic missiles. Pease's location provides less warning time for aircraft to launch during times of increased tension or international conflict.

This closure will have no negative impact on the environment. The cleanup of hazardous materials and waste contamination at Pease AFB is covered by the Defense Environmental Restoration Program. Cleanup is independent of the closure. The movement of units currently assigned to Pease will not significantly alter the environmental situation at gaining bases since comparable operations are presently under way at those locations.

This closure will have minimal impact on local employment.

The Commission recommends the following relocations of major units and related support activities:

The 509th Air Refueling Squadron (KC-135 aircraft) to Wurtsmith AFB, Michigan; Plattsburgh AFB, New York; Eaker AFB, Arkansas; Carswell AFB, Texas; and Fairchild AFB, Washington. These relocations will improve the efficiency of strategic-bomber operations by linking tankers with bombers, thus avoiding military construction by utilizing facilities that already exist at those locations.

The 132nd Air Refueling Squadron (Air National Guard (ANG) KC-135 aircraft) assigned to Pease to remain within its current cantonment area. The transfer of property ownership should include a memorandum of agreement that will permit the continued presence of the ANG and provide for the unit's future requirements. If local authorities do not elect to operate the facility as an airport, the ANG unit must be relocated. The Commission is aware

that Pease is high on the Federal Aviation Administration's list of military bases with potential civil use and believes that the ANG unit will likely be allowed to remain at Pease.

PETERSON

Peterson AFB
Colorado 80914-5000
USA

Phone:
(303) 554-7321

Autovon:
692-7011

Command:
Air Force Space Command

Date est:
1942

Named after:
1st Lt. Edward J. Peterson, who was killed in a crash at the base in 1942

Acreage:
1,176

Personnel:
4,500 military personnel (active duty), 1,000 (reserves), 1,700 civilians

Units:
3rd Space Support Wing; HQ Air Force Space Command; HQ North American Aerospace Defense Command; HQ US Space Command; Cheyenne Mountain Complex; 1st Space Wing; 302nd Tactical Airlift Wing; 2nd Space Wing*

Operational Aircraft:
731st Tactical Airlift Squadron (AFRES)
C-130B

Notes:
* The 2nd space wing is located 9 miles away at Falcon AFS. Peterson AFB is one of America's most prized possessions. It is the heart of a global network of radars and satellites which constantly supply information to safeguard the free world's boundaries

PITTSBURGH

Pittsburgh Greater International Airport
Pennsylvania 15231
USA

Phone:
ANG (412) 268-8402
AFRES (412) 269-8000

Autovon:
ANG 277-8402
AFRES 277-8441

Command:
Air Force Reserve

Date est:
1943

Acreage:
AFRES 165
ANG 90

Personnel:
AFRES: 1,071 military personnel, 342 civilians; ANG: 1,641 military personnel, 490 civilians

Units:
911th Tactical Airlift Gp (AFRES); 758th Tactical Airlift Sqdn (AFRES); 171st Air Refueling Wing (ANG); 147th Air Refueling Sqdn (ANG); 112nd Tactical Fighter Gp (ANG); 146th Tactical Fighter Sqdn (ANG)

Operational Aircraft:

C-130A	758th TAS
A-7D/K	146th TAS (PT)
KC-135E	147th ARS

PLATTSBURGH

  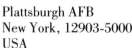

Plattsburgh AFB
New York, 12903-5000
USA

Phone:
(518) 565-5000

Autovon:
689-5000

Command:
Strategic Air Command

Date est:
1954*

Acreage:
4,879

Personnel:
4,077 military personnel, 450 civilians

Units:
380th Bomb Wing; 530th Strategic Bombing Training Wing; Det 18, 40th ARRS (MAC); FOL E, 71st Flying Training Wing (ATC) 2042nd Communications Sqdn (AFCC); 210th Field Training Det

Operational Aircraft:
380th Bombardment Wing (SAC)
FB-111A   528th BS
             529th BS
KC-135A/Q/R 310th ARS
             380th ARS

Notes:
* Plattsburgh AFB is second only to West Point as the oldest military establishment in America, being established in 1814

POPE

Pope AFB
North Carolina 28308-5000
USA

Phone:
(919) 394-0001

Autovon:
486-1110

Command:
Military Airlift Command

Date est:
1919

Named after:
1st Lt. Harley H. Pope, a WWI pilot who was killed when his JN-4 "Jenny" ran out of fuel and crashed in 1917

Acreage:
1,750

Personnel:
4,357 military personnel, 610 civilians

Units:
USAF Airlift Center; 317th Tactical Airlift Wing; 1st Aeromedical Evacuation Sqdn; 1943rd Communications Sqdn; 53rd Mobile Aerial Port Sqdn

Operational Aircraft:
317th Tactical Airlift Wing (MAC)
C-130E   39th TAS
          40th TAS
          41st TAS

Notes:
The base is situated next to the Fort Bragg, the home of the army's airborne forces

PORTLAND

Portland International Airport
Oregon 97218-2797
USA

Phone:
(503) 288-5611

Autovon:
891-1701

Command:
Air Force Reserve

Acreage:
273

Personnel:
1,794 military personnel, 515 civilians

Units:
142nd Fighter Interceptor Gp (ANG); 123rd Fighter Interceptor Sqdn (ANG); 939th Aerospace Rescue & Recovery Gp (AFRES); 304th Aerospace Rescue & Recovery Sqdn (AFRES); 244th Combat Communications Sqdn (ANG); 244th Combat Communications Flight (ANG); 116th Tactical Control Sqdn (ANG); Det 5, 2036th Communications Sqdn (AFCC); 12th Special Forces Gp (USAR); Oregon Wing (CAP); 83rd Aerial Port Sqdn (AFRES)

Operational Aircraft:
HC-130H   304th ARRS
HH-1H/UH-1N
F-4C   123rd FIS
The squadron will also get a C-130A for support duties

QUONSET

Quonset Point Airport
Rhode Island 02852
USA

Phone:
(401) 885-3960

Autovon:
476-3210

Command:
Air National Guard

Acreage:
ANG area 60

Units:
143rd Tactical Airlift Sqdn

Operational Aircraft:
C-130H   143rd TAS

RAF ALCONBURY

RAF Alconbury
Huntingdon
Cambs PE17 5DA
UK
APO New York 09238-5000

Phone:
(0480) 823000

Autovon:
223-1110

Command:
United States Air Forces in Europe

Units:
10th Tactical Fighter Wing (USAFE); 17th Reconnaissance Wing (SAC); 509th Tactical Fighter Sqdn (USAFE); 511th Tactical Fighter Sqdn (USAFE)

Operational Aircraft:
TR-1A   17th RW
A-10A   509th TFS
          511th TFS   (AR)

Center, far right: A squadron briefing of the 527th AS.

Far right: The crest of the 527th AMU based at Alconbury.

Two Aggressor F—5s take off
from RAF Alconbury.

The Aggressors of the 527th AS are prepared for an exercise at Alconbury. The 527th has now moved to RAF Bentwaters and changed its aircraft for F–16s.

RAF BENTWATERS

RAF Bentwaters
Eyke
Suffolk IP12 2RQ
UK
APO New York 09755-5000

Phone:
(03943) 433000

Autovon:
225-1110

Command:
United States Air Forces in Europe

Units:
81st Tactical Fighter Wing (USAFE);
78th Tactical Fighter Sqdn (USAFE);
91st Tactical Fighter Sqdn (USAFE);
92nd Tactical Fighter Sqdn (USAFE);
510th Tactical Fighter Sqdn (USAFE);
526th Aggressor Sqdn (USAFE)

Operational Aircraft:
RAF Bentwaters
A-10A   92nd TFS
           510th TFS
F-16C   5276 AS

RAF Woodbridge
A-10A   78th TFS
           91st TFS

The wing operates from 4 Forward
Operational Locations in Germany,
FOL1-Sembach, FOL2-Ahlorn, FOL3-
Leipheim and FOL4-Norvenich

RAF CHICKSANDS

RAF Chicksands
Shefford
Bedfordshire
UK
APO New York 09193-5000

Phone:
(0462) 812571

Autovon:
234-1110

Command:
United States Air Forces in Europe

Units:
7274th Air Base Gp (USAFE); 6950th
Electronic Security Gp (ESC)

Operational Aircraft:
None

RAF FAIRFORD

RAF Fairford
Fairford
Glos GL7 4DL
UK
APO New York 09125-5000

Phone:
(0285) 714000

Autovon:
247-1110

Command:
United States Air Forces in Europe

Date est:
1979

Units:
7020th Air Base Gp; 11th Strategic Gp
(SAC)

Operational Aircraft:
KC-135   11th SG

Notes:
The base acts as a forward operational
refueling base. From 1951 to June
1964, RAF Fairford was a US bomber
base

RAF GREENHAM COMMON

RAF Greenham Common
Newbury
Berks RG15 8HI
UK
APO New York 09150-5000

Phone:
(0635) 512000

Autovon:
266-1110

Command:
United States Air Forces in Europe

Units:
501st Tactical Missile Wing

Operational Aircraft:
None

Notes:
First operational ground launch cruise
missile site

RAF LAKENHEATH

RAF Lakenheath
Brandon
Suffolk IP27 9NP
UK
APO New York 09179-5000

Phone:
(0638) 523000

Autovon:
226-1110

Command:
United States Air Forces in Europe

Date est:
1951

Size:
1,800 acres

Units:
48th Tactical Fighter Wing (USAFE);
492nd Tactical Fighter Sqdn (USAFE);
494th Tactical Fighter Sqdn (USAFE);
495th Tactical Fighter Sqdn (USAFE)

Operational Aircraft:
F-111F   492nd TFS
            493rd TFS
            494th TFS
            495th TFS   (LN)

Side by side the Stars and
Stripes and the RAF Union
Jack. USAF bases in the United
Kingdom are operated by the
Royal Air Force and are on loan
to USAF units.

An RC–135 of the 306th SW based at RAF Mildenhall is refueled by a KC–135R of the 912th ARS based at Robins AFB on attachment to the 306th SW.

RAF MILDENHALL

RAF Mildenhall
Mildenhall
Suffolk IP28 8NF
UK
APO New York 09127-5000

Phone:
(0638) 513000

Autovon:
238-1110

Command:
United States Air Forces in Europe

Units:
HQ Third Air Force (USAFE); 513rd Tactical Airlift Wing (USAFE); 306th Strategic Wing (SAC); 313th Tactical Airlift Gp (MAC); 2147th Communications Wing (AFCC); 10th Airborne Control & Command Sqdn

Operational Aircraft:
EC-135H   10th ACCS

Right: RAF Mildenhall is familiar to many USAF personnel and their families. It is the main port of entry for Americans serving in the United Kingdom.

Far right: A Grumman technician and an electronic warfare NCO study the results of a test during servicing of an EF–111 EW system.

Notes:
RAF Mildenhall is the gateway to Great Britain, for US military personnel and their families. And each month it processes in excess of 8,000 passengers and 2,000 tons of cargo. Its ground crews have to have a vast working knowledge of NATO aircraft that pass through the base on a regular basis. It is also home for SILK PURSE the US Commander in Chief Europe's Airborne Command Post. The four EC-135H Stratotankers rotate in operation and are manned by the Silk Purse Control Group

RAF UPPER HEYFORD

RAF Upper Heyford
Oxfordshire
UK
APO New York 09194-5000

Protected in its hardened shelter, an EF–111 is checked by its ground crew at RAF Upper Heyford.

Phone:
(0869) 234000

Autovon:
263-1110

Command:
United States Air Forces in Europe

Units:
20th Tactical Fighter Wing (USAFE);
55th Tactical Fighter Sqdn (USAFE);
77th Tactical Fighter Sqdn (USAFE);
79th Tactical Fighter Sqdn (USAFE);
42nd Electronic Countermeasures
Sqdn (USAFE)

Operational Aircraft:
F-111E	55th TFS	
	77th TFS	
	79th TFS	
EF-111A	42nd ECS	(UH)

RAF WOODBRIDGE

RAF Woodbridge
Woodbridge
Suffolk
UK
APO New York 09755-5000

Phone:
(0394) 433000

Autovon:
225-1110

Command:
United States Air Forces in Europe

Units:
21st Special Operations Sqdn

Operational Aircraft:
HC-130H/N Hercules
MH-53J Jolly Green Giant

An A–10 pilot climbs into a Woodbridge-based aircraft. The A–10s also operate from forward locations in Germany.

RAMSTEIN

Ramstein AB
West Germany
APO New York 09012-5000

Phone:
(06371) 476558

Autovon:
480-1110

Command:
United States Air Forces in Europe

Units:
316th Air Divn (USAFE); 7455th
Tactical Intelligence Wing (USAFE);
86th Tactical Fighter Wing (USAFE);
417th Tactical Fighter Sqdn (USAFE);
512th Tactical Fighter Sqdn (USAFE);
526th Tactical Fighter Sqdn (USAFE);
377th Combat Support Wing (USAFE);
1856th Communications Gp (AFCC);
1964th Communications Gp (AFCC);
HQ European Electronic Security Divn
(ESC); 7th Air Divn (SAC); 322nd
Airlift Divn (MAC); 2nd Weather Wing
(MAC); 608th Military Airlift Gp
(USAFE); 58th Military Airlift Sqdn
(USAFE)

Operational Aircraft:
C-12F	58th MAS
C-21A	
C-135B	
C-140B	
F-16C/D	512th TFS
	526th TFS
	417th TFS

Far left: The dragon shield of the 81st TFW.

RANDOLPH

Randolph AFB
Texas 78150-5001
USA

Phone:
(512) 652-1110

Autovon:
487-1110

Command:
Air Training Command

Date est:
June 1930

Named after:
Capt. William M. Randolph who died when his AT-4 crashed on takeoff in 1928

Acreage:
2,901

Personnel:
5,445 military personnel, 3,002 civilians

Units:
HQ Air Training Command; 12th Flying Training Wing; Air Force Military Personnel Center; HQ USAF Recruiting Service; Civilian Personnel Management Center; Occupational Measurement Center

Operational Aircraft:
12th Flying Training Wing (ATC)
T-37B   559th FTS
T-38A   560th FTS

REESE

Reese AFB
Texas 79489-5000
USA

Phone:
(806) 885-4511

Autovon:
838-1110

Command:
Air Training Command

Date est:
1942

Named after:
1st Lt. Augustus F. Reese Jr, a P-38

pilot killed in action over Sardinia in May 1943

Acreage:
2,467

Personnel:
2,433 military personnel, 736 civilians

Units:
64th Flying Training Wing

Operational Aircraft:
64th Flying Training Wing (ATC)
T-37B   35th FTS
T-38A   54th FTS

Notes:
Reese AFB is home to the AF's officers basic flight training

RHEIN MAIN

Rhein Main AB
West Germany
APO New York 09057-5000

Phone:
(69) 699115

Autovon:
330-1110

Command:
United States Air Forces in Europe

Units:
8th Special Operations Sqdn (MAC); 435th Tactical Airlift Wing (MAC); 55th Tactical Airlift Sqdn (MAC); 7405th OS; 1868th Facility Checking Sqdn

Operational Aircraft:
MC-130E	8th SOS
C-9A	55th AAS
C-130E	37th TAS
	7405th OS
T-39A	1868th FCS

RICHARDS GEBAUR

Richards Gebaur AFB
Montana 64030-5000
USA

Phone:
(816) 348-2000

Autovon:
463-1110

Command:
Air Force Reserve

Date est:
Mar. 1944

Named after:
1st Lt. John F. Richards, killed while on an artillery spotting mission over France in Sep. 1918, and Lt. Col. Arthur W. Gebaur Jr, killed on his 99th mission in 1952 over North Korea

Acreage:
620 plus another 120 occupied by non-AF units

Personnel:
1,471 military personnel, 398 civilians

Units:
442nd Tactical Fighter Gp (AFRES); 303rd Tactical Fighter Sqdn (AFRES)

Operational Aircraft:
A-10A   303rd TFS (KC)

RICKENBACKER

Rickenbacker AFB
Ohio 43217
USA

Phone:
(614) 492-8211

Autovon:
950-1110

Command:
Air National Guard

Date est:
1942

Named after:
Capt. Edward V. Rickenbacker, the top WWI American ace and Medal of Honor recipient who died in 1973

A Beechcraft C-12 from the 58th Military Airlift Squadron at Ramstein.

Acreage:
2,016

Personnel:
1,836 military personnel, 406 civilians

Units:
121st Tactical Fighter Wing (ANG);
166th Tactical Fighter Sqdn (ANG);
356th Tactical Airlift Sqdn (AFRES);
907th Tactical Airlift Gp (AFRES);
160th Air Refueling Gp (ANG); 145th
Air Refueling Sqdn (ANG); 2032nd
Communications Sqdn (AFCC)

Operational Aircraft:

C-130A	356th TAS	
KC-135E	145th ARS	
A-7D/K	166th TFS	(OH)

Notes:
The base was transferred to the ANG
from SAC in Apr. 1980

ROBINS

Robins AFB
Georgia 31098
USA

Phone:
(912) 926-1110

Autovon:
468-1110

Command:
Air Force Logistics Command

Date est:
Mar. 1942

Named after:
Brig. Gen. Augustine Warner Robins,
an early Chief of the Material Divn of
the Air Corps, who died in 1940

Acreage:
8,863

Personnel:
3,889 military personnel, 16,742
civilians

Units:
HQ Warner Robins Air Logistics
Center; HQ Air Force Reserve
(AFRES); 2853rd Air Base Gp; 19th
Air Refueling Wing (SAC); 5th Combat
Communications Gp (AFCC); 3503rd
Recruiting Gp; 1926th
Communications Sqdn (AFCC)

Operational Aircraft:
19th Air Refueling Wing (SAC)

KC-135R	19th ARS

Home of the 435th TAW.

	22nd ARS
EC-135Y	19th ARWS

The EC-135Y is operated by the wing
on behalf of CinC Central Command

Notes:
The Center provides world-wide
logistics management for the B-52, C-
7A, C-130, C-140, C-141 and F-15. It
is tasked with the management of air-
to-air, air-to-ground and ground-to-air
missiles, RPVs and utility helicopters.
It is also responsible for the
management and repair of airborne
electronic components including
communications and navigation
equipment, bomb and gun directing
systems and all Air Force electronic
equipment

A C–130 of the 435th TAW
lines up ready for takeoff.

An example of NATO cooperation, C–130 air crews from the 435th TAW and the Portuguese Air Force plan a joint operation when the 435th deployed to Portugal.

Personnel:
1,510 military personnel, 348 civilians

Units:
151st Air Refueling Gp (ANG); 191st Air Refueling Sqdn (ANG); 130th Engineering Installation Sqdn (ANG); plus two ANG units

Operational Aircraft:
KC-135E   191st ARS

ROSECRANS

Rosecrans Memorial Airport
St Joseph
Missouri 64503
USA

Phone:
(816) 271-1300

Autovon:
720-9210

Command:
Air National Guard

Acreage:
ANG area 298

Personnel:
872 military personnel, 255 civilians

Units:
139th Tactical Airlift Gp (ANG); 180th Tactical Airlift Sqdn (ANG)

Operational Aircraft:
C-130A/H   180th TAS

ROSLYN

Roslyn ANG
New York 11576-2399
USA

Phone:
(516) 299-5201

Autovon:
456-5201

Command:
Air National Guard

Personnel:
466 military personnel, 22 civilians

Acreage:
ANG area 50

Units:
274th Combat Communications Sqdn; 213th Engineering Installation Sqdn

SALT LAKE CITY

Salt Lake City International Airport
Utah 84116
USA

Phone:
(801) 521-7070

Autovon:
790-9210

Command:
Air National Guard

Acreage:
ANG area 75

SAVANNAH

Savannah International Airport
Georgia 31402
USA

Phone:
(912) 964-1941

Autovon:
860-8210

Command:
Air National Guard

Acreage:
ANG area 232

Personnel:
1,197 military personnel, 274 civilians

Units:
165th Tactical Airlift Gp (ANG); 158th Tactical Airlift Sqdn (ANG)

Operational Aircraft:
C-130H   158th TAS

SCHENECTADY

Schenectady County Airport
New York 12302-9752
USA

Phone:
(518) 381-7300

Autovon:
974-9221

Command:
Air National Guard

Acreage:
ANG area 106

Personnel:
987 military personnel, 217 civilians

Units:
109th Tactical Airlift Gp (ANG); 139th Tactical Airlift Sqdn (ANG)

Operational Aircraft:
C/LC-130H

SCOTT

Scott AFB
Illinois 62225-5000
USA

Phone:
(618) 256-1110

Autovon:
576-1110

Command:
Military Airlift Command

Date est:
June 1917

Named after:
Corporal Frank S. Scott, the first enlisted man to be killed in an aircrash. His Wright Biplane crashed at College Park, Maryland, on 28 Sep. 1912

Acreage:
3,000

Personnel:
7,034 military personnel; 3,113 civilians

Units:
MAC; HQ Air Force Communications Command; 375th Aeromedical Airlift Wing; HQ 23rd Air Force; HQ Aerospace Rescue and Recovery Service; HQ Air Weather Service; Defense Commercial Communications Office; Environmental Technical Applications Center; Scott USAF Medical Center; 7th Weather Wing; 932nd Aeromedical Airlift Gp (AFRES Assoc.); Airlift Communications Divn; 375th Air Base Gp

Operational Aircraft:
375th Aeromedical Airlift Wing (MAC)
C-9A

1375th Military Airlift Sqdn (MAC)
C-12F
C-21A

1401st Military Airlift Sqdn (MAC)
C-12F
C-21A Det 1 Offutt AFB, Det 2 Wright Patterson AFB, Det 3 Barksdale AFB, Det 4 Peterson AFB

SELFRIDGE

Selfridge ANGB
Michigan 48045
USA

Phone:
(313) 466-4011

Autovon:
273-0111

Command:
Air National Guard

Date est:
July 1917

Named after:
1st Lt. Thomas E. Selfridge, the first army officer to fly and the first to die in an aircrash. He died on 17 Sep. 1908 when flying in an aircraft piloted by Orville Wright crashed.

Acreage:
3,727

Personnel:
2,014 military personnel, 1,063 civilians

Units:
127th Tactical Fighter Wing (ANG); 107th Tactical Fighter Sqdn (ANG); 191st Fighter Interceptor Gp (ANG); 171st Fighter Interceptor Sqdn (ANG); 927th Tactical Airlift Gp (AFRES); 63rd Tactical Airlift Sqdn (AFRES); 305th Aerospace Rescue & Recovery Sqdn (AFRES); plus Army, Navy and Marine Corps Units; Detroit US Coast Guard Air Station

Operational Aircraft:

C-130A	63rd TAS
HC/130H/N	305th ARRS (AFRES)
HH-3E	
A-7D/K	107th TFS
C-131	

The squadron's single C-131D is due to be replaced by a C-130A

F-4D	171st FIS (MI)

Notes:
The base was transferred to the Michigan ANG in July 1971

SEMBACH

Sembach AB
West Germany
APO New York 09130-5000

Phone:
(63) 02670

Autovon:
496-1110

Command:
United States Air Forces in Europe

Units:
HQ 17th Air Force (USAFE); 65th Air Division (USAFE); 66th Electronic Combat Wing (USAFE); 601st Tactical Control Wing (USAFE); 2005th Communications Wing (AFCC); Allied Tactical Operations Center

Operational Aircraft:

CH-53C	601st TCS

Notes:
The 601st Tactical Control Wing is responsible for radar control and surveillance of US and other NATO aircraft involved in operations over central Europe. Half of the Wing's personnel are located at over 50 different bases extending from the North Sea down to Italy

SEYMOUR JOHNSON

Seymour Johnson AFB
North Carolina 27531-5000
USA

Phone:
(919) 736-5400

Autovon:
488-1110

Command:
Tactical Air Command

Date est:
June 1942

Named after:
Lt. Seymour A. Johnson, a navy pilot killed in an aircrash in 1941

Acreage:
4,122

Personnel:
4,703 military personnel, 693 civilians

One of the first F–15Es to be delivered to Seymour Johnson AFB turns on its afterburners.

Right: The squadron emblem on a 16th Tactical Reconnaissance Squadron RF–4.

Far right: A pilot climbs into the cockpit of his F–16 at Shaw AFB.

Units:
4th Tactical Fighter Wing; 68th Air Refueling Wing (SAC); 2012th Communications Sqdn (AFCC); OL AD, 191st Fighter Interceptor Gp (MichANG)

Operational Aircraft:
4th Tactical Fighter Wing (TAC)

F-4E Phantom II	334th TFS
	335th TFS
F15-E	336th TFS

68th Air Refueling Gp (SAC)

KC-10A	911th ARS

Notes:
The 336th TFS is the first operational unit to receive the F-15E. It is planned that the unit will have completed its changeover from the F-4E by October 1989. The Wing will eventually receive 72 F-15Es as the Air Force continues its long-range interdiction capabilities. The F-4Es will be transferred to the Air National Guard and Air Force Reserve units.

SHAW

Shaw AFB
South Carolina 29152-5000
USA

Phone:
(803) 668-8110

Autovon:
965-1110

Command:
Tactical Air Command

Date est:
Aug. 1941

Named after:
2nd Lt. Ervin D. Shaw, one of the first Americans to see action in France during WWI. His Bristol fighter was shot down in 1918 while on a reconnaissance mission

Acreage:
3,363*

Personnel:
6,125 military personnel, 1,666 civilians

Units:
363rd Tactical Fighter Wing; HQ 9th Air Force (TAC); 507th Tactical Air Control Wing

Operational Aircraft:
21st Tactical Air Support Sqdn (TAC)

OT-37B	(SR)

363rd Tactical Fighter Wing (TAC)

RF-4C	16th TRS
F-16C/D	17th TFS
	19th TFS
	33rd TFS

Notes:
* Plus 8,078 leased acres at the Poinsett Bombing Range south west of Sumter

SHEMYA

Shemya AFB
Alaska (APO Seattle 98736-5000)
USA

Phone:
(907) 392-3000

Autovon:
(317) 392-3000

Command:
Alaskan Air Command

Date est:
1943

Size:
11.25 sq. miles

Personnel:
556 military personnel, 399 civilians

Units:
5073rd Air Base Gp

Notes:
The base is situated at the westernmost point of the United States; this meant that the International Date Line was bent around the island so that it would be in the same day as the rest of America. The island is home for the Cobra Dane AN/FPS-80 Phased Array Radar operated by AFSPACECOM. The radar monitors space and missile activities in eastern Siberia and Kamchatka. Its 10,000 ft runway built in WWII for B-29 operations is still used today as a forward operating base for AAC F-15s

SHEPPARD

Sheppard AFB
Texas 76311-5000
USA

Phone:
(817) 851-2511

Autovon:
736-1001

Command:
Air Training Command

Date est:
June 1941

Named after:
US Senator Morris E. Sheppard, a

F–4s line up on the flightline at Shaw AFB.

former chairman of the Senate Military Affairs Committee, who died in 1941

Acreage:
5,000

Personnel:
8,151 military personnel, 1,331 civilians

Units:
Sheppard Technical Training Center; 3700th Technical Training Wing; 3785th Field Training Wing; the School of Health Care Sciences; 80th Flying Training Wing; 205th Communications Sqdn (AFCC)

Operational Aircraft:
80th Flying Training Wing (ATC)
T-37B, T-38A 88th FTS,   89th FTS   90th FTS

Sheppard Technical Training Center (ATC)
various

Notes:
The 3700th TTW provides courses in aircraft maintenance, civil engineering, communications, comptroller, transportation and instructor training. The 3785th FTW provides training on specific weapons systems at bases scattered around the world. The 80th FTW undertakes pilot

and instructor training for the Euro-NATO Joint Jet Pilot Training Program and the 2054th Communications Squadron

SIOUX CITY

Sioux City Municipal Airport
Iowa 51110
USA

Phone:
(712) 255-3511

Autovon:
939-6210

Command:
Air National Guard

Acreage:
ANG area 114

Personnel:
931 military personnel, 253 civilians

Units:
185th Tactical Fighter Gp (ANG); 174th Tactical Fighter Sqdn (ANG)

Operational Aircraft:
A-7D/K   174th TFS   (HA)

SKY HARBOR

Sky Harbor International Airport
Phoenix 85034
Arizona
USA

Phone:
(602) 244-9841

Autovon:
853-9211

Command:
Air National Guard

Acreage:
ANG area 51

Personnel:
1,262 military personnel, 262 civilians

Units:
161st Air Refueling Gp (ANG); 197th Air Refueling Sqdn (ANG)

Operational Aircraft:
KC-135E   197th ARS

SMITH

Smith ANGB
Birmingham Municipal Airport
Alabama 35217
USA

Phone:
(205) 841-9200

Autovon:
694-2260

Command:
Air National Guard

Acreage:
ANG area 86

Personnel:
1,316 military personnel, 328 civilians

Units:
117th Tactical Reconnaissance Gp (ANG); 106th Tactical Reconnaissance Wing (ANG)

Operational Aircraft:
RF-4C   (BH)
C-131D

SOESTERBERG

Soesterberg AB
Camp New Amsterdam
Holland
APO New York 09292-5000

Phone:
(03404) 3422/Ext. 3142

Autovon:
Call Sembach Autovon 497-1110 and ask for Soesterberg AB

Command:
United States Air Forces in Europe

Units:
32nd Tactical Fighter Sqdn (USAFE)

Operational Aircraft:
F-15C/D   (USAFE)

SPANGDAHLEM

Spangdahlem AB
West Germany
APO New York 09123-5000

Phone:
Not available

Autovon:
452-1110

Command:
United States Air Forces in Europe

Units:
52nd Tactical Fighter Wing (USAFE);
23rd Tactical Fighter Sqdn (USAFE);
81st Tactical Fighter Sqdn (USAFE);
480th Tactical Fighter Sqdn (USAFE)

Operational Aircraft:
F-4G, F-16C/D   23rd TFS
                  81st TFS
                  480th TFS   (SP)

SPRINGFIELD

Springfield Municipal Airport
Ohio 45501-1780
USA

Phone:
(513) 323-8653

Autovon:
346-2311

Command:
Air National Guard

Acreage:
ANG area 113

Personnel:
1,133 military personnel, 270 civilians

Units:
178th Tactical Fighter Gp (ANG);
162nd Tactical Fighter Sqdn (ANG);
251st Combat Information Systems Gp (ANG)

Operational Aircraft:
A-7D/K   162nd TFS   (OH)

A C–21A of the 7005th Air Base Squadron based at Stuttgart International Airport.

STANDIFORD

Standiford Field
Louiseville
Kentucky 40213
USA

Phone:
(502) 566-9400

Autovon:
989-4400

Command:
Air National Guard

Acreage:
ANG area 65

Personnel:
1,238 military personnel, 310 civilians

Units:
155th Tactical Reconnaissance Gp
(ANG); 165th Tactical Reconnaissance
Sqdn (ANG)

Operational Aircraft:
RF-4C   165th TRS (KY)
C-12F

STEWART-NEWBURGH

Stewart-Newburgh Airport
New York 12550-6148
USA

Phone:
(914) 563-2000

Autovon:
247-2000

Command:
Air National Guard

Acreage:
ANG area 328

Personnel:
1,551 military personnel, 390 civilians

Units:
HQ New York ANG; 105th Military
Airlift Gp (ANG); 137th Military Airlift
Sqdn (ANG); USMA subpost airport

Operational Aircraft:
C-5A   137th MAS
C-131D

The C-131D will be replaced by a C-12J

Notes:
The base is used as an airport for the
United States Military Academy, West
Point

STUTTGART

Stuttgart International Airport
D-7000 Stuttgard 23
West Germany

Phone:
0711-79011

Autovon:
Not available

Command:
United States Air Forces in Europe

Units:
7005th Airbase Sqdn

Operational Aircraft:
C-21A

SUFFOLK COUNTY

Suffolk County Airport
New York 11978-1294
USA

Phone:
(516) 288-4200

Autovon:
456-7210

Command:
Air National Guard

Acreage:
ANG area 70

Personnel:
736 military personnel, 218 civilians

Units:
106th Aerospace Rescue & Recovery
Gp (ANG); 102nd Aerospace Rescue
& Recovery Sqdn (ANG)

Operational Aircraft:
HC-130H/P   102nd ARRS
HH-3E

SUWON

Suwon AB
South Korea

Phone:
Not available

Autovon:
284-4110

Command:
Pacific Air Forces

Units:
25th TFS, see OSAN AB

Operational Aircraft:
A-10A   25th TFS Suwon AB

TAEGU

Taegu AB
South Korea
APO San Francisco 96213-5000

Phone:
Not available

Autovon:
284-4110

Command:
Pacific Air Forces

Units:
497th TFS, see OSAN AB

Operational Aircraft:
F-4E   497th TFS

TEMPELHOF

Tempelhof Central Airport AS
West Berlin
APO New York 09611-5155

Phone:
30 81992: ask for Tempelhof

Autovon:
332-1100

Command:
United States Air Forces in Europe

Units:
7350th Air Base Group (USAFE)
6912th Electronic Security Group
(ESG)

THULE

Thule AB
Greenland
APO New York 09023-5000

Phone:
Not available

Autovon:
834-1211; ask for Thule AB

Command:
Air Force Space Command

TINKER

Tinker AFB
Oklahoma 73145-5900
USA

Phone:
(405) 732-7321

Autovon:
884-4360

Command:
Air Force Logistics Command

Date est:
Mar. 1941

Named after:
Maj. Gen. Clarence L. Tinker whose LB-30 aeroplane crashed as he led a bombing mission against Wake Island during WWII

Acreage:
4,775

Personnel:
7,400 military personnel, 19,825 civilians

Units:
HQ Oklahoma City Air Logistics Center; Engineering Installation Divn (AFCC); 3rd Combat Communications Gp (AFCC); 28th Air Divn (TAC); 507th Tactical Fighter Gp (AFRES)

Operational Aircraft:
465th Tactical Fighter Sqdn (AFRES)
F-4D   (SH)

8th Tactical Deployment Control Sqdn (TAC)
EC-135K

552nd Airborne Warning & Control Wing (TAC)
E-3A/B/C   963rd AW&CS
                964th AW&CS
                965th AW&CS
                966th AW&CS
All aircraft have been brought up to E-3C standard

Notes:
The Logistics Center provides logistics support bombers, electronics, instruments and jet engines

TOLEDO

Toledo Express Airport
Ohio 43558
USA

Phone:
(419) 866-2078

Autovon:
580-2078

Command:
Air National Guard

Acreage:
ANG area 79

Personnel:
966 military personnel, 253 civilians

Units:
180th Tactical Fighter Gp (ANG); 112th Tactical Fighter Sqdn (ANG)

Operational Aircraft:
A7D/K   112th TFS   (OH)

TONOPAH

Tonopah Test Range Airfield
Nellis AFB
Nevada 89191-5000
USA

Phone:
see Nellis AFB

Autovon:
see Nellis AFB

Command:
Tactical Air Command

Units:
4450th Tactical Group

Operational Aircraft:
F-117

Notes:
On 10 November 1988 the Air Force announced the existence of an operational stealth fighter aircraft, the Lockheed F-117. Tonopah is located deep in the vastness of Nellis AFB

TORREJON

Torrejon AB
Edif 105, Torrejon
Spain
APO New York 09283

Phone:
91205-6211

Autovon:
723-1110

Command:
United States Air Forces in Europe

Units:
HQ 16th Air Force (USAFE); 401st Tactical Fighter Wing (USAFE); 612nd Tactical Fighter Sqdn (USAFE); 613rd Tactical Fighter Sqdn (USAFE); 614th Tactical Fighter Sqdn (USAFE); JUSMG Madrid

Operational Aircraft:
F-16A/B   612th AFS
               613th AFS
               614th AFS   (TJ)
C-12A   JUSMUG Madrid

Notes:
The 401st Tactical Fighter Wing is due to be moved from Spain following the closing of the base in 1991. The base will be handed back to the Spanish and the 401st will move to Crotone in Italy.

TRAVIS

Travis AFB
California 94535-5000
USA

Phone:
(707) 438-4011

Autovon:
837-1110

Left: The camouflaged face of SRA Kelly McMahn, a member of the 60th Security Police Unit at Travis AFB.

Command:
Military Airlift Command

Date est:
May 1943

Named after:
Brig. Gen. Robert F. Travis who was killed in 1950 in a B-29 crash at the end of the local runway

Acreage:
7,580

Personnel:
12,797 military personnel, 4,037 civilians

Units:
HQ 22nd Air Force; 60th Military Airlift Wing; 349th Military Airlift Wing (AFRES); David Grant Medical Center

Operational Aircraft:
60th Military Airlift Wing (MAC)
C5A/B	22nd MAS	
	75th MAS	
C-141B	7th MAS	
	44th MAS	

Notes:
For many years Travis AFB has served as the gateway to the Pacific

TRUAX FIELD

Truax Field
Dane County Regional Airport
Wisconsin 53704-2591
USA

Phone:
(608) 2421-6200

Autovon:
273-8210

Command:
Air National Guard

Date est:
June 1942

Named after:
Lt. T. L. Truax, killed in a P-40 accident in 1941

Acreage:
ANG area 153

Personnel:
1,038 military personnel, 270 civilians

Units:
128th Tactical Fighter Wing (ANG); 176th Tactical Fighter Sqdn (ANG)

Operational Aircraft:
A-10A	176th TFS	
C-131E		(WI)

The C-131E will be replaced by a C-130A

Notes:
The base passed to the Wisconsin ANG in Apr. 1968

TUCSON

Tucson International Airport
Arizona 85734
USA

Phone:
(602) 573-2210

Autovon:
853-4210

Command:
Air National Guard

Acreage:
ANG area 49

Personnel:
1,187 military personnel, 600 civilians

Units:
162nd Tactical Fighter Gp (ANG); 152nd Tactical Fighter Training Sqdn (ANG); 195th Tactical Fighter Training Sqdn (ANG)

Operational Aircraft:
A-7D/K	152nd TFTS	(AZ)
F16A/B	195th TFTS	

TULSA

Tulsa International Airport
Oklahoma 74115
USA

Phone:
(918) 832-5208

Autovon:
956-5297

Command:
Air National Guard

Acreage:
ANG area 78

Personnel:
1,093 military personnel, 263 civilians

Units:
138th Tactical Fighter Gp (ANG);
125th Tactical Fighter Sqdn (ANG);
219th Electronic Installation

Operational Aircraft:
A7D/K   125th TFS   (OK)

TYNDALL

Tyndall AFB
Florida 32403-5000
USA

Phone:
(904) 283-1113

Autovon:
523-1113

Command:
Tactical Air Command

Date est:
Dec. 1941

Named after:
1st Lt. Frank B. Tyndall a WWI pilot
who was killed in 1930 flying a P-1

Acreage:
28,000

Personnel:
4,623 military personnel, 1,672
civilians

Units:
USAF Air Defense Weapons Center;
325th Tactical Training Wing; 475th
Weapons Evaluation Gp; 325th
Combat Support Gp; 23rd Air Div
(TAC); Air Force Engineering and
Services Center; 3625th Technical
Training Sqdn (ATC); 2021st
Communications Sqdn (AFCC);
4702nd Computer Services Sqdn
(TAC); Det 1, 48th Fighter Interceptor
Sqdn (TAC); TAC NCO Academy East

Operational Aircraft:
325th Tactical Training Wing (TAC)

F-15A/B   1st TFTS
           2nd TFTS   (TY)

Notes:
The Air Defense Weapons Center
provides the DoD with a central
location for operational and technical
on all matters relating to air defense. It
all provides management services for
all home-based aerial target
operations. Home of the William Tell
fighter weapons meet

US AIR FORCE ACADEMY

◼

US Air Force Academy
Colorado 80840-5000
USA

Phone:
(303) 472-3110

Autovon:
259-3110

Command:
US Air Force Academy

Date est:
1958*

Acreage:
18,000

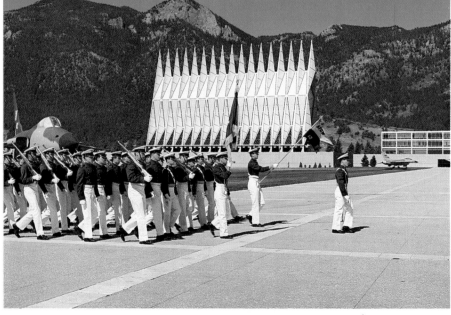

Top right: Whatever career a
cadet might wish to follow in the
Air Force, he or she will have to
go through a rigorous basic
training.

Center right: The Cadet Corp
parades during the graduation
ceremony.

Right: A Cadet squad parade in
front of the Academy chapel.

Graduation day at the Air Force Academy.

Personnel:
2,382 military personnel, 4,327 cadets, 1,750 civilians

Units:
US Air Force Academy; 1876th Information Systems Support Gp; Frank J. Seiler Research Lab (AFSC); DoD Medical Exam Review Board; Det 470, Air Force Audit Agency; 557th Flying Training Sqdn; 94th Air Training Sqdn

Operational Aircraft:
Air Force Academy (ATC)
T-41C

Notes:
* The Academy was originally formed at Lowry AFB, Colo. in 1954 and moved to its present site four years later

VANCE

Vance AFB
Oklahoma 73705-5000
USA

Phone:
(405) 237-2121

Autovon:
962-7110

Command:
Air Training Command

Date est:
Nov. 1941

Named after:
Lt. Col. Leon R. Vance, a Medal of Honor winner, who died in 1944 as the air-evac plane returning him home crashed off Iceland

Acreage:
1,811

Personnel:
1,300 military personnel, 1,320 civilians (1,200 contract employees)

Units:
71st Flying Training Wing

Operational Aircraft:
71st Flying Training Wing (ATC)
T-37B   8th FTS
T-38A   25th FTS

Notes:
The site of Vance AFB was bought by the US government from the city of Enid, Oklahoma for $1 in 1941. The training wing provides undergraduate pilot training

A Peacekeeper missile lifts off from a converted Minuteman silo at Vandenberg AFB. Test launches of SAC missiles are controlled at Vandenberg by the Space and Missile Test Organization.

VANDENBERG

Vandenberg AFB
California 93437-5000
USA

Phone:
(805) 866-1611

Autovon:
276-1110

Command:
Strategic Air Command

Date est:
Oct. 1941

Named after:
Gen. Hoyt S. Vandenberg, the Air Force's first full-term Chief of Staff between 1948 and 1953

Acreage:
98,400

Personnel:
3,971 military personnel, 1,487 civilians plus 7,913 civilian contractors

Units:
1st Strategic Aerospace Divn (SAC); 394th ICBM Test Maintenance Sqdn (SAC); 4315th Combat Crew Training Sqdn (SAC); 4392nd Aerospace Support Gp (SAC); 4392nd Security Police Gp (SAC); Space and Missile Test Organization (AFSC); Western Space and Missile Center (AFSC); Shuttle Test Gp (AFSC); Space and Missile Test Organization (SAMTO)

Notes:
The Air Force's own gateway to space. It was planned that Vandenberg would be used as the AF's launch site for Shuttle missions, but following the *Challenger* disaster modifications to the shuttle have meant that it is not possible to obtain earth orbit from the site

VAN NUYS

Van Nuys ANGB
California 91409
USA

Phone:
(213) 781-5980

Autovon:
873-6310

Command:
Air National Guard

Acreage:
ANG area 62

Personnel:
1,759 military personnel, 363 civilians

Units:
146th Tactical Airlift Wing (ANG); 115th Tactical Airlift Sqdn (ANG); 147th Combat Communications Sqdn (Contingency)

Operational Aircraft:
KC-135E
C-131D
The C-131D is to be replaced by a C-12J

WESTOVER

Westover AFB
Massachusetts 01022-5000
USA

Phone:
(413) 557-1110

Autovon:
589-1110

Command:
Air Force Reserve

Date est:
Apr. 1940

Named after:
Maj. Gen. Oscar Westover, Chief of the Air Corps, killed in an aircrash near Burbank, California in 1938

Acreage:
2,500

Personnel:
2,130 military personnel, 680 civilians

Units:
439th Tactical Airlift Wing (AFRES); 337th Tactical Airlift Sqdn (AFRES); plus Army, Navy and Marine Corps reserve units; Massachusetts National Guard

Operational Aircraft:
C-130E   337th TAS

WHEELER

Wheeler AFB
Hawaii 96854-5000
USA

Phone:
(808) 422-0531

Autovon:
449-0111

Command:
Pacific Air Forces

Date est:
Feb. 1922

Named after:
Maj. Sheldon H. Wheeler, CO of Luke Field, Hawaii, who was killed in a flying accident during an aerial exhibition in 1921

Acreage:
1,369

Personnel:
1,039 military personnel, 121 civilians

Units:
15th Air Base Sqdn; 326th Air Divn (Air Defense Control Center); 22nd Tactical Air Support Sqdn; 169th Aircraft Warning and Control

Left: An OV–10 Bronco of the 22nd TASS based at Wheeler AFB.

WILLIAMS

Williams AFB
Arizona 85240-5000
USA

Phone:
(602) 988-2611

Autovon:
474-1001

Command:
Air Training Command

Date est:
July 1941

Named after:
1st Lt. Charles D. Williams who died in a bomber crash in 1927

Acreage:
4,761

Personnel:
3,029 military personnel, 1,700 civilians

Units:
82nd Flying Training Wing; 1922nd Communications Sqdn; 425th Tactical Fighter Training Sqdn; Human Resources Lab/Flying Training Divn (AFSC)

Operational Aircraft:
82nd Flying Training Wing (ATC); T-37B 96th FTS; T-38A 97th FTS

Notes:
The free world's largest undergraduate pilot training base. The Human Resources Lab specializes in research on flight simulators

Far left: A 22nd TASS sign at Wheeler AFB.

Left: MSgt. Chip Sexton from the 22nd TASS at Wheeler AFB entertains a small South Korean girl while taking part in Team Spirit 87.

WILL ROGERS

Will Rogers World Airport
Oklahoma City
Oklahoma 73169-5000
USA

Phone:
(405) 686-5210

Autovon:
956-8210

Command:
Air National Guard

Acreage:
ANG area 71

Personnel:
1,122 military personnel, 215 civilians

Squadron (Hawaii Air National Guard–Air Defense Direction Center); 6924th Electronic Security Sqdn

Operational Aircraft:
22nd Tactical Air Support Sqdn (PACAF)
OV-10A   (WH)

Notes:
The army uses the base for helicopter training

WHITEMAN

Whiteman AFB
Missouri 65305
USA

Phone:
(816) 687-1110

Autovon:
975-1110

Command:
Strategic Air Command

Date est:
1942

Named after:
2nd Lt. George A. Whiteman, killed while trying to take off during the Japanese attack on Pearl Harbor, 7 Dec. 1941

Acreage:
3,384*

Personnel:
3,362 military personnel, 757 civilians

Units:
351st Strategic Missile Wing

Notes:
* Plus the missile site of 10,000 sq. miles

Operated by the 4950th Test Wing at Wright Patterson, the ARGUS is an airborne photo-documentation system incorporated in an NC–135A aircraft. The aircraft is used to monitor Strategic Defense Initiative Organization experiments.

Units:
137th Tactical Airlift Wing (ANG);
185th Tactical Airlift Sqdn (ANG)

Operational Aircraft:
C-130H   185th TAS

WILLOW GROVE

Willow Grove Air Reserve Facility
Pennsylvania 19090
USA

Phone:
ANG (215) 443-1500
AFRES (215) 443-1062

Autovon:
ANG 991-1500
AFRES 991-1062

Command:
ANG/AFRES

Date est:
Aug. 1958

Acreage:
ANG 41; AFRES 162

Personnel:
ANG: 907 military personnel, 229
civilians; AFRES: 856 military
personnel, 269 civilians

Units:
111th Tactical Air Support Gp (ANG);
103rd Tactical Air Support Sqdn
(ANG); 913th Tactical Airlift Gp
(AFRES); 327th Tactical Airlift Sqdn
(AFRES); plus Army, Navy and
Marine Corps Reserve units;
Philadelphia Defense Contract
Administration Service; 92nd Aerial
Port Sqdn (MAC) who are an off-base
tenant

Operational Aircraft:
OA-37B	103rd TASS	(PA)
C-131D		
C-130E	327th TAS	

W.K. KELLOGG

W. K. Kellogg Regional Airport
Battle Creek
Michigan 49015-1291
USA

Phone:
(616) 963-1596

Autovon:
476-6210

Command:
Air National Guard

Acreage:
ANG area 241

Personnel:
954 military personnel, 211 civilians

Units:
110th Tactical Air Support Gp (ANG);
172nd Tactical Air Support Sqdn
(ANG)

Operational Aircraft:
F-4D   (BC)

WRIGHT-PATTERSON

Wright-Patterson AFB
Ohio 45433
USA

Phone:
(513) 257-1110

Autovon:
787-1110

Command:
Air Force Logistics Command

Date est:
1948*

Named after:
Wilbur Wright and Lt. Frank Patterson

Acreage:
8,145

Personnel:
9,500 military personnel, 17,500
civilians

Units:
HQ Air Force Logistics Command; HQ
Aeronautical Systems Divn (AFSC);
Air Force Institute of Technology;
Wright-Patterson USAF Medical
Center; USAF Museum; Air Force
Acquisition Logistics Center; Logistics
Operations Center; Logistics
Management Systems Center; AFLC
International Logistics Center; 2750th
Air Base Wing (AFLC); 906th Tactical
Fighter Gp (AFRES); plus 90 other
DoD and other government agencies

Operational Aircraft:
4950th Test Wing/Aeronautical

Systems Divn (AFSC)
various

89th Tactical Fighter Sqdn (AFRES)
F-4D   (DO)

Notes:
The base employs more people than
any other air force base in the world. It
is the HQ for one of the world's most
complex logistics operations. Its
research and development center
spearheads USAF's future project
developments

WURTSMITH

Wurtsmith AFB
Michigan 48753-5000
USA

Phone:
(517) 739-2011

Autovon:
623-1110

Command:
Strategic Air Command

Date est:
1924

Named after:
Maj. Gen. Paul B. Wurtsmith who was
killed after his B-25 crashed near
Asheville, N.C. in 1946

Acreage:
5,223

Personnel:
3,033 military personnel, 615 civilians

Units:
40th Air Divn; 379th Bomb Wing

Operational Aircraft:
379th Bombardment Wing (SAC)
B-52G	524th BS
KC-135th	920th ARS

WUESCHHEIM

Wueschheim AB
Germany
APO New York 09109-5000

Phone:
(633) 286113

Autovon:
474-1110

Command:
United States Air Forces in Europe

Units:
38th Tactical Missile Wing, USAFE

YEAGER

Yeager Airport (formerly Kanawha)
Charleston
West Virginia 25311-5000
USA

Phone:
(304) 357-5100

Autovon:
366-9210

Command:
Air National Guard

Acreage:
ANG area 56

Personnel:
903 military personnel, 167 civilians

Units:
130th Tactical Airlift Sqdn Gp (ANG)

Operational Aircraft:
C-130H

YOKOTA

Yokota AB
Japan
APO San Francisco 96328-5000

Phone:
(425) 522511

Autovon:
248-1101

Command:
Pacific Air Forces

Units:
HQ US Forces Japan; HQ 5th Air
Force (PACAF); 475th Air Base Wing
(PACAF); 316th Tactical Airlift Gp
(MAC); 345th Tactical Airlift Sqdn;
1956th Communication Gp (AFCC)

Operational Aircraft:
345th Tactical Airlift Sqdn
C-130E
The 345th is assigned to the 347th
TAW based at Clark AB, but is
permanently based in Japan

475th Air Base Wing
UH-1N

1403rd Military Airlift Squadron
C-21A
C-12F Det 1 Clark AB Philippines,
Det 2 Kadena AB Okinawa, Japan Det
3 Osan AB, South Korea

1867th Facility Checking Sqdn

YOUNGSTOWN

Youngstown Municipal Airport
Ohio 44473-5000
USA

Phone:
(216) 392-1000

Autovon:
346-1000

Command:
Air Force Reserve

Date est:
1952

Acreage:
AFRES area 230

Personnel:
837 military personnel, 354 civilians

Units:
757th Tactical Airlift Sqdn (AFRES);
OL C, 2046th Communications Gp;
Defense Contract Administration
Services

Operational Aircraft:
C-130B   757th TAS

ZWEIBRUCKEN

Zweibrucken AB
West Germany
APO New York 09286-5000

Phone:
(633) 286113

A C–23 from Zweibrucken pays
a visit to RAF Gatow in West
Berlin during the 1988
commemoration celebrations of
the Berlin Airlift.

Left: Home to the Short's C–
23A, Zweibrucken AB is the
center of the European
Distribution System (EDS).

Autovon:
498-1110

Command:
United States Air Forces in Europe

Units:
10th Military Airlift Wing (MAC); 10th
Military Airlift Sqdn (MAC); 26th
Tactical Reconnaissance Wing
(USAFE)

Operational Aircraft:
C-23A   10th MAS
RF-4C   38th TRS   (ZR)
Extras

ZARAGOZA

Zaragoza AB
Spain
APO New York 09286

Phone:
976-214-600

Autovon:
724-1110

Command:
United States Air Forces in Europe

Units:
406th Tactical Fighter Training Wing

AIRCRAFT

Preceding pages: An SR-71 of the 9th SRW can overtake the setting sun. First flown in 1962, the Blackbird is able to operate at heights in excess of 85,000ft.

Right: Tank busters on patrol in South Korea. The Fairchild A-10 Warthog has been the Air Force's main close air support aircraft since the early 1970's but the Air Force is now looking for a replacement for service from the mid 1990's.

A-7D/K CORSAIR II

Contractor:
LTV Aerospace and Defense Company (formerly Vought Corporation)

Powerplant:
One Allison TF41-A-1 nonafterburning turbofan engine; 6,577kg (14,500 lb) thrust

Accommodation:
Pilot only

Dimensions:
Span 12.5m (38' 9")
Length 14m (46' 1.5")
Height 4.9m (16' 0.75")

Weights:
Empty 8,973kg (19,781 lb)
Gross 19,051.2kg (42,000 lb)

Performance:
Maximum speed at S/L 1,123km/h (698 mph)
Ferry range with external tanks 4,620km (2,871 miles)

Armament:
One M61A1 20mm (0.78") multibarrel gun; up to 6,804kg (15,000 lb) of air-to-air or air-to-surface missiles, bombs, Gator mines, rockets, or gun pods on six underwing and two fuselage attachments

Notes:
The A-7 has had a successful life; it entered service in 1966 and equipped a substantial number of USAF TAC wings. Today it is in service with the ANG but it is becoming increasingly vulnerable to emerging counter-air threats and has major logistics problems. To combat these problems the A-7 Upgrade (A-7 Plus) Program will provide the Air Force with a Close Air Support/Battlefield Air Interdiction which would support the Army's

An A-7 of the 112th TFS/ 180th TFG. The A-7 is expected to undergo a major upgrade following development work on two YA-7Fs which is being carried out by LTV.

AirLand battle concept into the 1990's and beyond. In May 1987 Congress authorized LTV Aerospace to build two prototype aircraft

Units:
107th TFS (MI); 112th TFS (OH); 120th TFS (CO); 124th TFS (IA); 146th TFS (PT); 149th TFS; 152nd TFTS (AZ); 162nd TFS (OH); 166th TFS (OH); 174th TFS (HA); 175th TFS (SD); 188th TFS; 198th TFS; 4450th TG (LV)

Service number:
380+

A-10 Thunderbolt II

Contractor:
Fairchild Republic Company, Division of Fairchild Industries

Powerplant:
Two General Electric TF34-GE-100 turbofan engines; each approx. 4,111kg (9,065 lb) thrust

Accommodation:
Pilot only

Dimensions:
Span 17.5m (57' 6")
Length 16.3m (53' 4")
Height 4.5m (14' 8")

Weights:
Empty 11,321kg (24,959 lb)
Maximum gross 22,680kg (50,000 lb)

Performance:
Combat speed at S/L, clean, 439 mph
Range with 4,309kg (9,500 lb) of weapons and 1.7 hr loiter, 20 min reserve, 463km (288 miles)

Armament:
One 30mm (1.18") GAU-8/A gun; eight underwing hard points and three under fuselage for up to 7,258kg (16,000 lb) of ordnance, including

Powerplant:
Four General Electric F101-GE-102 turbofan engines, each 13,608kg (30,000 lb) thrust class

Accommodation:
Four – pilot, copilot, and two systems operators (offensive and defensive)

Dimensions:
Span spread 41.7m (136′ 8.5″)
fully swept 23.8m (78′ 2.5″)
Length 44.8m (147′)
Height 10.4m (34′)

Weight:
Maximum T-O weight 216,367kg (477,000 lb)

Performance:
Maximum speed at low level high subsonic (supersonic at altitude)
Range intercontinental

Armament:
Three internal weapons bays capable of accommodating in a nuclear role 8 advanced cruise missiles, 24 AGM-69 SRAMs, 12 B-28 or 24 B-61 or B-83 free-fall nuclear bombs; in a non-nuclear role up to 84 MK 82 (226.8kg

Left: An A–10 of the 104th TFG at Myrtle Beach is prepared for a mission. The combination of the AGM–65 Maverick and the 30mm GAU–8/A gun mounted on the A–10 provides a very strong anti–tank combination.

various types of free-fall or guided bombs, combined effects munition (CEM) dispensers, gun pods, or six AGM-65 Maverick missiles, and jammer pods. Chaff and flares carried internally to counter radar or infrared-directed threats. The centerline pylon and the two flanking fuselage pylons cannot be occupied simultaneously. AIM-9L Sidewinder AAM dual rail adapters, to allow four missiles to be carried in pairs

Notes:
With its GAU-8/A Avenger 30mm seven-barrel gun able to fire 2,100 or 4,200 rds/min, the A-10 is designed to tackle armored vehicles in the Close Air Support role. It is itself heavily armored and its systems are duplicated; it is possible for it to carry on flying even with one engine, half the tail and other equipment shot away or damaged. Its Pave Penny pod provides the capability to fly both day and night missions and its laser target-designation offers extremely accurate targeting. It is in service with regular, AFRES and ANG units

Units:
23rd TFW, 74th TFS, 75th TFS, 76th TFS (EL); 45th TFS; 46th TFTS (BD); 47th TFS (BD); 51st TFW, 25th TFS; 104th TFS (MD); 118th TFS (CT); 131st TFS (MA); 138th TFS (NY); 176th TFS (WI); 303rd TFS (KC); 343rd TFW, 18th TFS (AK); 345th TFW, 353rd TFS, 355th TFS, 356th TFS (MB); 355th TTW, 333rd TFTS, 357th TFTS, 358th TFTS (DM); 81st TFW, 92nd TFS, 509th TFS, 510th TFS, 511th TFS (WR); 706th TFS (NO)

Service number:
650+

B-1B

◆

Contractors:
Rockwell International, North American Aircraft Operations; Eaton Corporation, AIL Division; Boeing Military Airplane Company; and General Electric

Pulling a high G turn a B–1B goes through its acceptance flight. The B–1B is designed to make high-subsonic flights at low level making full use of terrain to hide itself from enemy radar.

(500 lb)) or 24 MK 84 (907.2kg (2,000 lb)) bombs. Eight underfuselage stores stations can carry an additional 14 ALCMs or SRAMs, 8 B-28s, 14 B-43/B-61/B-83s, 14 Mk 84s, or 44 Mk 82s

Notes:
1988 saw the last B-1B delivered and all four Bombardment Wings operational. The B-1B provides SAC a new multi-role strategic bomber for the 1990's with improved range and payload delivery over the B-52. Initially it will operate in the penetration role and then later a cruise missile shoot-then-penetrate role

Units:
28th BW; 96th BW; 319th BW; 384th BW

Service number:
99

B-2

Contractors:
Prime contractor: Northrop; major subcontractors: Boeing Aerospace and LTV

Powerplant:
General Electric Engine Group. Four GE F118-GE-100 non-afterburning engines, each 8,618.4kg (19,000 lb) thrust

Accommodation:
Two, with a provision for a third

Dimensions:
Span 52.43m (172')
Length 21.03m (69')
Height 5.18m (17')

Weight:
Approx. take-off weight 136,080kg (300,000 lb)

Performance:
Approx. Mach 0.85, 1,040 km/h (647 mph) at low level
Service ceiling approx. 15,240m (50,000')
Range in excess of 6,000 nautical miles

Armament:
Approx. 18,144kg (8,230 lb) made up of two Common Strategic Rotary Launcher with mix of SRAM II and AGM-129A Advanced Cruise Missiles

Notes:
With an Initial Operational Capability set for some time in the early 1990's, the Northrop low observable technology bomber will provide SAC with a bomber which could operate at high altitudes over the Soviet Union as a counter to expected advances in Soviet defenses. The Air Force plans to deploy 132 ATBs in the 1990's at a program cost in the region of $60 billion or almost $500 million for each aircraft. First deliveries to Whiteman AFB, Montana are due in Fiscal Year 1991

B-52 Stratofortress

(information for B-52G)
Contractor:
Boeing Military Airplane Company

Powerplant:
Eight Pratt & Whitney J57-P-43WB turbojet engines, each 6,237kg (13,750 lb) thrust

Accommodation:
Two pilots, side by side, plus navigator, radar navigator, electronic warfare officer, and fire control system operator (gunner)

Dimensions:
Span 56.4m (185' 0")
Length 50m (160' 10.9")
Height 12.4m (40' 8")

Weight:
G/H models gross more than 221,360kg (488,000 lb)

Performance (approx):
Maximum level speed at high altitude 960 km/h (595 mph)
Service ceiling 16,765m (55,000')
Range more than 12,070km (7,500 miles)

Armament:
G model has 4 0.50-caliber guns in tail turret; H model has 20mm (0.78") gun. G/H models are adapted to carry 8 SRAMs and nuclear free-fall bombs internally and 12 AGM-86B ALCMs

Opposite: To thunderous applause the B-2 was unveiled to a select group of people in November 1988.

Left: The latest major aircraft to enter service with SAC is the Rockwell B–1B. Dyess AFB was the first B–1B base achieving IOC in September 1986 and completion of deliveries was in 1988.

A Boeing B–52 belches smoke as it climbs into the sky.

A B–52 crew is scrambled for a mission. The B–52 will see service well into the 21st century.

A Lockheed C–5 flies majestically over San Francisco bay.

C-5A/B GALAXY

(information for C-5B)

Powerplant:
Four General Electric TF39-GE-1C turbofan engines; each 18,600kg (41,100 lb) thrust

Accommodation:
Crew of 5, rest area for 15 (relief crew, etc.); 75 troops and 36 standard 463L pallets or assorted vehicles, or additional 270 troops

Dimensions:
Span 68m (222′ 8.5″)
Length 75m (247′ 10″)
Height 20m (65′ 1.5″)

Weights:
Empty 170,000kg (374,000 lb)
Maximum operational payload 132,000kg (291,000 lb)
Gross (for 2.0g) 380,000kg (837,000 lb)

Performance:
Maximum speed at 7,620m (25,000′) 920 km/h (571 mph)
Service ceiling (at 280,000kg (615,000 lb)) 10,900km (35,750′)
Range with 90,720kg (200,000 lb) payload 4,345km (2,700 miles)
Range with maximum payload 1,336km (830 miles)

Notes:
The largest aircraft flying in the Western world, the C-5 provides MAC with its major strategic airlift capability. In Dec. 1985 Lockheed was awarded a contract to re-wing the C-5A; this increased the maximum take-off weight from 348,810kg (768,980 lb) to 379,660kg (837,000 lb). The C-5B is equipped with the same wing plus updated avionics, and better fatigue and corrosion resistance. The fleet of C-5As can lift 30 per cent of the total intertheater airlift requirement. This will be increased to nearly 50 per cent when the last of the C-5Bs is delivered in 1989.

Units:
60th MAW, 22nd MAS, 75th MAS C5A/B; 68th MAS C-5A; 137th MAS C-5A; 436th MAW, 9th MAS, 20th MAS C5A/B; 443rd MAW, 56th MATS C5A/B

Service number:
77 C-5A, 50 C-5B

instead of SRAMs externally. There is provision for 8 more ALCMs instead of SRAMs internally on H model. Alternatively, modified G models can carry 8–12 Harpoons in underwing clusters

Notes:
The B-52 has been in service for a quarter of a century and should still be in service at the turn of the century, although by the 1990's it will have ceased its strategic role. Significant new capabilities will allow the B-52 to stand off from heavily defended areas and attack targets with conventional or nuclear weapons; 61 non-ALCM B-52Gs now have a major role in conventional warfare following the retirement of the B-52D; 30 aircraft are equipped to carry the AGM-84

Harpoon anti-ship missile. Two squadrons are equipped for this role based at Loring AFB, Me. for Atlantic operations and at Andersen AFB, Guam for operations in the Pacific

Units:
B-52G
2nd BW, 62nd BS, 596th BS; 42nd BW, 69th BS; 43rd BW, 60th BS; 93rd BW, 328th BS; 97th BW, 340th BS; 319th BW, 46th BS; 320th BW, 441st BS; 379th BW, 524th BS; 416th BW, 668th BS
B-52H
5th BW 23rd BS; 7th BW, 9th BS, 20th BS; 28th BW (B-1B/B-52H), 37th BS; 410th BW 644th BS

Service number:
B-52G 167, B-52H 95

C-9A NIGHTINGALE AND C-9C

(information for the C-9A)

Contractor:
Douglas Aircraft Company, Division of McDonnell Douglas Corporation

Powerplant:
Two Pratt & Whitney JT8D-9 turbofan engines; each 6,577kg (14,500 lb) thrust

Accommodation:
Crew of three; 40 litter patients or 40 ambulatory patients, or a combination of both, plus five medical staff

Dimensions:
Span 28.4m (93' 3")
Length 36.3m (119' 3")
Height 8.3m (27' 6")

Weights:
Gross 49,000kg (108,000 lb)

Performance:
Maximum cruising speed at 7,620m (25,000') 909 km/h (565 mph)
Ceiling 10,670m (35,000')
Range more than 3,218km (2,000 miles)

Notes:
Developed from the DC-9 series 30 airliner, the Nightingale is used as a dedicated aeromedical airlift transport and has been in service since Aug. 1988. Three aircraft have been designated as C-9Cs and are used as VIP (Presidential and US Government) transport aircraft operated by the 89th Military Airlift Wing

Units:
89th MAW C-9C; 375th AAW C-9A; 435th TAW, 55th AAS; 374th TAW, 20th AAS C-9A

Service number:
C-9A 20, C-9C 3

C-12A/E/F/J

Contractor:
Beech Aircraft Corporation

Powerplant:
Two Pratt & Whitney Canada PT6A-38 turboprop engines; each 750 shp (C-12F; 850 shp PT6A-42s)

Accommodation:
Crew of two; up to eight passengers or 2,160kg (4,764 lb) of cargo. Convertible to aeromedical evacuation configuration

Dimensions:
Span 16.5m (54' 6")
Length 13.2m (43' 9")
Height 4.6m (15'0")

Weights:
Gross 5,670kg (12,500 lb)

Performance:
Maximum speed at 4,267m (14,000') 484 km/h (301 mph)
Service ceiling 9,450m (31,000')
Range at maximum cruising speed 2,935km (1,824 miles)

Notes:
A total of 30 military versions of the Beechcraft Super have been flown by the USAF. The latest C-12 designation is the C-12F which is a Super King Air 200C and is used as an Operational Support Aircraft to provide support for time-sensitive, critical movement of people and cargo throughout the CONUS, PACAF and USAFE

Units:
58th MAS C-12-F; 89th MAW C-12A; 101st FIS C-12F; 110th TFS C-12F; 118th TFS; 165th TRS C-12F; 173rd TRS C-12F; 175th TFS; 616th MAG C-12F; 1375th MAS C-12F; 1400th MAS C-12F (these aircraft carry civilian numbers); 1401st MAS C-12F; 1403rd MAS C-12F; JUSMG Madrid

Service number:
75

C-17

Contractor:
Douglas Aircraft Company, Division of McDonnell Douglas Corporation

Powerplant:
Four Pratt & Whitney F117-PW-100 turbofan engines; each 17,055kg (37,600 lb) thrust

Accommodation:
Normal flight crew of two, plus loadmaster; provision for the full range of military airlift missions

Built by McDonnell Douglas, the C-9A Nightingale is used as a casualty lift aircraft. It is capable of carrying 40 stretcher cases and five medical staff.

The McDonnell Douglas C–17 will, during the 1990's, provide MAC with a medium lift aircraft able to operate into small landing areas following a trans-continental flight. MAC is due to receive a total of 210 aircraft starting in FY '92. The first unit to receive the C–17 will be the 437th MAW based at Charleston AFB.

Dimensions:
Span 50m (165′)
Length 53.4m (175′ 2.4″)
Height 16.8m (55′ 3.6″)

Weights:
Maximum payload 78,000kg (172,200 lb)
Gross 260,000kg (570,000 lb)

Performance (estimated):
Normal cruising speed at height 834 km/h (518 mph) (Mach 0.77)
Range with 75,750kg (167,000 lb) payload 4,450km (2,765 miles)

Notes:
The C-17 will fill a major gap in MAC's airlift capability, providing a tactical outsize airland and airdrop capability. The C-17 will be the USAF's first airlift aircraft capable of covering the full spectrum of airlift missions, from intercontinental movement of personnel and cargo to low-altitude parachute extraction of outsize equipment into the forward battle area. Procurement began in FY 1988 with an initial operational capability in FY 1992

Units:
The 437th MAW will be the first unit

Service number:
210 planned

C-20 GULFSTREAM

Contractor:
Gulfstream Aerostream Corporation

Powerplant:
Two Rolls-Royce F113-RR-100 turbofan engines, each rated at 5,170kg (11,400 lbs) thrust

Accommodation:
Five crew, 14–18 passengers

Dimensions:
Span 23.5m (77′ 10″)
Length 25.3m (83′ 1″)
Height 7.4m (24′ 4.5″)

Weights:
Gross 31,615kg (69,700 lb)

Performance:
Maximum cruising speed 928 km/h (577 mph)
Service ceiling 13,868m (45,500′)
Range 6,518km (4,050 miles)

Notes:
Based on the twin turbofan Gulfstream Biz jet, the C-20 is used as a VIP transport and operational support aircraft. The Air Force acquired 11 C-20s under a leasing agreement and then later purchased them outright

Units:
58th MAS (C-20A); 89th MAW (C-20B)

Service numbers:
C-20A 3, C-20B 8

C-21A LEARJET

Contractor:
Gates Learjet Corporation

Powerplant:
Two Garrett TFE731-2A turbofan engines; each 1,588 kg (3,500 lb) thrust

Accommodation:
Crew of two and up to eight passengers or 1,430kg (3,153 lb) cargo. Convertible to aeromedical evacuation configuration

Dimensions:
Span 11.9m (39′ 6″)
Length 14.7m (48′ 8″)
Height 3.7m (12′ 4″)

Weights:
Gross 8,392kg (18,500 lb)

Performance:
Cruising speed Mach 0.81
Service ceiling 13,716m (45,000′)
Range with maximum passenger load 3,895km (2,420 miles), with maximum cargo load 2,660km (1,653 miles)

Notes:
A conversion of the Learjet 35A, the C-21A operates from 16 bases for the movement of time-crucial people and equipment that have a sensitive movement requirement throughout America, the Pacific and Europe

Units:
58th MAS; 1375th MAS; 1400th MAS; 1401st MAS; 1402nd MAS; 1403rd MAS; 7005th AS

Service number:
84

A C–21A Learjet operated by the 1375th MAS based at Scott AFB, Illinois.

C-23 SHERPA

Contractor:
Short Brothers Plc

Powerplant:
Two Pratt & Whitney Canada PT6A-45R turboprop engines; each 1,198 shp

Accommodation:
Crew of three; up to 3,175kg (7,000 lb) of freight, including four LD3 containers, and engines the size of the F100 series

Dimensions:
Span 22.6m (74′ 8″)
Length 17.7m (58′ 0.5″)
Height 4.9m (16′ 3″)

Weights:
Gross 10,387kg (22,900 lb)

Performance:
Maximum cruising speed at 3,050m (10,000′) 350 km/h (218 mph)
Range 1,240 km/h (770 miles) with 1,996kg (4,400 lb) payload

Notes:
Since its introduction to MAC in Nov. 1984, the C-23 has been dedicated to USAFE. It has consistently won awards for its performance in carrying cargo for the European Distribution System. Based at Zweibrucken, W. Germany it can be seen operating from bases throughout USAFE. It has meant that supplies can be delivered much more quickly, often taking days off the old time schedules

Units:
10th MAS

Service number:
18

C-130 HERCULES

(information for C-130H)

Contractor:
Lockheed-Georgia Company

Powerplant:
Four Allison T56-A-15 turboprop engines; each 4,508 ehp

Accommodation:
Crew of five; up to 92 troops, 64 paratroops, 74 litter patients, or up to five 463L standard freight pallets, etc.

Dimensions:
Span 40.3m (132′ 7″)
Length 29.6m (97′ 9″)
Height 11.6m (38′ 3″)

Weights:
Operating 36,300kg (80,000 lb)
Maximum payload 22,680kg (50,000 lb)
Gross 79,380kg (175,000 lb)

Performance:
Maximum speed at 6,096km (20,000′) 555 km/h (345 mph)
Service ceiling (at 79,380kg (175,000 lb) 7,010m (23,000′)
Range with maximum payload 1,352km (840 miles)

Notes:
The four turboprop Hercules certainly lives up to its name. It has provided the Air Force with its tactical airlift for over thirty years and will see service well into the next century. It has been converted to meet any different special roles, all of which it has carried out successfully. The latest additions ordered in Apr. 1987 are for an AC-130U for the Special Operations Force and eight C-130Hs for the Air Force Reserve. The Air Force uses six different types of C-130, and there are four variants of the basic C-130 tactical transport. There are also three COIN variants – the AC130A/H/U. Three variants are currently used in the SAR role; two variants for tactical ECM; two variants for Special Operations, plus the WC-130 Weather Reconnaissance aircraft

Units:
C-130A
63rd TAS; 64th TAS; 95th TAS; 105th TAS; 107th TFS; 150th ARS; 152nd TFTS; 155th TAS; 178th FIS; 180th TAS (C130-A/H); 199th FIS; 356th TAS; 758th TAS; 4950th TW/ AD
C-130B
135th TAS; 156th TAS; 158th TAS; 164th TAS; 167th TAS; 187th TAS; 303rd TAS; 731st TAS; 757th TAS;
C-130E
62nd MAW; 96th TAS; 109th TAS; 115th TAS; 314th MAS; 317th MAW; 327th TAS; 337th TAS; 345th TAS; 374th TAW (C-130E/H); 435th TAW; 616th MAG
C-130H
130th TAS; 181st TAS; 185th TAS; 147th TAS; 357th TAS; 463rd MAW; 700th TAS
HC/NC-130H
6514th Test Sqdn
C/LC-130H

The need to supply heavy fire support to Special Forces will be met by the Rockwell AC–130U. The illustration shows Lockheed's concept for the new gunship.

An army unit deploys into the rear of an Air Force Reserve C–130.

The C–130's rough terrain landing capability is well illustrated in this photo as a C–130 lands in a cloud of dust.

Performance:
Maximum cruising speed at 6,096m (20,000″) 885 km/h (550 mph)
Ceiling above 13,716m (45,000′)
Range with reserves 3,670km (2,280 miles)

Notes:
The C-140As are used by the Air Force Communications Command to evaluate landing systems, navigation aids etc. The other eight C-140Bs are split with four based at Andrews AFB and four which operate in Europe

Units:
58th MAS; 89th MAW; AFCC

Service number:
C-140A 4, C-140B 8

C-141 STARLIFTER

(information for the C-141B)

Contractor:
Lockheed-Georgia Company

Powerplant:
Four Pratt & Whitney TF33-P-7 turbofan engines; each 9,526kg (21,000 lb) thrust

Accommodation:
Crew of five; cargo on 13 standard 463L pallets. Alternative freight or vehicle payloads, 200 fully equipped troops, 155 paratroops, or 103 litter patients plus attendants

Dimensions:
Span 48.8m (159′ 11″)
Length 51.2m (168′ 3.5″)
Height 11.9m (39′ 3″)

The Lockheed C–141B is capable of airlifting a 94,508-lb payload with a cargo capacity of 322.78m³ (11,399 cubic feet).

139th TAS
EC-130E/H
41st ECS (DM); 193rd ECS;
MC-130E/H
1st SOS; 8th SOS
AC-130A/H
711th SOS; 16th SOS
HC-130N/P
31st ARRS; 41st ARRS; 55th ARRS; 67th ARRS; 71st ARRS; 102nd ARRS; 301st ARRS; 304th ARRS;
1550th CCTW
WC-130E/H
53rd WRS; 815th WRS

Service number:
C-130 A/B/D/E/H 600+, AC-130A/H/U 20+, EC-130E/H 18, HC-130H/N/P 50+, MC-130E/H, WC-130 17

C-137 STRATOLINER AIR FORCE ONE

Contractor:
The Boeing Company

Powerplant:
Four Pratt & Whitney JT3D-3 turbofan engines; each 8,165kg (18,000 lb) thrust

Dimensions:
C-137B span 39.7m (130′ 10″)
Length 43.9m (144′ 6″)
Height 12.8m (42′ 0″)
C-137C span 44.2m (145′ 9″)
Length 46.4m (152′ 11″)
Height 12.8m (42′ 5″)

Weights:
C-137B gross 116,575kg (257,000 lb)
C-137C gross 146,000kg (322,000 lb)

Performance (C-137C):
Maximum speed 1,009 km/h (627 mph)
Service ceiling 12,800m (42,000′)
Range 8,288km (5,150 miles)

Notes:
The two Presidential aircraft, designated Air Force One while the President is aboard, have been in service for 15 years and 25 years respectively and are due to be replaced because they do not meet FAA noise standards nor the requirements for communications, range, performance or payload

Units:
89th MAW

Service number:
2 C-137C plus 3 C-137B

C-140 JETSTAR

Contractor:
Lockheed-Georgia Company

Powerplant:
Four Pratt & Whitney J60-P-5A turbojet engines; each 1,360kg (3,000 lb) thrust

Accommodation:
C-140A crew of five; C-140B crew of four and eight passengers

Dimensions:
Span 16.7m (54′ 11″)
Length 18.3m (60′ 5′)
Height 6m (20′ 5″)

Weights:
Gross 18,560kg (40,920 lb)

Weights:
Operating 676,000kg (149,000 lb)
Maximum payload 40,370kg
(89,000 lb)
Gross 155,585kg (343,000 lb)

Performance:
Maximum cruising speed 910 km/h
(566 mph)
Range with maximum payload
3,690km (2,293 miles) (range
significantly increased if air refueling
used)

Notes:
Currently providing for the middle
range of airlift tasks, the C-141 is used
both for passengers, cargo and
paratroop drops. The C-141A entered
service in Apr. 1965 and was
immediately flying supply missions to
South-east Asia. It became clear that
the aircraft could carry far more if it
was lengthened and Lockheed
extended the 264 airframes by 7m (23′
4″). At the same time they received an
in-flight capability. The increased lift
capability was large, providing the
equivalent of 90 extra C-141s. The C-
141 is flown by regular, AFRES and
ANG units.

Units:
60th MAW, 7th MAS, 44th MAS; 63rd
MAW, 14th MAS, 15th MAS, 53rd
MAS; 183rd MAS; 172nd TAG, 183rd
MAS; 437th MAW, 3rd MAS, 4th
MAS, 76th MAS; 443rd MAW, 57th
MATS; 459th TAW, 756th MAS;
AFSC

Service number:
267

CH-3E and HH-3E

Contractor:
Sikorsky Aircraft, Division of United
Technologies Corporation

Powerplant:
Two General Electric T58-GE-5
turboshaft engines; each 1,500 shp

Accommodation:
Crew of two or three; 25 fully equipped
troops, 15 litters, or 2,270kg
(5,000 lb) of cargo

Dimensions:
Rotor diameter 18.9m (62′ 0″)
Length of fuselage 17.4m (57′ 3′)
Height 5.5m (18′ 1″)

Far right: The CV-22A will form
an important part of the Air
Force's Special Operations
Force when it enters service in
late 1992, following first
deliveries to the Marine Corps.

Weights:
Empty 6,012kg (13,255 lb)
Gross 10,000kg (22,050 lb)

Performance:
Maximum speed at S/L 260 km/h
(162 mph)
Service ceiling 3,383m (11,100′)
Maximum range, with 10% reserve,
750km (465 miles)

Armament:
General Electric 7.62mm (0.3″)
machine gun

Notes:
Based on the Navy's SH-3A Sea King it
is an amphibious transport helicopter it
is used for Special Operations and
SAR. The HH-3E Jolly Green Giant it
is fitted with extra equipment and an
in-flight refueling probe. It is operated
by Aerospace Rescue and Recovery
squadrons in the regular Air Force and
reserve units

Units:
703rd TASS (CH-3E); 1550th CCTW,
1551st FTS (CH/HH-3E); 31st ARRS
(CH/HH-3E); 71st ARRS (CH/HH-
3E); 102nd ARRS (HH-3E); 129th
ARRS (HH-3E); 305th ARRS (HH-
3E); 6514th TS (CH-3E)

Service number:
80+

CT-39 SABRELINER

Contractor:
Sabreliner Division of Rockwell
International Corporation

Powerplant:
Two Pratt & Whitney J60-P-3 turbojet
engines, each 1,360kg (3,000 lb)
thrust

Accommodation:
Crew of two; four to seven passengers

Dimensions:
Span 13.5m (44′ 5″)
Length 13.4m (43′ 9″)
Height 4.9m (16′ 0″)

Weights:
Empty 4,220kg (9,300 lb)
Gross 8,055kg (17,760 lb)

Performance:
Maximum speed at 11,000m (36,000′)
958 km/h (595 mph)
Service ceiling 12,000m (39,000′)
Range 3,140km (1,950 miles)

Notes:
The last few Sabreliners still in service
are operated by AFCC, AFSC and
ATC. Both the AFCC and AFSC use
the CT-39 for facility checking and
ATC use if for communications and
navigation aid checking

Units:
4950th TW/ASD

Service number:
25+

CV-22A OSPREY

Contractor:
Bell/Boeing

Powerplant:
Two Alison T406-AD-400 turboshafts
each 5,890 shp

Dimensions:
Rotor diameter (each) 11.58m (38′ 0″)
Length fuselage 17.47m (57′ 4″)
Height over tail fins 5.38m (17′ 8″)

Weights:
STO 24,947kg (55,000 lb), VTO
21.545kg (47,500 lb)

Performance:
Maximum cruising speed at S/L in
helicopter made 100 knots (185km/h;
115mph)
at S/L in aeroplane made 275 knots
(556km/h; 345mph)

Notes:
The CV-22A is the linchpin of the Air
Force Special Operations Force in the

1990's. It combines medium-speed cruise efficiency with vertical takeoff and landing

Service number:
The Air Force has a requirement for 55, originally 80. Deliveries are due to start in late 1992 with initial operational capability (six aircraft) scheduled for Fiscal Year 1995

EF-111A RAVEN

Contractor:
Grumman Aerospace Corporation

Powerplant:
Two Pratt & Whitney TF30-P-3 turbofan engines, each 83,900kg (18,500 lb) thrust with afterburning

Accommodation:
Crew of two, side-by-side in escape module

Dimensions:
Span spread 19.2m (63′ 0″)
Fully swept 9.7m (31′ 11.4″)
Length 23.2m (76′ 0″)
Height 6.1m (20′ 0″)

Weights:
Empty 25,072kg (55,275 lb)
Gross 40,347kg (88,948 lb)

Performance:
Maximum combat speed 2,216 km/h (1,377 mph)
Service ceiling with afterburning at combat weight 13,700m (45,000′)
Combat radius with reserves 370–1,495 km (230–929 miles), according to mission

Notes:
The EF-111 was developed by Grumman Aerospace from the General Dynamics F-111 using mostly off-the-shelf components. It was first deployed to RAF Upper Heyford in Feb. 1984. The ALQ-99E is a development of the

Navy's ALQ-99 which was used in the EA-6B. The ALQ-99E is itself now undergoing further modification. The ALQ-99E Tactical Jamming System is designed to deny enemy command and control units the necessary range, azimuth and altitude information used to guide their interceptors, SAMs and anti-aircraft artillery. The success of the Raven was proved during the raid on Libya when it cut an electronically sanitized path through the Libyan defenses for the F-111 bombers

Armament:
None

Units:
346th TFW, 390th ECS; 42nd ECS

Service number:
42

E-3 B/C SENTRY (AWACS)

Contractor:
Boeing Aerospace Company

Powerplant:
Four Pratt & Whitney TF33-PW-100/100A turbofan engines, each 9,526kg (21,000 lb) thrust

Accommodation:
Basic operational crew of 20, including 16 AWACS mission specialists

Dimensions:
Span 44.2m (145′ 9″)
Length 46.4m (152′ 11″)
Height 12.5m (41′ 9″)

Weights:
Gross 147,420kg (325,000 lb)

Far left: A Grumman EF-111 of the 42nd Electronic Countermeasures Squadron at RAF Upper Heyford. It was the 42nd's EF-111 that led the F-111 attack on Libya in 1986, creating complete confusion in the Libyan defenses.

Below: The interior of an AWACS with a number of mission specialist operators.

Bottom: A Boeing E-3 AWACS flies high over the cloud tops but its powerful Westinghouse AN/APY-1 radar can track multiple targets over a huge area.

Performance:
Maximum speed 850 km/h (530 mph)
Service ceiling above 8,840m (29,000').
Endurance 6 hr on station 1,600km (1,000 miles) from base

Notes:
The E-3 provides tactical commanders with real-time battle management information in support of tactical air operations. The first E-3A AWACS entered service in March 1977. Over the years it has gone through a number of changes. Ten E-3As are being upgraded to the E-3C configuration by the addition of five more consoles and extra communications systems. Twenty-four other E-3As are being upgraded to E-3B standard by the upgrading of communications equipment, which includes JTIDS and fitting extra consoles. Chaff/flare dispensers can now be fitted

Units:
552nd AW&CW, 963rd AW&CS, 964th AW&CS, 966th AW&CS

Service number:
34

E-4B

Contractor:
Boeing Aerospace Company

Power plant:
Four General Electric CF6-50E2 turbofan engines, each 23,800kg (52,500 lb) thrust

Dimensions:
Span 59.5m (195' 8")
Length 70.4m (231' 4")
Height 19.2m (63' 5")

Weights:
Gross 362,880kg (800,000 lb)

Performance:
Unrefueled endurance in excess of 12 hours

Notes:
The Four E–4B National Emergency Airborne Command Post aircraft in conjunction with the EC–135 Airborne Command Post form the basis of the National Emergency Airborne Command Post. The E–4 is a development of the Boeing 747 airframe.

Originally three were built to E–4A standard and those three, plus another airframe, have been brought up to the current E–4B standard. They are hardened to withstand the effects of a nuclear explosion including electromagnetic pulse. They are able to handle a wide variety of communications systems and if necessary can link into even commercial telephone and radio networks. Major modernization is planned including Milstar transition satellite communications terminals

Units:
55th SRW, 1st ACCS

Service number:
4

F-4 PHANTOM II

(information for F-4E)

Contractor:
McDonnell Aircraft Company, Division of McDonnell Douglas Corporation

Powerplant:
Two General Electric J79-GE-17A turbojets, each 8,120kg (17,900 lb) thrust with afterburning

Accommodation:
Pilot and weapons systems operator in tandem

Dimensions:
Span 11.6m (38' 7.5")
Length 19.2m (63' 0")
Height 4.9m (16' 5.5")

Weights:
Empty 13,757kg (30,328 lb)
Gross 28,030kg (61,795 lb)

Performance:
Maximum speed at 12,700m (40,000') Mach 2.0 class, range with typical tactical load 700 miles

Armament:
One 20mm (0.79") M61A1 multibarrel gun; provision for up to four AIM-7E Sparrow, AGM-45A Shrike, AGM-88A HARM, or AIM-9 Sidewinder missiles on four underfuselage and four underwing mountings, or up to 7,258kg (16,000 lb) external stores

Right: F–4s of the 3rd TFW based at Clark AB while on deployment to South Korea.

Below: An E–4B Airborne Command Post is refueled by a KC–135. The Air Force operates and supports the E–4B for the National Command Authorities, the Joint Chiefs of Staff and Commanders–in–Chief of nuclear forces.

Notes:

For many years the workhorse of the tactical air commands, the F-4 still has major tasks in the Wild Weasel and Recce roles. With its APR-38 Radar Attack and Warning System, the F-4G can detect, identify and accurately locate, engage and destroy hostile radars. The APR-38 Product Upgrade Program (PUP) will update the warning/location Wild Weasel System to handle the advanced threat radars it may encounter in the 1990's. The PUP upgrade is divided into two sections: Phase I increases the on-board computer memory and processing speed while Phase II extends the frequency range. Phase I will have achieved an Initial Operational Capability in July 1988. Following problems with the first Phase II receiver prototype during FY 1987, the second part of the program is being extended to tackle the problems. As the F-4E is replaced in regular units by the F-15 and F-16 it is being transferred to the ANG. The RF-4 provides a vital tactical photo reconnaissance platform equipping two air wings

Units:

F-4C
160th TFS; 199th FIS (The F-4Cs are due to be replaced by F-15A/B) (HF); 113th TFS (HF); 114th TFTS; 196th TFS F-4C/E; 123rd FIS;
F-4D
121st TFS (DC); 704th TFS (TX); 170th TFS (SI); 457th TFS (TH); 179th FIS (AL); 179th FIS; 184th TFS; 111th FIS; F-4C/D; 194th FIS; 178th FIS; 27th TFW, 307th TFS, 113th TFS; 127th TFS; 177th TFTS; 136th FIS; 171st FIS (MI); 465th TFS (SH); 172nd TASS; 89th TFS (DO)
F-4E/G
163rd TFS (FW); 3rd TFS; 90th TFS (PN); 35th TTW; 20th TFTS, 21st TFTS (GA); 37th TFW, F-4E&G, 561st TFS, 562nd TFS, 563rd TFS (WW); 37th TFW, F-4E&G, 561st TFS, 562nd TFS, 563rd TFS (WW); 110th TAS? (SL); 141st TFS (NJ); 347th TFW, 68th TFS (the wing is converting to the F-16s); 4th TFW, 334th TFS, 335th TFS, 336th TFS; 51st TFW, 36th TFS (OS), 497th TFS (GU)
RF-4C
10th TRW, 1st TRS (AR); 26th TRW RF-4C (ZR)

Service Number:
F-4/D/E 1200+, RF-4C 325+

F-5E/F TIGER II

(information for the F-5E)

Contractor:
Northrop Corporation, Aircraft Division

Powerplant:
Two General Electric J85-GE-21B turbojet engines; each 2,268kg (5,000 lb) thrust with afterburning

Accommodation:
Pilot only (two seats in tandem in F-5F)

Dimensions:
Span 7.9m (26′ 8″)
Length 14.3m (47′ 4.75″)
Height 3.9m (13′ 4.25″
(F-5F length 15.5m (51′ 4″)
Height 3.9m (13′ 2″)

Weights:
Empty 4,410kg (9,723 lb)
Gross 11,214kg (24,722 lb)

Performance
(at 6,055kg (13,350 lb)):
Maximum level speed at 11,000m (36,000′) Mach 1.64
Service ceiling 15,789m (51,800′)
Range with maximum fuel, with reserve fuel for 20 min maximum endurance at S/L (with external tanks retained), 2,483km (1,543 miles)

Armament:
Two AIM-9 Sidewinder missiles on wingtip launchers; two M39-A2 20mm cannon in nose, with 280 rounds per

gun (one 20mm (0.79″) in F-5F); up to 3,175kg (7,000 lb) or mixed ordnance on four underwing attachments and one underfuselage station. Optional armament and equipment include AGM-65 Maverick, laser-guided bombs, and centerline multiple ejector rack

Notes:
Anyone who has flown a Red Flag exercise knows the F-5 flown by the Agggressors of the 57th FWW or their counterparts in Europe the 10th TRW Aggressors from Alconbury, Great Britain. The F-5 is used now by the USAF as a dissimilar trainer posing as a Soviet Fighter

Units:
26th TFTAS, F-5E (PN); 405th TTW, 425th TFS, F-5B/E/F (LA); 57th FWW, 64th AS, 65th AS, F-5E (WA)

Service number:
90+/4

An F–5 of the 527th AS sits and waits in the early dawn at RAF Alconbury. The Air Force is now withdrawing its F–5 Aggressors and replacing them with F–16s.

F-15 EAGLE

(information for the F-15C)

Contractor:
McDonnell Aircraft Company, Division of McDonnell Douglas Corporation

Now entering service, the F-15E dual role fighter is designed to operate long-range missions at night and in poor weather. It is shown here with its Martin Marietta LANTIRN pods and conformal tanks. The LANTIRN (Low Altitude Navigation and Target Infrared for Night) pods enable the F-15 crew to carry out precise attacks at night.

Powerplant:
Two Pratt & Whitney F100-PW-100 turbofan engines; each approx. 10,800kg (23,830 lb) thrust. Improved F100-PW-220 will equip new F-15s

Accommodation:
Pilot only

Dimensions:
Span 12.9m (42' 9.75")
Length 19.5m (63' 9")
Height 5.5m (18' 5.5")

Weights:
Empty 12,383kg (27,300 lb)
Gross 308,45kg (68,000 lb)

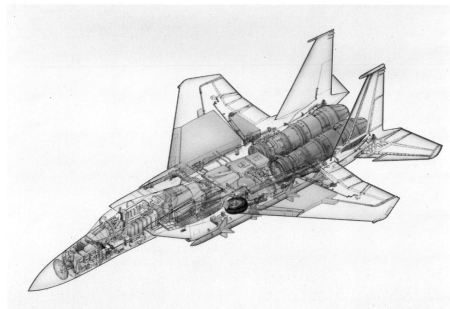

Performance:
Maximum speed Mach 2.5
Service ceiling 18,288m (60,000')
Ferry range, with external fuel tanks, more than 4,632km (2,878 miles) with CFTs, 5,745km (3,570 miles)

Armament:
One internally mounted M61A1 20mm (0.79") multibarrel cannon; 4 AIM-9L/M Sidewinder and 4 AIM-7F/M Sparrow air-to-air missiles, or 8 AMRAAMs, carried externally. Provision for carrying up to 10,705kg (23,600 lb) of ordnance on weapon stations

Right: The McDonnell Douglas F-15 provides the tactical air commands with one of the finest fighters ever built.

Below: An F-15 of 555th TFTS based at Luke AFB, Arizona, the largest fighter training base in the Western world.

Notes:
The F-15E, the latest in the F-15 family, provides a long-range, large payload capability to strike second echelon targets at night and in any weather condition while retaining a superior air-to-air capability. Although the F-15E has less range while carrying a similar load than the F-111 (11,113kg (24,500 lbs)), it is capable of carrying a much wider mix of air-to-surface munitions. It will be equipped with the Low Altitude Navigation and Targeting Infrared System for Night (LANTIRN) and the beyond visual range Advanced Medium Range Air-to-Air Missile (AMRAAM). The F-15E is due to enter IOC in mid-1989 service. The existing F-15s are being upgraded to increase their air superiority and the earlier F-15A/Bs are being transferred to Reserve units. The first ANG unit to receive the F-15 was the 159th TFG in 1985. In FY 1988 the Air Force received 42 F-15Es, bringing the total up to 92 aircraft. They have requested another 36 F-15 aircraft in FY 1989 with a total delivery number of 392 aircraft

Units:

F-15A/B

5th FIS; 21st TFW, 43rd TFS (AK); 48th FIS; 49th TFW, 7th TFS, 8th TFS, 9th TFS; 318th FIS; 325th TTW, 1st TFTS, 2nd TFTS (TY); 405th TTW, 426th TFTS

F-15C/D

1st TFW, 27th TFS, 71st TFS, 94th TFS (FF); 32nd TFS (CR); 33rd TFW, 58th TFS, 59th TFS, 60th TFS (EG); 36th TFW, 22nd TFS, 53rd TFS; 525th TFS (BT); 128th TFS; 18th TFW, 12th TRS, 44th TRS, 67th TRS (ZZ); 57th FIS (IS); 57th FWW (WA); 405th TTW, 426th TFTS, 555th TFTS

F-15E

4th TFW, 336th TFS

Service number:

A total of 1,266 airframes.

F-16 FIGHTING FALCON

(information for the F-16C)

Contractor:

General Dynamics Corporation

Powerplant:

One Pratt & Whitney F100-PW-200(3) turbofan engine; approx. 11,340kg (25,000 lb) thrust with afterburning. General Electric F110-GE-100 and Pratt & Whitney F100-PW-220 augmented turbofans will be alternative standard engines in future production aircraft

Accommodation:

Pilot only

Dimensions:

Span over missiles 10m (32' 10")
Length overall 15m (49' 3")
Height 4.9m (16' 8.5")

Weights:

Empty 7,618kg (16,794 lb)
Gross with external loads 17,010kg (37,500 lb)

Performance:

Maximum speed Mach 2 class
Service ceiling more than 15,240m (50,000')
Ferry range more than 3,200km (2,000 miles)

Armament:

One M61A1 20mm (0.79") multibarrel cannon, with 500 rounds, mounted in fuselage; wingtip-mounted infrared missiles; seven other external stores stations for fuel tanks and air-to-air and air-to-surface munitions

Notes:

With its exceptional air-to-air performance and a potent air-to-surface capability the F-16 is the major tactical aircraft in the Air Force inventory and is replacing the much older F-4 in both the regular and

Below: High above the desert the AFTI/F-16 goes through its paces.

Bottom: An F-16 of the 363rd TFW, based at Shaw AFB, South Carolina, with a pair of Maverick air-to-surface missiles.

reserve fleets; 27 regular air wings will have received the F-16 by the end of FY 1988, plus 4 Air Force Reserve Wings and 9 Air National Guard Wings. The AMRAAM integration program is well under way and certification for the High Speed Anti-Radiation Missile (HARM) and Shrike Missile is progressing. Integration of these systems on the newest F-16 C/D block 40 aircraft will be tested in FY 1989. The F-16 is also undergoing a pre-planned product improvement for its electronic countermeasures system. The F-16 Agile Falcon program is looking into ways to develop further the derivative F-16s in the 1990's and beyond

Units:
F-16A/B
8th TFW, 35th TFS, 80th TFS; 56th TTW, 61st TFTS, 62nd TFTS, 63rd TFTS, 72nd TFTS (MC); 57th FWW F-16A/B/C/D (WA); 58th TTW, 310th TFTS, 311th TFTS F-16A/B, 312th TFTS, 314th TFTS F-16C/D (LF); 134th TFS; 157th TFS (SC); 159th FIS; 161st TFTS: 182nd TFS (SA); 195th TFTS; 347th TFW, 69th TFS, 70th TFS (MY); 388th TFW, 4th TFS, 34th TFS, 421st TFS (HL); 401st TFW, 612th AFS, 613th AFS, 614th AFS (TJ); 466th TFS; 474th TFW, 428th TFS, 429th TFS, 430th TFS (HM) the wing was due to disband in 1988; Air Demonstration Squadron (the Thunderbirds)
F-16C/D
50th TFW, 10th TFS, 313th TFS, 496th TFS (HR); 86th TFW, 512th TFS, 526th TFS, 417th TFS (RS); 363rd TFW, 17th TFS, 19th TFS, 33th TFS (SW); 432nd TFW, 13th TFS, 14th TFS (MF)

Service number:
F-16A/B: 735+, F-16C/D: 1936 Req.; delivery in progress

F-106 DELTA DART

(information for F–106A)

Contractor:
Convair Division of General Dynamics

Powerplant:
One Pratt & Whitney J75-P-17 turbojet engine; 11,113kg (24,500 lb) thrust with afterburning

Accommodation:
Pilot only

Dimensions:
Span 11.6m (38' 3.5")
Length 21.6m (70' 8.75")
Height 6m (20' 3.33")

Weights (approx):
Empty 11,476kg (25,300 lb)
Gross 19,233kg (42,400 lb)

Performance approx:
Maximum speed at 12,192m (40,000')
Mach 2.0
Service ceiling 19,812m (65,000')
Range 1,930km (1,200 miles)

Armament:
Four AIM-4F/G Falcon air-to-air missiles carried internally; a 20mm (0.79") cannon on most F-106As

Notes:
1988 saw the end of Convair F-106 air defense fighter. This mighty aircraft, built in the 1950's, has provided sterling service in the defense of the United States. The remaining airframes will continue to serve the Air Force as they are being converted into QF-106 aerial target drones

Service number:
50+

F-111

Contractor:
General Dynamics Corporation

Powerplant:
F-111A/E: two Pratt & Whitney TF30-P-3 turbofan engines; each 8,390kg (18,500 lb) thrust with afterburning. F-111D: two TF30-P-9 turbofan engines; each 19,600 lb thrust with afterburning. F-111F: two TF30-P-100 turbofan engines; each approx. 11,400kg (25,100 lb) thrust with afterburning

Accommodation:
Crew of two side-by-side in escape module

Dimensions:
Span spread 19.2m (63' 0")
Fully swept 9.7m (31' 11.4")
Length 22.4m (73' 6")
Height 5.2m (17' 1.4")

Weights (F-111F):
Maximum speed at S/L Mach 1.2
Maximum speed at altitude Mach 2.5
Service ceiling more than 18,000m (59,000')
Range with maximum internal fuel more than 4,700km (2,925 miles)

Armament:
Two nuclear bombs in internal weapon bay; four swiveling wing pylons

Opposite: A head-on view of an F–106 Delta Dart. Following many years of service the F–106 was finally removed from the active service list in 1988. All the surviving airframes will be converted into QF–106 aerial target drones.

Leading a flight of F–111Es from the 79th TFS, 77th TFS and 55th TFS is a 42nd ECS EF–111A.

carrying total external load of up to 11,340kg (25,000 lb) of bombs, rockets, missiles, or fuel tanks

Notes:

The world's first blind first-pass precision attack aircraft when it entered service in June 1967, it is still the Air Force's only long-range, day-and-night interdiction fighter. This will change when the F-15E comes into full service. The F-111Fs of the 48th TFW at RAF Lakenheath carried out a retaliatory raid against Libya in April 1986. Fitted with the Pave Tack system which provides a day/night capability to acquire, track and designate ground targets for laser, infrared, and optically guided weapons, they were able to hit their targets accurately. To provide increased self-protection the ALR-62 radar warning receiver and the ALQ-94/137 self-protection jammer system are to be replaced. The ALR-621 is now in full-scale development and it is due to enter service in July 1989. The Air Force also intends to procure ALQ-131/184 jammer pods for the F-111 fleet. Developed by ASD's Dynamics Laboratory and built by Boeing Military Aircraft Company the AFTI/F-111 is fitted with the Mission Adaptive Wing. This advanced wing does not have conventional flaps, slats, ailerons, or spoilers; instead the wing changes its camber by using hydraulic actuators to alter the shape of the flexible composite skin

Centre right: The first photograph of the Lockheed F-117. Its unique multi-faced design will produce almost no radar signal.

Units:

20th TFW, F-111E, 55th TFS, 77th TFS, 79th TFS (UH); 27th TFW, F-111D, 522nd TFS, 523rd TFS, 524th TFS (CC); 57th FWW F-111D/F (WA); 48th TFW, F-111F, 492nd TFS, 493rd TFS, 494th TFS, 495th TFS (LN); 366th TFW F-111A 389th TFTS, 391st TFS (MO)

Service number:
325+

F-117

Contractor:
Lockheed Corporation

Powerplant:
Two General Electric F404-GE-400 turbofans each rated at 4,899 kg (10,800 lb) without afterburners

Accommodation:
Pilot

Dimensions (provisional):
Span 9.65m (31′ 8″), wings folded 5m (16′ 5″)
Length 6.7m (22′)
Height 3.98 (13′ 1″)

Weights (provisional):
Empty 22,050lb Gross 33,070 lb

Performance (provisional):
Cruising speed at SL 645 mph Combat radius 345–360 miles

Armaments:
not known

Notes:
It is believed that Lockheed first flew an XST (Experimental Stealth Technology) demonstrator in 1977. It is possible that a total of seven of these small aircraft were built for testing and that two crashed. The operational F-117 was first flown in 1982.

The existence of a stealth fighter has been known for several years but was only revealed on 10 November 1988. The fighter has been in service since October 1983. The announcement was given as the aircraft will now be flying in daylight and will also operate abroad. The Air Force has released almost no information on the aircraft and the above figures must be taken as provisional.

Units:
4450th Tactical Test Group

Service number:
52 delivered with a further 7 on order

FB-111A

Contractor:
General Dynamics Corporation

Powerplant:
Two Pratt & Whitney TF30-P-7 turbofan engines; each 9,230kg (20,350 lb) thrust with afterburn

Accommodation:
Two, side-by-side

Dimensions:
Span spread 21.3m (70′ 0″)
Fully swept 10.4m (33′ 11″)
Length 23.3m (73′ 6″)
Height 5.2m (17′ 1.4″)

Weight (approx):
Gross 45,000kg (100,000 lb)

Performance:
Maximum speed at 11,000m (36,000′) Mach 2.5
Service ceiling more than 18,000m (60,000′)
Range 6,600km (4,100 miles) with external fuel

Armament:
Up to 4 AGM-69A SRAM air-to-surface missiles on external pylons, plus 2 in the weapons bay, or 6 nuclear bombs, or combinations of these weapons; provision for up to 14,000kg (31,500 lb) or conventional bombs

Notes:
The FB-111 which are flown by two SAC Wings will be handed over to Tactical Air Command in the early 1990's and will undertake long-range tactical bombing missions

Units:
509th BW, 393rd BS, 713th BS; 380th BW, 528th BS, 529th BS

Service number:
60+

HH-53B SUPER JOLLY AND HH-53C/CH-53C

Contractor:
Sikorsky Aircraft, Division of United Technologies Corporation

Powerplant:
Two General Electric T64-GE-7 turboshaft engines; each 3,925 shp

Accommodation:
Crew of 5; basic accommodation for 38 combat-equipped troops or 24 litters and 4 attendants

Dimensions:
Rotor diameter 22m (72′ 3″)
Length of fuselage (without refueling

probe) 20.4m (67′ 2″)
Height 7.6m (24′ 11″)

Weights:
Empty 10,500kg (23,125 lb)
Gross 19,000kg (42,000 lb)

Performance:
Maximum speed at S/L 300 km/h
(186 mph), service ceiling 5,600m
(18,400′), maximum range, with 10%
reserve, 870km (540 miles)

Notes:
A larger and faster variant of the HH-
3E it has twin engines. The HH-53B
was first delivered to the Air Force in
June 1968. The HH-53C quickly
followed; it can transport 38
passengers or 8,390kg (18,500 lbs) of
cargo. The CH-53C are used to carry
the Air Force mobile Tactical Air
Control System. The MH-53J PAVE
LOW is a highly modified C/HH-53
equipped with an integrated digital
avionics suite including terrain
following/terrain avoidance radar,
precision navigation, secure
communications and defensive systems
capability. Deliveries began at the end
of 1987 and all 41 of the H-53s will
have been converted by the end of
1991.

Units:
67th ARRS (HH-53C); 601st TCW
(CH-53C) 1550th CCTW, 1551st FTS
(HH-53B/C, CH-53C)

Service number:
41

HH-1H IROQUOIS, TH/UH-1F and UH-1P

Contractor:
Bell Helicopter Textron

Powerplant:
One General Electric T58-GE-3
turboshaft engine; 1,272 shp (derated
to 1,100 shp)

Accommodation:
One pilot and 10 passengers; or 2 crew
and 900kg (2,000 lb) or cargo

Dimensions:
Rotor diameter 14.6m (48′ 0″)
Length of fuselage 11.9m (39′ 7.5″)
Height 4.4m (14′ 8″)

An HH–53 Super Jolly

Weights:
Gross 4,000kg (9,000 lb) (4,300kg
(9,500 lb for HH-1H))

Performance
Maximum speed 222 km/h (138 mph)
Service ceiling at mission gross weight
4,010m (13,450′)
Maximum range, no allowances, at
mission gross weight 558km (347
miles)

Notes:
Developed from the Bell Model 204,
the basic UH-1F was used for missile
site support duties. The HH-1N is a
larger variation of the Bell 205

Units:
1st TFW (UH-1P); 35th TTW (UH-1F);
56th TTW (UH-1P); 405th TTW (UH-
1P); 37th ARRS, Det-2 (TH-1F, UH-
1F), Det-3 (HH-1H), Det-4 (HH-1F),
Det-5 (TH-1F), Det-6 (HH-1F), Det-7
(HH-1F), Det-9 (HH-1N), Det-10 (TH-
1F, UH-1F); 40th ARRS; 1550th
CCTW, 1550th FTS (TH-1F); 304th
ARRS (HH-1N)

Service number:
60+

KC-10A EXTENDER

Contractor:
Douglas Aircraft Company; Division of
McDonnell Douglas Corporation

Powerplant:
Three General Electric CF6-50C2
turbofan engines, each 23,800kg
(52,500 lb) thrust. Design fuel
capacity 161,500kg (356,065 lb)

Accommodation:
Crew of three on flight deck; seating for
limited number of essential support
personnel; maximum 25/27 pallets;
maximum cargo payload is 76–
4,268kg (168–9,409 lb)

Dimensions:
Span 50.3m (165′ 4.4″)
Length 55.2m (181′ 7″)
Height 17.7m (58′ 1″)

Weights:
Gross 268,000kg (590,000 lb)

Performance:
Maximum speed at 12,800m (42,000′)
850 km/h (528 mph)
Service ceiling 12,800m (42,000′)
Maximum range with maximum cargo
7,033km (4,370 miles); or delivery of
90,720kg (200,000 lb) of transfer fuel
to a receiver 3,540km (2,200 miles)
from its home base and return

Notes:
The KC-10 provides the capability to
deploy tactical fighter forces and their
support equipment simultaneously.
Additionally the KC-10 significantly
expands the US strategic airlift
capability, particularly with respect to
the long-range movement of oversize
cargo, when the aircraft is not required
for tankering operations. It is equipped
with both an air refueling boom and a

hosereel system for probe and drogue refueling. This is an important feature because it now means that the AF is able to refuel Navy, Marine Corps and Nato aircraft. The last KC-10 was delivered to the Air Force in Dec. 1988.

Units:
2nd BW, 32nd ARS, 78th ARS (Associate); 22nd ARW, 9th ARS, 79th ARS (Associate); 68th ARG, 911th ARS, 77th ARS (Associate)

Service number:
60

KC-135 STRATOTANKER

(information for KC-135A)

Contractor:
Boeing Military Airplane Company

Powerplant:
Four Pratt & Whitney J57-P-59W turbojet engines; each 6,240kg (13,750 lb) thrust

Accommodation:
Crew of four or five; up to 80 passengers

Dimensions:
Span 39.9m (130' 10")
Length 41.4m (136' 3")
Height 11.6m (38' 1")

Weights:
Empty 44,664kg (98,466 lb)
Gross 135,000kg (297,000 lb)

Performance:
Maximum speed at 9,000m (30,000')
940 km/h (585 mph)
Service ceiling 15,240m (50,000')
Range with 55,000kg (120,000 lb) of transfer fuel 1,850km (1,150 miles)
Ferry mission 14,800km (9,200 miles)

Notes:
The KC-135 is still the AF's primary strategic aerial refueling tanker. Built between 1955 and 1964 the Stratotanker proved the case for aerial refueling during the Vietnam war, and the lessons learnt have been acted upon. Today the KC-135 can be called upon to refuel almost all of the Air Force's aircraft. The KC-135 is undergoing a major re-engine upgrade by being converted to the KC-135R

configuration using the CFM56 high by-pass turbofan engine. This provides a 50 per cent increase in load.

Units:
2nd BW, 71st ARS KC-135A; 5th BW, 906th ARS KC-135A; 7th BW, 7th ARS KC-135A; 9th SRW, 349th ARS, 350th ARS KC-135Q; 19th ARW, 19th ARS, 912th ARS; 22nd ARW, 22nd ARS KC-135A; 28th BW, 28th ARS KC-135R; 42nd BW, 42nd ARS, 407th ARS KC-135A; 55th SRW KC-135A; 72nd ARS KC-135E; 93rd BW, 93rd ARS, 924th ARS KC-135A; 96th BW 917th ARS KC-135A; 116th ARS KC-135E; 126th AFS KC-135E; 132nd ARS KC-135E; 133rd ARS KC-135E; 145th ARS KC-135E; 147th ARS KC-135E; 150th ARS KC-135E; 305th ARW, 70th ARS, 305th ARS KC-135A; 314th ARS KC-135A/E; 319th BW, 905th ARS KC-135A; 320th BW, 904th ARS KC-135A; 336th AFS KC-135A/E; 340th ARW, 11th ARS, 340th ARS KC-135A; 379th BW, 920th ARS KC-135A; 376th SR, 906th ARS KC-135A/Q; 380th BW, 920th ARS KC-135A/Q/R; 410th BW, 46th ARS, 307th ARS KC-135A; 416th BW, 41st ARS KC-135A; 509th BW, 509th ARS KC-135A

Service number:
640+

OA-37B DRAGONFLY

Contractor:
Cessna Aircraft Company

Powerplant:
Two General Electric J85-GE-17A turbojet engines, each 1,290kg (2,850 lb) thrust

Accommodation:
Two, side-by-side

Dimensions:
Span over tip-tanks 10.9m (35' 10.5")
Length excluding fuel probe 8.5m (28' 3.25")
Height 2.7m (8' 10.5")

Weights:
Empty 2,817kg (6,211 lb)
Gross 6,350kg (14,000 lb)

Performance:
Maximum level speed at 4,875m (16,000') 816 km/h (507 mph)
Service ceiling 12,730m (41,765')
Range with maximum payload, including 1,860kg (4,100 lb) ordnance, 740km (460 miles)

Armament:
One GAU-2B/A 7.62mm Minigun installed in forward fuselage, four

Right: A KC-135A of the 509th ARS based at Pease AFB, operating from RAF Fairford.

pylons under each wing able to carry various combinations of rockets and bombs

Notes:
The Dragonfly is used in both the COIN and FAC roles

Units:
23rd TASS (NF); SAD; 103rd TASS (PA); 169th TASS (IL); 172nd TASS (BC)

Service number:
85+

OV-10A BRONCO

Contractor:
Rockwell International Corporation, Aircraft Operations

Powerplant:
Two Garrett T76-G-416/417 turboprop engines; each 715 hp

Accommodation:
Two, in tandem

Dimensions:
Span 12.5m (40′ 10″)
Length 12.6m (41′ 7″)
Height 4.6m (15′ 2″)

Weights:
Empty 3,127kg (6,893 lb)
Overload gross weight 6,552kg (14,444 lb)

Performance:
Maximum speed at S/L, without weapons, 452 km/h (281 mph)
Service ceiling 7,315m (24,000′)
Combat radius with maximum weapon load
No loiter, 367km (228 miles)

Armament:
Four fixed forward-firing M60C 7.62mm (0.27″) machine guns; four external weapon attachment points under short sponsons, for up to 1,000kg (2,400 lb) of rockets, bombs,

etc.; fifth point, capacity 540kg (1,200 lb), under centre fuselage. Provision for carrying one Sidewinder missile on each wing and, by use of a wing pylon kit, various stores, including rocket and flare pods and free-fall ordnance. Maximum weapon load 1,630kg (3,600 lb)

Notes:
Built for counterinsurgency operations it is now used in the Forward Air Control role

Units:
19th TASS (OS); 22nd TASS (WH); 27th TASS (VV); 549th TASS (FL)

Service number:
75+

Top: The A–37 Dragonfly built by Cessna is operated in the Forward Air Control role.

Left: A 22nd TASS, OV–10 based at Wheeler AFB, taking part in an exercise in South Korea.

Overleaf: The sci-fi outline of the world's fastest aircraft, an SR–71 of the 9th SRW at Beale AFB.

SR-71A/B "BLACKBIRD"

(Strategic Air Command)

Contractor:
Lockheed Corporation

Powerplant:
Two Pratt & Whitney JT11D-20B (J58) turbojet engines; each 10,000kg (24,000 lb) thrust with afterburning

Accommodation:
Crew of two in tandem

Dimensions:
Span 16.8m (55′ 7″)
Length 32.6m (107′ 5″)
Height 5.5m (18′ 6″)

Weights (estimated):
Empty 27,000kg (60,000 lb)
Gross 77,000kg (170,000 lb)

Performance (estimated):
Maximum speed at 24,000m (78,750′)

more than Mach 3
Operational ceiling above 24,000m
(80,000')

Armament:
None

Notes:
The aircraft which beat all the records,
the SR-71, is still the fastest
production aircraft ever built.
Designed in the 1960's, it set the
World Absolute Speed record of
2193.167 mph in July 1976. Its

sophisticated battlefield surveillance
systems can cover 260,000sq.km
(100,000 sq. miles) in a single hour.
Based at Beale AFB, California the
SR-71s also operate from forward
bases around the world

Units:
9th SRW

Service number:
6

TR-1 and U2

(information for the TR-1A)

Contractor:
Lockheed Corporation

Powerplant:
One Pratt & Whitney J75-P-13B
turbojet engine; 7,700kg (17,000 lb)
thrust

Dimensions:
Span 31.4m (103′ 0″)
Length 19.2m (63′ 0″)
Height 4.9m (16′ 0″)

Weights:
Gross 18,000kg (40,000 lb)

Performance:
Maximum cruising speed at over
20,000m (70,000′) more than 690
km/h (430 mph)
Range more than 4,800km (3,000
miles)

Armament:
None

Notes:
The TR-1 first flew on 1 August 1981
and deliveries started to Beale AFB a
month later. Operated primarily in
Europe the TR-1A with its Side-
Looking airborne radar is able to look
deep into enemy territory without
having to leave friendly airspace. It is
a direct descendant of the U-2R which
first flew in the 1960's. Although the
TR-1s operate from RAF Alconbury
they are SAC aircraft and not
controlled by USAFE. Some of the TR-
1s are to be converted to take the
Precision Location Strike System
(PLSS). PLSS missions require the use
of three aircraft to detect and locate
enemy emitters and then to direct
friendly forces to attack them.

Units:
9th SRW TR-1A U-2CT/R; 17th RW
TR-1A

Service number:
25+

T-37B TWEET

Contractor:
Cessna Aircraft Company

Powerplant:
Two Continental J69-T-25 turbojet
engines; each 465kg (1,025 lb) thrust

Accommodation:
Two, side-by-side

Dimensions:
Span 10.2m (33′ 9.3″)
Length 8.9m (29′ 3″)
Height 2.8m (9′ 2.3″)

Weights:
Empty 1,755kg (3,870 lb)
Gross 3,000kg (6,600 lb)

Performance:
Maximum speed at 7,620 (25,000′)
685 km/h (426 mph)
Service ceiling 10,700m (35,100′)
Range at 580 km/h (360 mph) with
standard tankage 1,400 km (870
miles)

The most difficult aircraft to
land in the inventory is the TR–
1, with habits more renowned to
the gliding fraternity than fast-
jet jocks.

Notes:
Introduced in the 1950's, the Cessna T-37 was the first jet designed specifically for training. Following the demise of the Fairchild T-46 the Air Force has had to go back to the drawing-board to decide on a future trainer. This has given the T-37 an extended lease of life which will include structural improvements

Units:
12th FTW, 559th FTS; 14th FTW, 37th FTS; 47th FTW, 85th FTS; 64th FTW, 35th FTS; 71st FTW, 8th FTS; 80th FTW, 88th FTS, 89th FTS, 90th FTS; 82nd FTW, 96th FTS; 323rd FTW, 454th FTS

Service number:
685+

The new "Air Force One", a B–747–200B, was due to enter service in November 1988, but will enter service during 1989.

Units:
475th TTW, 433rd TFTS, 434th TFTS, 435th TFTS, 436th TFTS, 12th FTW, 560th FTS; 14th FTW, 38th FTS; 47th FTW, 86th FTS; 71st FTW, 25th FTS; 80th FTW, 97th FTS; 3246th TW/AD

Service number:
870+

Training Command in 1964. The more powerful T-41C is used for cadet flight training at the Air Force Academy

Units:
AFA, 557th FTS; OTS

Service number:
100

T-38A TALON and AT-38B

Contractor:
Northrop Corporation

Powerplant:
Two General Electric J85-GE-5 turbojet engines; each 1,210kg (2,680 lb) thrust dry, 1,750kg (3,850 lb) thrust with afterburning

Accommodation:
Student and instructor, in tandem

Dimensions:
Span 7.6m (25′ 3″)
Length 14.1m (46′ 4.5″)
Height 3.9m (12′ 10.5″)

Weights:
Empty 3,250kg (7,164 lb)
Gross 5,485kg (12,093 lb)

Performance:
Maximum level speed at 11,000m (36,000′) more than Mach 1.23 (1,300 km/h (812 mph))
Ceiling above 16,765m (55,000′)
Range, with reserves, 1,760km (1,093 miles)

Notes:
First flown in 1959 the Talon has proved an excellent twin jet trainer. It is used by ATC, SAC and TAC and in its AT-38B configuration is fitted with a gunsight and practice bomb dispensers. The T-38 is being rewired to allow it to carry on into the next century

T-41 MESCALERO

(information for the T-41A)

Contractor:
Cessna Aircraft Company

Powerplant:
One Continental 0-300-C piston engine; 145 hp (210 hp Continental 0-360-D in T-41C)

Accommodation:
Crew of two, side-by-side

Dimensions:
Span 10.6m (35′ 1″)
Length 8.3m (26′ 11″)
Height 2.5m (8′ 9.5″)

Weights:
Empty 583kg (1,285 lb)
Gross 1,040kg (2,300 lb)

Performance:
Maximum speed at S/L 224 km/h (139 mph)
Service ceiling 4,000m (13,100′)
Range 1,160km (720 miles)

Notes:
The T-41 is a standard Cessna Model 172 and entered service with the Air

T-43A

Contractor:
Boeing Aerospace Company

Powerplant:
Two Pratt & Whitney JT8D-9 turbofan engines, each 6,600kg (14,500 lb) thrust

Accommodation:
Crew of 2, 12 students, 5 advanced students, 3 instructors

Dimensions:
Span 28m (93′ 0″)
Length 30.5m (100′ 0″)
Height 11.3m (37′ 0″)

Weights:
Gross 52,390kg (115,500 lb)

Performance:
Econ. cruising speed at 10,700m (35,000′) Mach 0.7
Operational range 4,820km (2,995 miles)

Notes:
The T-43 is used for navigation training, and was developed from the Boeing 737-200

Units:
323rd FTW, 455th FTS; HANGB
(Western Divn)

Service number:
18

UH-1N IROQUOIS

Contractor:
Bell Helicopter Textron

Powerplant:
Pratt & Whitney Canada T400-CP-400
Turbo "Twin-Pac," consisting of two
PT6 turboshaft engines coupled to a
combining gearbox with a single output
shaft; flat-rated to 1,290 shp

Accommodation:
Pilot and 14 passengers or cargo; or
external load of 1,800kg (4,000 lb)

Dimensions:
Rotor diameter (with tracking tips)
14.6m (48' 2.25")
Length of fuselage 12.8m (42' 4.75")
Height 4.5m (14' 10.25")

Weights:
Gross and mission weight 5,080kg
(11,200 lb)

Performance:
Maximum cruising speed at S/L

185 km/h (115 mph)
Service ceiling 4,000m (13,000')
Maximum range, no reserves, 420km
(261 miles)

Armament (optional):
Two General Electric 7.62mm (0.3")
Miniguns or two 40mm (1.57") grenade
launchers; two seven-tube 2.75 rocket
launchers

Notes:
Used in the combat rescue role, the
UH-1N is a twin-engined variant of the
UH-1

Units:
57th FWW; SAD; 37th ARRS, Det-8;
89th MAW; 67th ARRS; 1550th FTS;
304th ARRS; 475th ABW; 3246th
TW/AD

Service number:
70+

UH-60A BLACK HAWK

Contractor:
Sikorsky Aircraft, Division of United
Technologies Corporation

Powerplant:
Two General Electric T700-GE-700
turboshaft engines; each 1,560 shp

Accommodation:
Crew of two or three; 11–14 troops, up
to six litters, or internal or external
cargo

Dimensions:
Rotor diameter 16.2m (53' 8")
Length of fuselage 15.2m (50' 0.75")
Height 5.2m (16' 10")

Weights:
Empty 4,820kg (10,624 lb)
Gross 7,375–9,000kg (16,260–
20,250 lb)

Performance:
Maximum speed 296 km/h (184 mph)
Service ceiling 5,800m (19,000')
Maximum range, with reserves, 600km
(373 miles) (internal fuel), 2,220km
(1,380 miles) (external tanks)

Notes:
The Air Force originally received ten
basic UH-60As and it was planned that
they would receive more of the Night
Hawk variant at a later stage. The
Night Hawk program was cancelled
and so the Air Force is converting the
UH-60s through the Credible Hawk
program. Each helicopter will be fitted
with an aerial refuelling probe,
auxiliary fuel tank and fuel
management panel

Units:
55th ARRS

Service number:
10

UV-18B TWIN OTTER

Contractor:
The de Havilland Aircraft of Canada
Ltd

Powerplant:
Two Pratt & Whitney Canada PT6A-27
turboprop engines; each 620 ehp

Accommodation:
Crew of 2 and up to 20 passengers

Dimensions:
Span 19.8m (65' 0")
Length 15.6m (51' 9")
Height 5.8m (19' 6")

The Sikorsky UH–60A Black
Hawk is in service with MAC
ARRS units. The Air Force is
modifying their UH–60As to
MH–60G Pave Hawk standard
with precision low-level
navigation.

The Air Force Academy uses
two de Havilland Canada UV–
18Bs for parachute training.

X-29 FORWARD SWEPT WING DEMONSTRATOR

Contractor:
Grumman Corporation

Powerplant:
One General Electric F404-GE-400
turbofan engine; 7,260kg (16,000 lb)

Accommodation:
Pilot only

Dimensions:
Span 8.3m (27' 2.5")
Length overall 16.4m (53' 11.25")
Height 4.3m (14' 3.5")

Weights:
Empty 6,260kg (13,800 lb)
Gross 8,000kg (17,800 lb)

Performance:
Maximum level speed approx. Mach
1.6

Notes:
The X-29 is designed to test a wide
range of aeronautic technology. It first
flew supersonic in Dec. 1985 and has
undergone a vigorous set of flight tests
since then, including low-speed, high
angle-of-attack trials. The information
that the X-29 has produced will have a
significant effect on the next
generation of military aircraft

Units:
DARPA/USAF/NASA test aircraft

Service Number:
There are two X-29 aircraft flying

Performance:
Maximum cruising speed 338 km/h
(210 mph)
Service ceiling 8,138m (26,700')
Range with 1,134kg (2,500 lb)
payload 1,297km (806 miles)

Notes:
Two of these aircraft were bought in FY
1977 to provide parachute training at
the Air Force Academy

Units:
AFA

Service Number:
2

VC-25A

♦

Contractor:
Boeing Military Airplane Company

Powerplant:
Four General Electric CF6-80C2-B1
turbofan engines; each 25,700kg
(56,700 lb) thrust

Accommodation:
Crew of 23; up to 70 passengers

Dimensions:
Span 59.5m (195' 8.5")
Length 70.7m (231' 10")
Height 19.5m (64' 3")

Weights:
Gross 370,000kg (814,000 lb)

Performance:
Maximum cruising speed Mach 0.91
Normal cruising speed Mach 0.84
Service ceiling 13,700m (45,000')
Unrefueled range 11,600km (7,215
miles)

Notes:
These two aircraft are due to replace
the existing pair of Air Force Ones.

Units:
1402nd MAS

Service number:
2

The Grumman X–29 is being
used to push forward research
into new areas of aeronautical
design.

MISSILES AND SPACE LAUNCHERS

Preceding pages: Seen on the wing of an aircraft, the sidewinder looks quite small. It is only when you realize it takes three people to carry it that its true size is revealed.

Right: Armorers load an AIM–9 Sidewinder onto an F–15C of the 18th TFW at Kadena AB, Japan.

AIM-7 SPARROW

Contractor:
Raytheon Company/General Dynamics Pomona Division

Powerplant:
Hercules Mk 58 Mod O boost-sustain rocket motor

Guidance:
Raytheon semiactive Doppler radar homing system

Warhead:
High-explosive, blast fragmentation, weighing 40kg (86 lb)

Dimensions:
Length 3.6m (11′ 10″)
Body diameter 31.5mm (8″)
Wing span 0.9m (3′ 4″)

Weights:
Launch weight 228kg (504 lb)

Performance (estimated):
Maximum speed more than Mach 3.5
Range AIM-7E 14 miles, AIM-7F more than 25 miles

Aircraft types:
F-4, F-15

AIM-9 SIDEWINDER

Contractor:
Raytheon Company/Ford Aerospace and Communications Corporation

Powerplant:
Thiokol Hercules Mk 36 Mod 11 solid-propellant motor

Guidance:
Solid-state infrared homing guidance

Warhead:
High-explosive, weighing 9.4kg (20.8 lb)

Dimensions:
Length 2.7m (9′ 5″)
Body diameter 20mm (5″)
Fin span 0.6m (2′ 1″)

Weights:
Launch weight 87kg (191 lb)

Performance:
Maximum speed above Mach 2

Aircraft types:
A-7, A-10, F-4, F-15, F-111

An F–4E of the 52nd TFW armed with two AGM–45A Shrikes for ground defense suppression and three AIM–7 Sparrows for air defense.

AIM-120A AMRAAM

Contractor:
Hughes Aircraft Company/Raytheon
Company

Guidance:
Inertial midcourse, with active radar
terminal homing

Dimensions:
Length 3.6m (11' 9")
Body diameter 17.8cm (7")
Span of tail control fins 0.64m (2' 1")

Weights:
152kg (335 lb)

Performance:
Cruising speed approx Mach 4

Aircraft types:
F-15, F-16

AGM-45A SHRIKE

Contractor:
Naval Weapon Center

Powerplant:
Rocketdyne Mk 39 Mod 7 or Aerojet
Mk 53 solid-propellant rocket motor

Guidance:
Passive homing head by Texas
Instruments

Warhead:
High-explosive fragmentation,
weighing 65kg (145 lb)

Dimensions:
Length 3m (10' 0")
Body diameter 20cm (8")
Span 91cm (3' 0")

Weights:
Launch weight 180kg (400 lb)

Performance (estimated):
Range more than 5km (3 miles)

Aircraft types:
F-4G/E

AGM-65 MAVERICK

Contractor:
GM-Hughes, Missile Systems Group

Powerplant:
Thiokol TX-481 solid-propellant
rocket motor

Guidance:
Self-homing electro-optical guidance
system

Warhead:
High-explosive, shaped charge

Dimensions:
Length 2.4m (10' 2")
Body diameter 30cm (1' 2")
Wing span 71cm (2' 4.5")

Weights:
Launch weight 209kg (462 lb)

Performance:
Range of 1–22km (0.6 to 14 miles)

Aircraft types:
A-7D, A-10, F-4D/E/G, F-5E/F, F-
111 and F-16

A Hughes Aircraft AIM–120A
AMRAAM destroys a QF–100
drone during tests over the
White Sands Missile Range,
New Mexico.

AGM-69A SRAM

Contractor:
Boeing Aerospace Company

Powerplant:
Lockheed Propulsion Company LPC-415 restartable solid-prolid-propellant two-pulse rocket engine

Guidance:
General Precision/Kearfott inertial system, permitting attack at high or low altitude and dogleg courses

Warhead:
Nuclear, of similar yield to that of single Minuteman III warhead

Dimensions:
Length 4.3m (14' 0")
Body diameter 43cm (1' 5.5")

Weights:
Launch weight approx 1,010kg (2,230 lb)

Performance:
Speed up to Mach 2.5
Range 160km (100 miles) at high altitude
56km (35 miles) at low altitude

Units:
B-52H/G Wings and FB-111 Wings

Service number:
1,500

Right: High over the Pacific a B–52G releases a Boeing AGM–86B Air Launched Cruise Missile during missile acceptance trials.

AGM-84 HARPOON

Contractor:
McDonnell Douglas Astronautics Company

Powerplant:
Teledyne CAE J402-CA-400 turbojet engine, 300kg (660 lb) thrust

Guidance:
Sea-skimming cruise monitored by radar altimeter, active radar terminal homing

Warhead:
Penetration high-explosive blast type, weighing 220kg (488 lb)

Dimensions:
Length 3.7m (12' 7.5")
Body diameter 33cm (1' 1.5")
Wing span 0.9m (3')

Right: An F–4G "Wild Weasel" of the 37th TFW, based at George AFB, is shown carrying (front to back) an AGM–88A HARM, AGM–65D Maverick, ALW–119 jammer pod, AGM–78 Standard ARM and an AGM–45 Shrike.

Weights:
520kg (1,145 lb)

Performance:
Speed high subsonic, range over 92km (57 miles)

Aircraft types:
B-52G

AGM-86B ALCM

Contractor:
Boeing Aerospace Company

Powerplant:
Williams International Corporation/Teledyne CAE F107-WR-100 turbofan engine; 270kg (600 lb) thrust

Guidance:
Inertial plus tercom, by Litton

Warhead:
W80-1 nuclear

Dimensions:
Length 6.4m (20' 9")
Body diameter 68.5cm (2' 3.3")
Wing span 3.6m (12')

Weights:
1,450kg (3,200 lb)

Performance (approx):
Speed 800km/h (500 mph)
Range 2,400km (1,500 miles)

Aircraft types:
B-1, B-52

Units:
2nd BW; 7th BW; 92nd BW; 97th BW; 416th BW; 379th BW; 319th BW

Service number:
1,715

AGM-88A HARM

Contractor:
Texas Instruments Inc

Powerplant:
Thiokol smokeless dual-thurst solid-propellant rocket motor. Hercules second source

Guidance:
Passive homing guiding system, using seeker head that homes on enemy radar emissions

Warhead:
High explosive

Dimensions:
Length 4m (13′ 8.5″)
Body diameter 25cm (10″)
Wing span 1.1m (3′ 8.5″)

Weights:
366kg (807 lb)

Performance:
Cruising speed supersonic
Altitude limits S/L to 12,000m (40,000′)
Range more than 16km (10 miles)

Aircraft types:
F-4G also a number of other types could be converted

AGM-136A TACIT RAINBOW

Contractor:
Northrop

Powerplant:
Williams International WR36-1 turbofan

Guidance:
Pre-programmed plus passive homing system

Dimensions:
Length 2.53m (8′4″)
Body diameter 33.5cm (1′2″)
Span 155.4cm (5′1″)

Weights:
200 kg (441 lb)

Performance:
not announced

A BGM–109G Ground Launched Cruise Missile is launched from its Transporter Erector Launcher at the Dunway range in western Utah. This GLCM is being phased out following the ratification of the INF Treaty in 1988 and all missiles will be out of service by 1991.

BGM-109G TOMAHAWK GLCM

Contractor:
General Dynamics (Convair)/
McDonnell Douglas Astronautics

Powerplant:
Williams International Corporation/
Teledyne CAE F107-WR-400 turbofan engine; 270kg (600 lb) thrust Atlantic Research corporation solid-propellant booster

Guidance:
Intertial plus Tercom, by Litton

Warhead:
W84 nuclear

Dimensions:
Length 6.2m (20′ 6″)
Body diameter 82.5cm (1′ 8.5″)
Wing span 2.6m (8′ 7″)

Weights:
With booster, 1,475kg (3,250lb)

Performance:
Maximum speed high subsonic, range 2,400km (1,500 miles)

Units:
303rd TMW; 487th TMW; 485th TMW; 486th TMW; 501st TMW

Service number:
464 missiles deployed

GBU-15 AND AGM-130A

Contractor:
Rockwell International Corporation

Dimensions:
Length 3.9m (12′ 10.5″)
Body diameter 45cm (1′ 6″)
Wing span 1.5m (4′ 11″)

Weights:
1187kg (2,617lb)

Performance:
Cruising speed subsonic

Aircraft types:
F-4, F-111

Guidance:
TV or imaging infrared seeker

Warhead:
Mk 84 bomb (900kg (2,000lb) unitary)

LGM-30F/G MINUTEMAN II III

Assembly and checkout:
Boeing Aerospace Company

A Rockwell GBU–15 is mounted under the wing of an F–4. The GBU–15 is an air-launched cruciform-wing guided bomb capable of destroying heavily protected targets.

A test launch of an LGM–30 Minuteman ICBM from Vandenberg AFB. The LGM–30F/G has for many years been SAC's main nuclear weapon.

Powerplant:
First stage: Thiokol M-55E solid-propellant motor, 950,000kg (210,000lb) thrust; second stage: Aerojet-General SR19-AJ-1 solid propellant motor, 27,350kg (60,300lb) thrust; third stage: LGM-30F: Hercules, Inc., solid-propellant motor; LGM-30G: Thiokol SR73-AJ-1 solid-propellant motor: 7,700kg (17,000lb) thrust (LGM-30F), 15,600kg (34,400lb) thrust (LGM-30G)

Guidance:
Autonentics Division of Rockwell International inertial guidance system

Dimensions:
Length GM-30F 17m (55′ 11″)
      LGM-30G 18m (59′ 10″)
Diameter of first stage 1.6m (5′ 6″)

Weights:
Launch weight (approx) LGM-30F 33,000kg (73,000lb), LGM-30G 35,000kg (78,000lb)

Performance:
Speed at burnout more than 24,000km/h (15,000mph), highest point of trajectory approx 1,125km (700 miles), range with max operational load LGM-30F more than 9,650km (6,000 miles); LGM-30G more than 11,250km (7,000 miles;

Units:
44th SWM (MM II); 90th SMW (MM III); 91st SMW (MM III); 321st SMW (MM III); 341st SMW (MM II/III); 351st SMW (MM II)

Right: An LGM–118A Peacekeeper missile is cold launched during the missile's acceptance flights. A total of 50 missiles have been based in existing Minuteman III silos in the missile complex at F.E. Warren AFB.

Service Number:
450 MM IIs, 500 MM IIIs

LGM-118A PEACEKEEPER

Basing:
Boeing Aerospace Company

Assembly and test:
Martin Marietta, Denver Aerospace

Powerplant:
First three stages solid-propellant, fourth stage storable liquid; by Thiokol, Aerojet, Hercules, and Rocketdyne, respectively

Guidance:
Intertial; integration by Rockwell, IMU by Northrop

Warheads:
10 Avco Mk21 re-entry vehicles

Dimensions:
Length 21.6m (71′)
Diameter 2.2m (7′ 8″)

Weights:
Approx 88,000kg (195,000lb)

Units:
90th SMW

Service number:
100 planned

The British Aerospace Rapier air defense missile seen here in operation at RAF Upper Heyford. It is in use at nine USAFE bases in Britain and Turkey. It was battle proven during the Falklands War.

RAPIER

Contractor:
British Aerospace Plc, Army Weapons Division

Powerplant:
IMI two-stage solid-propellant motor

Guidance:
Racal-Decca surveillance radar and command to line-of-sight guidance, Optional Marconi DN181 Blindfire radar or optical target tracking, according to conditions

Warhead:
Semi armor-piercing, with impact fuse

Dimensions:
Length 14.4m (7′ 4″)
Body diameter 12.7cm (5″)
Wing span 43cm (1′ 5″)

Weights:
Approx 43kg (94lb)

Performance:
Maximum speed more than Mach 2, range 6km (4 miles)

Bases:
Seven USAF bases in Great Britain (operated by the RAF Regiment), two bases in Turkey

ROLAND

Contractor:
Euromissile GIE

Powerplant:
Two stage solid-propellant motor

Guidance:
Pulse-Doppler surveillance radar on launch vehicle and command to line-of-sight guidance. Radar or optical target tracking, according to conditions

Warhead:
High-explosive with proximity and impact fuses, weighing 6.5kg (14.3lb)

Dimensions:
Length 2.4m (7′ 10.5″)
Body diameter 16cm (6.3″)
Wing span 50cm (1′ 7.75″)

Weights:
67kg (147lb)

Performance:
Speed Mach 1.5, range 6km (3.7 miles)

Bases:
A total of 27 Roland units guard three USAF bases in West Germany (operated by the W. Germans)

SMALL ICMB (SICBM)

Contractor:
Martin Marietta Aerospace Corporation

Powerplant:
Stage one Morton Thiokol solid propellant, stage two Aerojet solid propellant, stage three Hercules solid propellant

Guidance:
Stella inertial

Warhead:
Single warhead and decoy aids

Dimensions:
Length 13.8m (55′ 3″)
Diameter approx 115cm (1′ 2″)

Weights:
16,800 kg: (37,038 lb)

Performance:
11,100 km (6,835 miles)
Diameter approx 115m (1′ 2″)

Bases:
Not known

SPACE LAUNCHERS

ATLAS LAUNCHERS

Prime contractor:
General Dynamics Corporation,
Convair Division

Powerplant:
Uprated Rocketdyne MA-5 propulsion
system, comprising central sustainer
motor and two boosters. Total thrust
(Atlas E) 178,000kg (392,000lb);
(Atlas G by itself is 22m (72'));
maximum body diameter 3m (10' 0")

Launch weight:
(Atlas G/Centaur) 163,000kg
(360,000lb)

Performance:
(Atlas H) capable of putting payload of
1,995kg (4,400lb) into low-earth polar
orbit, but has no provisions for
geosynchronous transfer orbit; (Atlas
G/Centaur) capable of putting 6,125kg
(13,500lb) into low-earth polar orbit
and a payload of 2,400kg (5,300lb)
into geosynchronous transfer orbit

Service number:
7

CENTAUR

Prime contractor:
General Dynamics Corporation,
Convair Division

Powerplant:
Two Pratt & Whitney RL10A/3 liquid
oxygen/liquid hydrogen engines; each
7,500kg (16,500lb) thrust

Guidance:
Inertial guidance system

Dimensions:
(Centaur D-1A only):
Length 9.1m (30' 0")
Diameter 3m (10' 0")

Launch weight:
(D-10A, approx) 16,000kg (35,000lb)

INERTIAL UPPER STAGE (IUS)

Prime contractor:
Boeing Aerospace Company

Powerplant:
Aft-stage solid rocket motor 9,700kg
(21,400lb) thrust; forward-stage solid
rocket motor 8,400kg (18,500lb) thrust

Guidance:
Inertial, plus star tracker

Dimensions:
Length 5m (17')
Diameter 2.7m (9' 2.25")

Launch weight:
14,750kg (32,500lb)

SCOUT

Prime contractor:
LTV Aerospace and Defense Company
(subsidiary of LTV Corporation)

Powerplant:
First stage: CSD Algol IIIA, 49,000kg
(109,000lb) thrust; second stage:
Thiokol Castor IIA solid-propellant
motor, 29,000kg (64,000lb) thrust;
third stage: Thiokol Antares IIIA solid-
propellant motor, 8,500kg (18,700lb)
thrust; fourth stage: Thiokol Altair IIIA
solid-propellant motor, 2,630kg
(5,800lb) thrust

Guidance:
Simplified Honeywell gyro guidance
system

Dimensions:
Height overall 23m (75' 5")
Maximum body diameter 1m (3' 9")

Launch weight:
21,600kg (47,619lb)

Service number:
10

SPACE TRANSPORTATION SYSTEM

Prime contractors:
Rockwell International (Orbiter),
Martin Marietta (propellant tank),
Thiokol (boosters), Lockheed Space
Operations (Shuttle processing)

Powerplant:
Three Rocketdyne main engines, each
170,000kg (375,000lb) thrust at liftoff.
Two Thiokol solid-propellant rocket
boosters, each 1,500,000kg
(3,300,000lb) thrust at liftoff

Guidance:
Automatic and manual control

Dimensions:
(Orbiter):
Length 37m (122')
Wing span 23.8m (78' 7")
Height 17m (56' 7")

Launch weights:
Shuttle complete approx 2,000,000kg
(4,500,000lb). Orbiter (empty)
68,000kg (150,000lb), external tank
(full) 750,000kg (1,655,600lb),
boosters (2) each 586,000kg
(1,292,000lb)

Service number:
3

TITAN 34D AND TITAN IV (CELV)

Prime contractor:
Martin Marietta Denver Aerospace

Powerplant:
First and second stages: Aerojet
liquid-propellant engines: first stage
243,000kg (536,000lb) thrust; second
stage 102,000lb thrust; Transtage:
Aerojet twin-chamber liquid-
propellant engine; 16,000lb thrust; two

CSD five and one-half segment solid-propellant booster rocket motors; each more than 520,000kg (1,150,000lb) thrust. (Titan IV: first stage 248,000kg (546,000lb) thrust; second stage 47,000kg (104,000lb) thrust; two SRBs total 1,236,000kg (2,725,000lb) thrust).

Dimensions:
First and second stages of core:
Height 31m (101′)
Diameter 3m (10′)

Transtage:
Height 4.3m (14′ 8″)
Diameter 3m (10′)

Launch weight (approx):
635,312kg (1,400,600lb)

Performance (Titan 34D/Transtage):
1,800kg (4,000lb) to geosynchronous orbit.

Service number:
4

Overleaf: A 1/20th scale model of the new Grumman E–8A JSTARS (Joint Surveillance Target Attack Radar System) undergoing tests in Grumman's anechoic chamber.

An artist's impression of the Air Force's new McDonnell Douglas Delta III rocket.

BUDGETS

Department of the Air Force
FY 1990/1991 RDT & E Program

Thousands of Dollars

	FY 1988	FY 1989	FY 1990	FY 1991
Summary Recap of Research Categories				
Research	200,167	196,388	220,094	223,775
Exploratory Development	572,892	573,868	579,707	591,781
Advanced Development	4,257,448	2,331,852	2,503,591	1,743,788
Engineering Development	3,866,624	5,393,655	5,280,073	5,378,859
Management and Support	645,986	554,426	600,643	615,946
Research and Development (FVDP Program 6)	9,543,117	9,050,189	9,184,108	8,554,149
Operational Systems Development	5,514,445	5,628,574	5,588,092	5,230,151
Total: Research Development Test & Evaluation AF	15,057,562	14,678,763	14,772,200	13,784,300
Summary Recap of Budget Activities				
Technology Base	773,059	770,256	799,801	815,556
Advanced Technology Development	789,350	764,711	785,338	900,969
Strategic Programs	5,743,174	5,374,252	4,658,451	3,630,964
Tactical Programs	3,942,780	4,121,674	4,660,224	4,649,529
Intelligence and Communications	2,135,782	2,064,445	2,086,660	2,119,467
Defensewide Mission Support	1,673,417	1,583,425	1,781,726	1,667,815
Total: Research Development Test & Evaluation AF	15,057,562	14,678,763	14,772,200	13,784,300
Summary Recap of FVDP Programs				
Strategic Forces	496,125	473,859	526,928	353,388
General Purpose Forces	917,185	988,129	1,135,826	1,127,562
Intelligence and Communications	3,792,870	3,798,127	3,700,747	3,501,014
Airlift/Sealift	26,968	12,808	14,784	12,845
Guard and Reserve	59,414	82,560	29,945	4,932
Research and Development (FVDP Program 6)	9,543,117	9,050,189	9,184,108	8,554,149
Central Supply and Maintenance	101,602	117,021	97,958	99,585
Administration and Assoc Activities			4,148	4,360
Support of Other Nations	3,066	3,114	3,177	3,750
Special Operations Forces	117,215	152,958	74,579	122,715
Total: Research Development Test & Evaluation AF	15,057,562	14,678,763	14,772,200	13,784,300

Budget Activities

Thousands of Dollars

Item Nomenclature	FY 1988	FY 1989	FY 1990	FY 1991
In-House Laboratory Independent Research	14,966	7,000	7,657	8,114
Defence Research Sciences	185,201	189,388	187,555	190,783
University Research Initiatives			24,882	24,878
Geophysics	37,702	34,645	36,025	36,434
Materials	53,727	58,071	59,313	59,717
Aerospace Flight Dynamics	70,482	68,885	67,650	69,074
Human Systems Technology	51,473	51,017	50,181	51,732
Aerospace Propulsion	60,658	64,173	64,921	65,735
Aerospace Avionics	62,193	64,109	68,457	72,014
Personnel, Training and Simulation	30,835	30,853	29,018	28,990
Civil Engineering and Environmental Quality	6,512	6,816	6,051	5,885
Rocket Propulsion	41,167	34,324	37,740	38,505
Advanced Weapons	35,407	34,492	32,880	34,029
Conventional Munitions	44,509	43,763	44,459	45,266
Command Control and Communications	78,227	82,720	83,012	84,400
Technology Base	773,059	770,256	799,801	815,556
Logistics Systems Technology	8,316	14,862	9,616	13,469
INEWS/ICNIA	85,129	37,079	36,364	31,788
Advanced Materials for Weapon Systems			13,116	14,673
Aerospace Propulsion Subsystems Integration	19,394	20,905	23,152	27,771
Advanced Avionics for Aerospace Vehicles	12,151	24.882	26,994	32,582
Aerospace Vehicle Technology	21,358	21,242	19,150	21,858
Aerospace Structures	24,497	27,665	18,087	18,705
Aerospace Propulsion and Power Technology	26,628	32,365	34,923	39,256
DoD Common Programming Language (Ada) Advanced Development	14,591			
Personnel, Training and Simulation Technology	7,504	8,038	7,829	8,997
Crew Systems and Personnel Protection Technology	19,344	20,272	22,606	21,906
Advanced Fighter Technology Integration	22,138	23,759	22,775	23,268
Lincoln Laboratory	25,999	23,003	25,603	26,988
Advanced Avionics Integration	3,085	11,000	14,732	18,240
National Aero Space Plane Technology Program	182,780	230,767	299,742	389,524
EW Technology		35,470	38,342	42,959
Space and Missile Rocket Propulsion	6,183	8,995	11,594	12,285
Hypervelocity Missile	6,605	5,577	9,306	7,189
Advanced Spacecraft Technology	3,972	7,995	9,998	12,730
Space Systems Environmental Interactions Technology	3,353	3,930	3,965	4,148

Model of a Westinghouse Rail
Garrison for Peacekeeper.

Item Nomenclature	FY 1988	FY 1989	FY 1990	FY 1991
Very High Speed Integrated Circuits	89,539	43,680		
Conventional Weapons	15,454	25,069	25,521	28,834
Advanced Weapons Technology	69,477	88,671	70,324	58,751
Weather Systems – Adv Dev	4,798	5,304	5,551	5,619
Civil and Environmental Engineering Technology	6,062	9,934	9,146	9,971
C3I Subsystem Integration	5,166	8,026	7,878	9,215
Advanced Computer Technology	4,081	7,239	10,027	10,851
Training Systems Technology	273	470		
DoD Software Engineering Institute	18,704			
Balanced Technology Initiative	51,332			
C3 Advanced Development	31,437	18,512	8,997	9,392
Advanced Technology Development	789,350	764,711	785,338	900,969

	FY 1988	FY 1989	FY 1990	FY 1991
Olympic				
Special Evaluation Program				
Meridian				
Advanced Strategic Missile Systems	129,193	141,768	99,352	99,272
Advanced Concepts				
Bell Weather				
Short Range Attack Missile II (SRAM II) – Adv Dev	139,955	197,018		
Relocatable Target Capability Program	9,859	19,534	6,398	6,972
Space Surveillance Technology			4,968	9,928
Technical On-site Inspection Program	10,573	9,245		
B-1B	359,040	218,284		
Common Strategic Rotary Launcher	5,546			
B-2 Advanced Technology Bomber				
Short Range Attack Missile II (SRAM II) – Eng Dev			217,011	212,759
ICBM Modernization	1,058,547	871,447	789,010	551,546
Strategic Conventional Standoff Capability (SCSC)	7,874	9,950		
Air Launched Cruise Missile (ALCM)	3,410	953	1,347	
Space Defense System	111,627			
Systems Survivability (Nuclear Effects)	11,467	8,291	7,675	8,743
Advanced Cruise Missile				
KC-135 Squadrons	3,979	3,161	2,203	3,533
Minuteman Squadrons	44,545	59,678	100,910	40,632
PACCS and WWABNCP System EC-135 Class V Mods	927	1,204	1,186	1,245
War Planning Automated Data Processing (ADP) – SAC		15,168	13,811	15,779
NCMC – TW/AA Systems	55,867	69,620	118,320	102,569
NCMC – Space Defense Systems	26,226	22,540		
Ballistic Missile Tactical Warning/Attack Assessment System	2,226	2,521		

Thousands of Dollars

Item Nomenclature	FY 1988	FY 1989	FY 1990	FY 1991
Joint Surveillance System	2,119	1,689	1,626	1,674
Surveillance Radar Stations/Sites	5,136	1,566	6,376	8,198
Distant Early Warning (DEW) Radar Stations	8,333			2,847
Over-the-Horizon Backscatter Radar	28,076	18,479	20,399	18,145
Ballistic Missile Early Warning System (BMEWS)	18,904	24,806	19,314	22,962
SPACETRACK	9,901	12,295	15,747	15,520
Defense Support Program	87,256	96,979	134,004	61,516
Submarine-Launched Ballistic Missile (SLBM) Radar Warning System	11,178	9,980	4,599	3,891
NUDET Detection System	7,272	10,806	6,735	3,131
Command Center Processing and Display System	29,050	26,417		
Minimum Essential Emergency Communications Network (MEECN)	49,680	40,420	15,798	2,670
World-Wide Military Command and Control Systems, Information System	5,020	2,307	3,435	3,700
WWMCCS Information System Joint Program Management Office	19,124	64,439	73,009	68,572
Milstar Satellite Communications System (AF Terminals)	196,156	302,975	210,193	104,915
Milstar Satellite Communications System	384,779	272,778		
Special Applications Progam				
BERNIE				
Special Analysis Activities				
Military Airlift Group (IF)	11,481	193		
Strategic Programs	5,743,174	5,374,252	4,658,451	3,630,964
Technical Evaluation System				
Advanced Tactical Fighter	492,255	684,566	1,111,492	206,563
Intelligence Advanced Development	3,973	4,969	6,699	7,273
Air Base Operability Advanced Development	4,136	5,073	2,794	3,832
Low Cost Anti-Radiation Seeker	13,325	12,391	7,632	
Command, Control, and Communication Applications			7,876	8,016
DoD Physical Security Equipment – Exterior	908			
Combat Identification Technology		1,940	1,959	1,973
Special Programs				
Aircraft Avionics Equipment Development	16,641	19,531	14,557	12,943
Aircraft Equipment Development	2,826	1,134	2,481	2,869
Engine Model Derivative Program (EMDP)	956	953	994	994
Nuclear Weapons Support	4,666	2,167	2,246	2,311
Alternate Fighter Engine	74,688	27,811	63,758	4,977
C-17 Program	1,090,539	932,022	915,227	498,426
Tanker, Transport, Bomber Training System		4,478	3,625	2,374
Infrared Search and Track System	13,814	4,621	2,449	
Variable Stability In-Flight Simulator Test Aircraft	6,022	7,895	12,445	3,896
Advanced Tactical Fighter – Eng Dev				1,411,565

Test-firing a Hughes aircraft
AMRAAM missile.

Thousands of Dollars

Item Nomenclature	FY 1988	FY 1989	FY 1990	FY 1991
Consolidated EW Programs	166,248			
Advanced Tactical Aircraft		34,571		
Short Range Attack Missile – Tactical (SRAM-T)			58,602	114,518
Close Air Support			66,000	55,000
Modular Automatic Test Equipment	14,636	11,151	13,926	12,701
Night/Precision Attack	19,291	4,662	3,514	
Integrated EW/CNI Development	7,684	121,162	106,194	47,968
Aircraft Engine Component Improvement Program	91,009	92,993	112,494	137,325
EW Development		97,218	150,456	195,613
Advanced Medium-Range, Air-to-Air Missile (AMRAAM)	23,467			
Advanced Short Range Air-to-Air Missile (ASRAAM)	996	996	4,987	6,472
Joint Tactical Fusion Program	14,049	7,960		
Hardened Target Munitions	1,474	6,248	3,408	
Ground-Launched Cruise Missile (GLCM)	296			
Chemical/Biological Defense Equipment	14,290	18,638	9,145	9,449
Armament/Ordnance Development	13,844	18,992	23,236	25,029
Submunitions	4,583	7,289	7,349	7,406
Wide-Area, Anti-Armor Munitions	21,994	26,519	27,625	
Air Base Operability	11,758	13,772	17,154	17,014
Aeromedical Systems Development	6,005	6,067	6,038	7,667
Common Support Equipment Development	1,617	1,620	6,967	8,485
Life Support Systems	12,501	16,767	13,020	13,315
Other Operational Equipment	7,478	7,258	2,230	2,135
Reconnaissance Equipment	194			
DoD Physical Security Equipment – Exterior	9,265			
Combat Identification Systems	30,961	83,359	111,389	104,406
Joint Standoff Weapon Systems			24,711	34,611
Surface Defense Suppression	9,745	39,213	15,422	7,149
Protective Systems	34,557			
Computer Resources Management Technology	10,415	13,020	11,736	12,295
Intelligence Equipment	5,846	4,852	3,522	3,808
Joint Tactical Information Distribution System (JTIDS)	21,814	49,315	44,351	43,683
Side Looking Airborne Radar	1,800	3,632	8,155	4,026
Joint Surveillance/Target Attack Radar System (JSTARS)	337,311	235,988	153,483	58,864
Joint Interoperability of Tactical Command & Control Systems (JINTACCS)	5,563	5,850	6,271	6,456
SR-71 Squadrons				
US Central Command – Communications	3,999			
F-111 Squadrons	16,822	21,300	22,369	9,028
F-15A/B/C/D Squadrons	99,199	87,610	2,749	2,842
F-16 Squadrons	25,067	26,229	33,458	176,961
F-15E Squadrons			121,894	98,950
F-4G WILD WEASEL Squadrons	7,621	4,487	3,149	12,085
CONSTANT HELP F-117A Squadrons			69,409	68,854

Item Nomenclature	FY 1988	FY 1989	FY 1990	FY 1991
Tactical AGM Missiles	2,044	3,881	2,485	497
Advanced Medium Range Air-to-Air Missile (AMRAAM) (Procurement)			14,929	24,878
F-111 Self Protection Systems	73		10,560	11,609
SEEK CLOCK				
TR-1 Squadron	70,517	100,775	110,710	53,311
Follow-On Tactical Reconnaissance System	44,789	56,067	104,048	89,524
AF TENCAP	312	322	335	345
TACIT RAINBOW	81,076	39,124	20,997	9,754
Standoff Land Attack Missile			5,062	10,076
Overseas Air Weapon Control System	8,729	5,707	3,524	4,110
Tactical Air Control Systems	15,733	13,290	22,322	28,648
Airborne Warning and Control System (AWACS)	96,527	116,124	139,632	126,231
Advanced Communications Systems	29,490	10,378	11,228	6,950
Copper Coast				
Tactical Air Intelligence System Activities	1,930		462	472
Tactical Improvement Program				
Tactical Reconnaissance Imagery and Exploitation	1,123	1,525		
Advanced Systems Improvements				
SEEK SPINNER		19,900		
Seek Eagle			16,797	17,807
OMEGA				
Mission Planning Systems			2,485	6,950
Joint Tactical Communications Program (TRI-TAC)	6,430	4,234	3,536	4,713
Electronic Combat Support			2,490	2,697
HAVE FLAG				
Satellite Communications Terminals	13,596	17,738	5,915	5,910
CENTENNIAL				
Electronic Combat Intelligence Support			1,744	1,793
THEME CASTLE				
Senior Citizen				
MAC Command and Control System	6,486	8,907	10,989	11,446
A-7 Squadrons (ANG)	59,414	82,560	29,945	4,932
Force Enhancements-Active	117,215	152,956	74,579	122,715
Tactical Programs	3,942,780	4,121,674	4,660,224	4,649,529

Intelligence Production Activities

Foreign Technology Division

Defense Dissemination Program

Infrared/Electro-Optical/Dir. Energy Weapons
Processing and Exploitation

Missile and Space Technical Collection

SENIOR YEAR Operations

| | | | Thousands of Dollars |
| | | | |

Item Nomenclature	FY 1988	FY 1989	FY 1990	FY 1991
FOREST GREEN				
NUDET Detection System				
Defense Satellite Communications System	43,325	33,733	28,105	15,579
Long-Haul Communications (DCS)	5,064	4,728	3,235	3,481
Inter-Service/Agency Automated Message Processing Exchange	472			
Electromagnetic Compatibility Analysis Center (ECAC)	8,083	8,395	8,746	9,101
Communications Security (COMSEC)				
Special Activities	1,587,813	1,476,221		
Traffic Control, Approach, and Landing System (TRACALS)	25,791	29,050	23,409	20,573
Defense Reconnaisance Support Activities				
NAVSTAR Global Positioning System (User Equipment)	38,239	47,005	35,555	32,916
NAVSTAR Global Positioning System (Space and Control Segments)	26,204	47,538	33,310	30,669
Intelligence and Communications	2,135,782	2,064,445	2,086,660	2,119,467
Space Test Program	48,399	44,304	74,589	77,005
Satellite Systems Survivability	3,170	5,003	10,361	10,554
Advanced Aerial Target Development	7,905	3,693	6,955	7,179
Flight Simulator Development	50,501	65,798	65,186	45,764
Manpower, Personnel and Training Development			497	695
Advanced Launch System			99,352	99,272
R&M Maturation/Technology Insertion	13,984	18,500	22,531	23,014
Weather Systems – Eng Dev	12,244	8,658	4,821	5,358
Range Improvement	54,654	19,893	118,069	102,195
Electromagnetic Radiation Test Facilities	5,869	5,207	4,447	4,728
Improved Capability for Development Test and Evaluation	53,113	49,565	52,599	56,407
Project Air Force	22,020	21,881	23,320	24,658
Ranch Hand II Epidemiology Study	5,754	1,740	1,419	1,476
Small Business Innovative Research	79,286			
Navigation/Radar/Sled Track Test Support	24,122	20,394	26,568	26,433
Test and Evaluation Support	299,105	297,106	304,352	321,319
Advanced Systems Engineering/Planning	16,957	13,204	14,036	14,914
DYCOMS	7,471	9,146	4,968	3,177
RDT&E Aircraft Support	51,999	52,364	60,448	62,153
Real Property Maintenance – RDT&E	78,464	78,710	97,752	96,452
Base Operations – RDT&E	60,808	59,881	67,780	65,364
Satellite Control Facility	91,884	88,255	68,579	117,717
Space Boosters	451,697	473,225	405,948	272,650
Consolidated Space Operations Center	38,836	34,913	24,533	24,762
Defense Meteorological Satellite Program (DMSP)	41,770	52,220	52,641	49,647
Space Shuttle Operations	48,737	39,630	64,692	47,227
Inventory Control Point Operations	4,326	4,455	4,621	4,752
Depot Maintenace (Non-IF)		969	2,428	2,668

Thousands of Dollars

Item Nomenclature	FY 1988	FY 1989	FY 1990	FY 1991
Industrial Preparedness	82,770	96,430	70,751	71,513
Productivity, Reliability, Availability, Maintain. Prog Ofc (PRAMPO)	14,506	15,167	20,158	20,652
Civilian Compensation Program			4,148	4,360
International Activities	3,066	3,114	3,177	3,750
Defensewide Mission Support	1,673,417	1,583,425	1,781,726	1,667,815
Total: Research Development Test & Eval AF	15,057,562	14,678,763	14,772,200	13,784,300

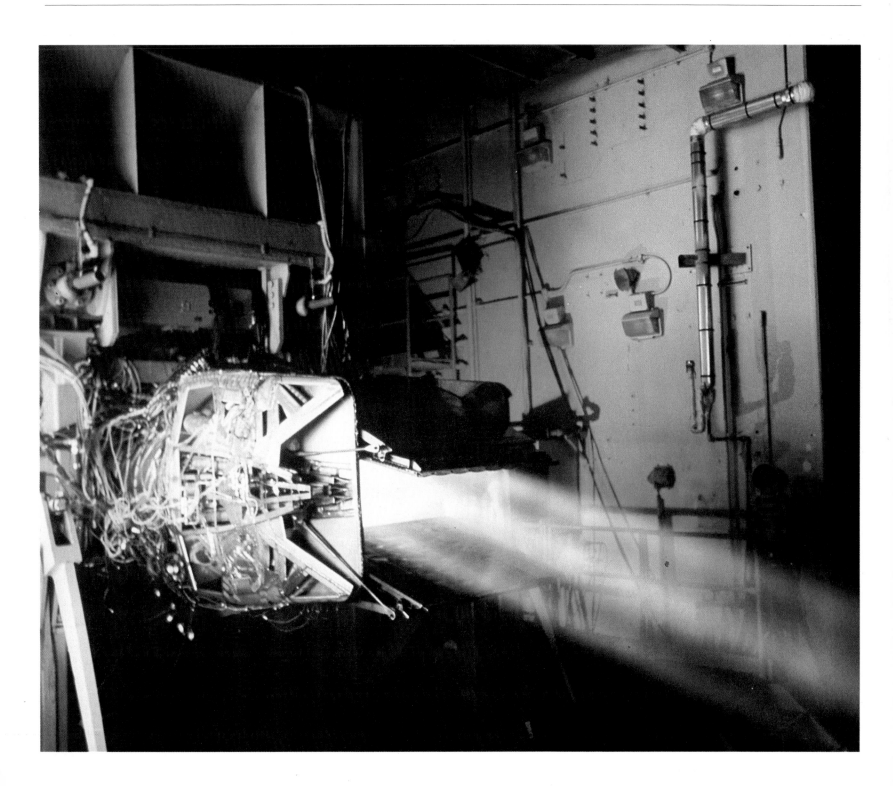

Department of the Air Force
FY 1990/1991 Procurement Program

SUMMARY   **Date: 9 Jan 1989**

Millions of Dollars

Appropriation	FY 1988	FY 1989	FY 1990	FY 1991
Aircraft Procurement	12,830.5	15,619.5	17,975.0	20,628.4
Missile Procurement	7,206.3	7,120.4	7,690.0	10.371.9
Other Procurement	7,941.2	8,153.5	8,735.8	9,256.0
Total	27,978.1	30,893.4	34,400.8	40,256.3

Appropriation: Aircraft Procurement

Millions of Dollars

Activity	FY 1988	FY 1989	FY 1990	FY 1991
01. Combat Aircraft	4,362.3	7,635.6	8.365.9	10,752.4
02. Airlift Aircraft	654.2	995.2	1,766.0	2,421.4
03. Trainer Aircraft		9.5	147.4	178.3
04. Other Aircraft	87.2	89.8	54.8	90.3
05. Modification of Inservice Aircraft	1,933.2	2,275.5	2,245.0	2,183.5
06. Aircraft Spares and Repair Parts	2,348.2	2,994.1	3,967.0	3,680.9
07. Aircraft Support Equipment and Facilities	3,445.5	1,619.3	1,428.9	1,321.7
Total	12,830.5	15,619.5	17,975.0	20,628.4

Preceding page: Testing the "2-dimensional" efflux of the STOL F–15 demonstrator P&W F100 engine.

Millions of Dollars

Item Nomenclature	(Dollars) FY 1990 Unit cost	FY 1988 Quantity	FY 1988 Cost	FY 1989 Quantity	FY 1989 Cost	FY 1990 Quantity	FY 1990 Cost	FY 1991 Quantity	FY 1991 Cost
Budget Activity 01: Combat Aircraft									
Strategic Offensive									
B1-B							10.0		9.9
B-2A Less: Advance Procurement									
B-2A Advance Procurement									
Tactical Forces									
F-15 D/E Less: Advance Procurement	37,108,777	42	(1398.6) (−139.4)	36	(1434.6) (−154.2)	36	(1335.9) (−100.7)	36	(1458.9) (−167.0)
			1259.2		1280.4		1235.2		1291.9
F-15 D/E Advance Procurement			154.2		100.7		230.5		147.8
F-16 C/D Less: Advance Procurement	18,434,073	180	(2633.9) (−534.0)	180	(3215.1) (−646.1)	150	(2765.1) (−309.1)	150	(2841.8) (−424.1)
			2100.0		2569.0		2456.0		2417.7
F-16 C/D Advance Procurement			475.9		462.7		556.1		437.4
Other Combat Aircraft									
MC-130H-SOF Less: Advance Procurement	118,374,000	7	(353.8) (−14.8)	4	(348.8) (−15.8)	2	(236.7)		(43.8)
			339.0		333.0		236.7		43.8
MC-130H – SOF Advance Procurement			15.8						
AC-130U Gunship – SOF Less: Advance Procurement	53,708,000			6	(305.0) (−18.2)	5	(268.5) (−29.5)		
					286.8		239.0		
AC-130U Gunship – SOF Advance Procurement			18.2		29.5				
Classified Programs									
Multi-Year Offset									
Multi-Year Offset					−81.8				
Total: Combat Aircraft			4,362.3		7,635.6		8,365.9		10,752.4

Millions of Dollars

Item Nomenclature	(Dollars) FY 1990 Unit cost	FY 1988 Quantity	Cost	FY 1989 Quantity	Cost	FY 1990 Quantity	Cost	FY 1991 Quantity	Cost
Budget Activity 02: Airlift Aircraft									
Tactical Airlift									
C-17	270,639,333	2	(622.7)	4	(962.0)	6	(1623.8)	10	(2177.8)
Less: Advance Procurement			(−34.8)		(−66.3)		(−99.9)		(−167.6)
			587.9		895.7		1524.0		2010.2
C-17 Advance Procurement			66.3		99.9		167.6		335.0
Other Airlift									
C-27A	14,877,200					5	74.4	5	76.2
Total: Airlift Aircraft			654.2		995.6		1,766.0		2,421.4
Budget Activity 03: Trainer Aircraft									
Tanker, Transport, Trainer System	10,530,357			1	9.5	14	147.4	28	178.3
Total: Trainer Aircraft					9.5		147.4		178.3
Budget Activity 04: Other Aircraft									
Helicopters									
MH-60G	13,205,500			9	75.4	4	52.8	4	33.0
Mission Support Aircraft									
Civil Air Patrol A/C	52,631	38	1.5	38	1.8	38	2.0	38	1.8
Other Aircraft									
C-29A		6	75.0						
E-8B Advance Procurement									55.5
TR-1/U-2			10.7		12.6				
Total: Other Aircraft			87.2		89.8		54.8		90.3
Budget Activity 05: Modification of Inservice Aircraft									
Strategic Aircraft									
B-52			247.2		209.6		218.7		74.3
FB-111			2.1						108.7
B-1B			14.5		24.5		73.3		108.7
Tactical Aircraft									
A-7			10.7		25.2		56.7		22.5
A-10			15.2		22.9		53.3		20.6
F/RF-4			9.1		16.5		94.7		107.9
F-5			2.4		.2				
F-15			120.3		174.2		254.8		254.6
F-16			73.3		167.5		228.1		300.7
F-111			250.3		124.3		83.8		134.2
TR-1A			9.9		20.3		22.3		18.8

Millions of Dollars

Item Nomenclature	(Dollars) FY 1990 Unit cost	FY 1988 Quantity	Cost	FY 1989 Quantity	Cost	FY 1990 Quantity	Cost	FY 1991 Quantity	Cost
T/AT-37			8.5		12.9		16.9		19.6
Airlift Aircraft									
C-5			16.9		99.9		55.7		56.3
C-9			.2		6.7		5.7		1.4
C-21							3.9		.1
C-137			1.8		2.0		1.7		1.7
C-141			.9		20.1		31.2		42.7
SOF C141			16.2		20.7				
Trainer Aircraft									
T-38			16.6		19.8		12.7		21.8
T-43			.6		4.9		10.2		.3
Other Aircraft									
KC-10A (ATCA)			11.9		26.0		12.1		6.6
C-12							3.5		1.0
C-18							.2		.2
C-20 MODS							.2		.2
VC-25A MOD					1.0				
C-130			100.9		121.3		118.3		128.2
SOF C130			121.0		106.8		118.1		63.5
C-135 (MYP)			762.2		784.8		485.5		497.1
E-3			21.8		16.4		36.5		104.2
E-4					49.0		18.2		37.8
E-8							.8		
H-1			.7		.4				
H-3 Aircraft System			.2				.7		.6
HH-53 Aircraft			.4		30.3		31.0		6.9
SOF HH-53					8.5				
H-60							7.2		4.6
Other Aircraft			43.9		57.4		120.9		79.0
SOF Other Aircraft							6.7		5.0
OV-10							2.1		3.8
Other Modifications									
Classified Projects			42.0		83.3		49.9		49.3
SOF Classified Projects			11.5		18.0		9.4		9.4
Total: Modification of Inservice Aircraft			1,933.2		2,275.5		2,245.0		2,183.5

Budget Activity 06: Aircraft Spares And Repair Parts

Aircraft Spares and Repair Parts

Item Nomenclature	(Dollars) FY 1990 Unit cost	FY 1988 Quantity	Cost	FY 1989 Quantity	Cost	FY 1990 Quantity	Cost	FY 1991 Quantity	Cost
Spares and Repair Parts (B-2A MYP EOQ)			2348.2		2994.1		3967.0 (13.2)		3680.9 (6.8)
Total: Aircraft Spares and Repair Parts			2,348.2		2,994.1		3,967.0		3,680.9

Millions of Dollars

Item Nomenclature	(Dollars) FY 1990 Unit cost	FY 1988 Quantity Cost	FY 1989 Quantity Cost	FY 1990 Quantity Cost	FY 1991 Quantity Cost
Budget Activity 07: Aircraft Support Equipment and Facilities					
Common Age (Associated Ground Equipment)		194.1	234.7	298.5	347.6
Industrial Responsiveness		41.4	23.2	57.6	43.3
War Consumables		29.0	20.4	51.9	53.7
Other Production Charges		2977.3	1075.6	673.5	657.8
Common ECM Equipment		197.4	248.5	228.8	195.6
Common Ground Equipment		4.0	14.3	109.2	14.1
Other Production Charges – SOF		2.3	2.6	9.4	9.6
Total: Aircraft Support Equipment and Facilities		3,445.5	1,619.3	1,428.9	1,321.7
Total: Aircraft Procurement		**12,830.5**	**15,619.5**	**17,975.0**	**20,628.4**

Night shot of a Rockwell B–1B being marshalled out to the runway.

Appropriation: Missile Procurement

Millions of Dollars

Activity	FY 1988	FY 1989	FY 1990	FY 1991
01. Ballistic Missiles	912.1	851.5	1,140.9	2,015.3
02. Other Missiles	1,916.4	1,469.2	1,566.3	2,233.1
03. Modification of Inservice Missiles	95.2	144.0	117.1	234.6
Spares and Repair Parts	154.1	231.0	469.4	607.2
05. Other Support	4,128.5	4,424.7	4,396.3	5,281.8
Total	7,206.3	7,120.4	7,690.0	10.371.9

Millions of Dollars

Item Nomenclature	(Dollars) FY 1990 Unit cost	FY 1988 Quantity	Cost	FY 1989 Quantity	Cost	FY 1990 Quantity	Cost	FY 1991 Quantity	Cost
Budget Activity 01: Ballistic Missiles									
Strategic									
Peacekeeper (M-X) Less: Advance Procurement	76,533,333	12	(864.0)	12	(794.9)	12	(918.4)	12	(2004.7) (−163.6)
			864.0		794.9		918.4		1841.1
Peacekeeper (M-X) Advance Procurement							163.6		133.9
Missile Replacement Equipment-Ballistic									
Missile Replacement Equipment-Ballistic			48.1		56.5		58.9		40.3
Total: Ballistic Missiles			912.1		851.5		1,140.9		2,015.3
Budget Activity 02: Other Missiles									
Strategic									
Advanced Cruise Missile Less: Advance Procurement									
Advanced Cruise Missile Advance Procurement									
HAVE FLAG									
Tacit Rainbow			55.1		70.5				190.5
SRAM II Less: Advance Procurement							(4.4)	25	(80.0) (−6.4)
							4.4		73.6
SRAM II Advance Procurement							6.4		5.7
HAVE NAP	987,772			6	8.3	22	21.7	26	22.4
Air Launch Cruise Missile			2.3						
Tactical									
AIM-7F/M Sparrow		558	66.0	174	25.0				
AIM-9L/M Sidewinder		1106	40.1	760	37.1		.5		.4
AGM-65D Maverick Less: Advance Procurement	78,175	2875	(290.0)	2820	(258.3)	2270	(177.5)	2020	(178.0) (−10.8)
			290.0		258.3		177.5		167.2

	(Dollars) FY 1990 Unit cost	FY 1988		FY 1989		FY 1990		Millions of Dollars FY 1991	
Item Nomenclature		Quantity	Cost	Quantity	Cost	Quantity	Cost	Quantity	Cost
AGM-65D Maverick									
Advance Procurement							10.8		7.8
AGM-88A HARM	243,371	1531	360.5	893	212.3	326	79.3	200	45.3
Rapier			4.1						
AMRAAM	622,673	400	(712.2)	874	(795.4)	1450	(902.9)	2200	(892.9)
Less: Advance Procurement			(−42.2)						
			670.0		795.4		902.9		892.9
Grd Launch Cruise Missile			4.1		.6				
Target Drones									
Target Drones	459,122	24	11.0	48	23.9	49	22.5	49	22.8
Industrial Facilities									
Industrial Preparedness			15.8		10.7		13.9		14.0
Missile Replacement Equipment – Other									
Missile Replacement Equipment – Other			4.8		4.9		2.0		2.5
Total: Other Missiles			1,916.4		1,469.2		1,566.3		2,233.1
Budget Activity 03: Modification of Inservice Missiles									
Class IV									
Advanced Cruise Missile									
Classified Programs									
HAVE NAP							1.0		
AIM-9L/M Sidewinder					49.8				
MM II/III Modifications			83.5		69.1		92.7		217.5
AGM-45A Shrike					14.9				
AGM-65D Maverick							10.0		3.1
AGM-88A HARM			2.2		2.2		1.4		2.0
Air Launch Cruise Missile			5.2		6.0		3.9		3.6
Peacekeeper (M-X)					1.7		3.4		3.4
Modifications Under $2.0m			.2		.2		.2		.3
Total: Modification of Inservice Missiles			95.2		144.0		117.1		234.6
Budget Activity 04: Spares and Repair Parts									
Missile Spares and Repair Parts									
Spares and Repair Parts			154.1		231.0		469.4		607.2
Total: Spares and Repair Parts			154.1		231.0		469.4		607.2
Budget Activity 05: Other Support									
Space Programs									
Spaceborne Equipment (COMSEC)			23.7		19.7		20.5		7.3
Global Positioning Less: Advance Procurement		4	(206.2) (−114.8)		(74.6)		(70.3)		(67.1)
			91.4		74.6		70.3		67.1

Millions of Dollars

Item Nomenclature	(Dollars) FY 1990 Unit cost	FY 1988 Quantity	Cost	FY 1989 Quantity	Cost	FY 1990 Quantity	Cost	FY 1991 Quantity	Cost
Global Positioning Advance Procurement									133.7
Space Shuttle Operations Less: Advance Procurement			(98.4) (−4.9)		(6.6)		(46.1)		(38.4)
			93.5		6.6		46.1		38.4
Milstar Advance Procurement									
Defense Meteorological Satellite Program Less: Advance Procurement	126,845,000		(5.7)	1	(123.1) (−34.3)	1	(126.8) (−46.5)	1	(155.5) (−69.0)
			5.7		88.8		80.4		86.5
Defense Meteorological Satellite Program Advance Procurement			63.0		69.0		57.0		63.7
Defense Support Program Less: Advance Procurement	431,730,000	1	(362.7) (−72.4)	1	(505.1) (−111.0)	1	(431.7) (−72.4)	1	(373.2) (−72.3)
			290.3		394.1		359.3		300.9
Defense Support Program Advance Procurement			63.1		36.4		12.3		241.9
Defense Satellite Communications System Less: Advance Procurement		1	(94.7) (−25.7)		(53.9)		(49.1)		(62.9)
			69.0		53.9		49.1		62.9
Space Boosters Less: Advance Procurement	161,427,000	9	(484.3) (−152.5)	3	(505.1) (−293.6)	3	(484.3) (−297.8)	2	(414.6) (−178.5)
			331.8		211.5		186.5		236.1
Space Boosters Advance Procurement			168.0		130.0		61.0		
Medium Launch Vehicle Less: Advance Procurement	44,096,500	7	(182.6)	8	(255.5) (−15.7)	4	(176.4) (−16.4)	5	(232.2) (−39.4)
			182.6		239.8		160.0		192.8
Medium Launch Vehicle Advance Procurement			15.7		16.4		39.4		27.3
Special Programs									
Other Programs			*						
Defense Reconnaisance Support Activities Advance Procurement									65.8
FOREST GREEN							.5		.6
IONDS		4	22.5						
IONDS Advance Procurement									32.8
Special Programs			2087.1		2818.3		3139.7		3441.5
Special Update Programs			621.2		265.7		114.2		198.1
Total: Other Support			4,128.5		4,424.7		4,396.3		5.281.8
Total: Missile Procurement			**7,206.3**		**7,120.4**		**7,690.0**		**10,371.9**

* Items under $50,000

Appropriation: Other Procurement

				Millions of Dollars
Activity	FY 1988	FY 1989	FY 1990	FY 1991
01. Munitions and Associated Equipment	589.4	592.5	421.2	696.3
02. Vehicular Equipment	231.4	272.5	226.1	241.4
03. Electronics and Telecommunications Equipment	1,899.1	1,909.8	2,387.6	2,374.1
04. Other Base Maintenance and Support Equipment	5,221.2	5,378.8	5,701.0	5,944.2
Total	7,941.2	8.153.5	8.735.8	9.256.0

Millions of Dollars

Item Nomenclature	(Dollars) FY 1990 Unit cost	FY 1988 Quantity	Cost	FY 1989 Quantity	Cost	FY 1990 Quantity	Cost	FY 1991 Quantity	Cost
Budget Activity 01: Munitions and Associated Equipment									
Rockets and Launchers									
2.75 inch Rocket Motor	227	91002	17.3	50370	10.0	68491	15.6	65841	15.2
2.75 inch Rocket Head – WP	75	94512	7.2	96926	6.5	80078	6.0	119763	9.1
Light Anti-tank Tactical AT-4	848	1066	2.1	3637	3.0	3516	3.0	3022	2.8
Items less than $2,000,000			2.5		5.5		5.8		7.1
Cartridges (thousands)									
9mm Parabellum		4546	.5	14933	1.5				
5.56mm	146	18944	2.9	30000	4.3	39997	5.9	42538	6.5
20mm Combat	3,478	3067	15.5	2112	9.7	1341	4.7	1743	6.1
20mm Training	2,875	5649	14.0	9822	22.6	9389	27.0	12637	36.5
30mm Training	8,294	8057	60.8	8160	63.0	7082	58.7	7086	58.7
40mm TP Grenades				754	1.0			1214	1.9
40mm HE Grenades	11,368	236	2.0	191	1.4	190	2.2	143	1.6
Cartridge Chaff RR-170			3.4	1700	3.7				
Signal Mk-4 mod 3	1,160	1300	1.3	1252	1.2	1516	1.8	1576	1.8
MXU-4A/A Engine Starter		53	4.9	45	5.3			60	7.8
Cart Imp 3000 ft/lb		1586	3.4	1563	3.8				
Item less than 2.0m Cartridges-SOF					.5				
Items less than $2,000,000			13.5		9.8		11.3		13.2
Bombs									
MK-82 Inert/BDU-50				70578	19.8			58861	17.0
Timer Actuator Fin Fuze		14000	4.1						
BSU-49 Inflatable Retarder	375	3924	1.6	46128	16.9	14969	5.6	14981	5.6
BSU-50 Inflatable Retarder		5036	4.3	7000	7.6				
Bomb 2000lb High Explosive		3400	5.8						
Bomb Hard Target 2000lb		2990	32.6	2610	30.8			2037	27.2
GBU-15									15.0
Bomb Practice 25lb	15	1255632	16.4	1160000	14.0	1584086	24.2	1538518	23.5

Millions of Dollars

Item Nomenclature	(Dollars) FY 1990 Unit cost	FY 1988 Quantity	Cost	FY 1989 Quantity	Cost	FY 1990 Quantity	Cost	FY 1991 Quantity	Cost
Bomb Practice BDU-38	4,190			668	2.3	846	3.5	846	3.6
MK-84 Bomb Empty		1766	2.9					15321	23.3
SKEET/Sensor Fuzed Weapon								65	118.7
CBU-87 (Combined Effects Munition) (MYP)	11,842	18451	(267.1)	16562	(252.9)	11537	(136.6)	10425	(136.6)
Less: Advance Procurement (PY)									(−10.0)
			267.1		252.9		136,6		126.6
CBU-87 (Combined Effects Munition) (MVP) Advance Procurement (CY)							20.0		15.0
Big Eye					9.7		6.9		60.7
Items less than $2,000,000					1.0		.3		.3
Targets									
Items less than $2,000,000					1.3				
Other Items									
Flare, IR MJU-7B	36	315960	9.0	326040	9.8	182311	6.6	91279	3.2
Parachute Flare LUU-2 B/B	440	9566	3.7	10000	3.8	3818	1.7	3860	1.7
Flare IR (B1B)	996			1275	1.9	5990	6.0	6094	6.0
MJU-10B		239179	10.8	206309	9.4			152243	7.3
Spares and Repair Parts			4.2		4.0		8.1		7.7
Modifications			29.6		.8		.2		.2
Items less than $2,000,000			10.6		21.7		17.1		20.1
Fuzes									
FMU-139	694	38766	28.8	41348	30.1	36213	25.1	47392	44.0
Items less than $2,000,000			*		*		1.3		1.3
Other Weapons									
M-203 Grenade Launcher		40	*	145	.1				
Machine Gun, 7.62mm, M-60		18	.1						
9mm Handgun		20000	4.2	9000	1.9				
Host Nation Support Weapons	216,216	259	2.1			74	16.0		
Total: Munitions and Associated Equipment			589.4		592.5		421.2		696.3

* Items under $50,000

Budget Activity 02: Vehicular Equipment

Passenger Carrying Vehicles

Item Nomenclature	Unit cost	FY 1988 Qty	Cost	FY 1989 Qty	Cost	FY 1990 Qty	Cost	FY 1991 Qty	Cost
Sedan, 4 dr 4x2	7,487	409	3.2	120	.9	117	.9	84	.6
Station Wagon, 4x2	7,901	235	1.8	91	.7	61	.5	58	.5
Bus, 28 passenger	39,375	123	4.8	22	.9	16	.6	16	.6
Bus Intercity	171,750	8	1.3	3	.5	4	.7	1	.2
Bus, 44 passenger	65,035	29	2.3	60	4.2	56	3.6	67	4.3
Ambulance, Bus	91,800	17	1.5			5	.5	8	.8
Modular Ambulance	40,490	112	4.0	44	1.7	51	2.1	44	1.8
14-20 passenger Bus	34,363	17	.5	16	.5	11	.4	4	.1
Law Enforcement Vehicle	10,369	141	1.4	161	1.6	130	1.3	55	.6

Item Nomenclature	(Dollars) FY 1990 Unit cost	FY 1988 Quantity	Cost	FY 1989 Quantity	Cost	FY 1990 Quantity	Cost	FY 1991 Quantity	Cost
Cargo and Utility Vehicles									
Truck, Stake/Platform	14,226	632	10.6	454	5.8	517	7.4	366	5.1
Truck, Cargo-Utility, ¾ ton, 4x4	16,356	448	6.8	201	3.4	255	4.2	206	3.5
Truck, Cargo-Utility, ½ ton, 4x2	14,398	304	3.9	187	2.7	286	4.1	213	3.1
Truck, Pickup, ½ ton, 4x2	11,248	880	6.5	632	6.6	435	4.9	388	4.0
Truck, Pickup, Compact		616	4.3						
Truck Multi-stop, 1 ton, 4x2	19,782	514	8.2	250	4.6	410	8.1	452	8.5
Truck, Panel, 4x2		349	3.2	193	2.3				
Truck Carryall	16,690	516	7.3	295	4.5	210	⁊	189	3.1
Commercial Utility Cargo Vehicle	16,000					34	5		
Truck, Cargo, 2½ ton, 6x6, M-35		335	17.4	177	9.4				
Truck, Cargo, 5t, M-923m M-925 (MYP)	57,233	75	5.2	73	4.6	137	7.8	67	4.7
High Mobility Vehicle (MYP)		139	3.4	186	4.4				
Truck Tractor, over 5 ton	44,811	97	3.5	91	3.9	69	3.1	77	3.7
Truck, Dump, 5 ton	38,064	143	6.1	52	2.2	77	2.9	96	3.7
Truck, Utility		346	4.7						
CAP Vehicles			.8		.8				
Items less than $2,000,000			16.4		9.1		16.7		11.7
Special Purpose Vehicles									
Truck Maintenance 4x2		320	3.4						
Truck, Telephone Maintenance		15	2.0						
Truck, Tank, 1200 gallon	36,833	56	2.1			48	1.8	71	2.7
Truck Tank Fuel R-11 (R-9)	96,085			567	53.5	350	33.6		
Truck Tank Fuel M-49	71,647	48	3.8			68	4.9	31	2.3
Truck Tank Water Waste								41	4.1
Tractor, A/C Tow, MB-4	50,333	87	2.0			3	.2	145	3.7
Tractor, Tow, Flightline	21,666	192	3.7	388	6.6	3	.1	303	5.6
Tractor, Dozer		76	5.0						
Mobile Maintenance Unit				13	7.0			9	4.5
Mobile Arm Reconnaissance Vehicle				20	18.2			40	26.2
Mos Marking Vehicle				36	2.7				
Items less than $2,000,000			18.5		15.2		16.8		13.2
Fire Fighting Equipment									
Truck Crash P-19	189,500					2	.4		
Truck Crash P-23 (P-2)	456,595			18	8.2	42	19.2	48	21.9
Truck Water P-18	119,333	57	6.5	9	1.6	9	1.1	46	5.8
Truck Pumper P-24 (P-8)	130,444			30	3.9	36	4.7	50	6.5
Truck Pumper P-22 (P-12)	113,444			26	2.9	36	4.1	35	4.0
Items less than $2,000,000			3.6		4.3		2.7		2.5
Materials Handling Equipment									
Truck, F/L 4000lb GED/DED 144 inch	28,559	179	2.6	274	7.5	220	6.3	293	7.3
Truck, F/L 6000lb	23,425	36	1.2	71	2.4	80	1.9	103	2.8
Truck, F/L 10,000lb	42,368	89	5.4	115	8.1	163	6.9	331	18.4
60K A/C Loader		3	3.1						

							Millions of Dollars	
Item Nomenclature	(Dollars) FY 1990 Unit cost	FY 1988 Quantity	Cost	FY 1989 Quantity	Cost	FY 1990 Quantity	Cost	FY 1991 Quantity	Cost

Item Nomenclature	(Dollars) FY 1990 Unit cost	FY 1988 Quantity	FY 1988 Cost	FY 1989 Quantity	FY 1989 Cost	FY 1990 Quantity	FY 1990 Cost	FY 1991 Quantity	FY 1991 Cost
25K A/C Loader	139,545			14	2.0	11	1.5	18	2.5
Tactical Cargo Loader								2	1.7
Container, Lift, Truck		15	2.8						
Items less than $2,000,000			5.1		11.3		9.9		6.5
Base Maintenance Support									
Loader, Scoop	62,224	73	5.0	93	4.9	116	7.2	103	6.4
Distributor, Water 1500 gallon		35	1.8						
Cleaner, Runway/Street	60,883	149	12.4	180	17.7	86	5.2	119	8.5
Crane, 7-50 ton	161,400	7	.8	21	5.5	10	1.6	12	.8
Excavator, Ded, PT	139,000					40	5.6	25	3.6
Spares and Repair Parts			1.9		3.2		3.0		2.8
Modifications			.4		1.1		1.2		1.0
Items less than $2,000,000			9.2		9.2		12.5		15.4
Total: Vehicular Equipment			231.4		272.5		226.1		241.4

Budget Activity 03: Electronics and Telecommunications Equipment

Item Nomenclature	FY 1988 Cost	FY 1989 Cost	FY 1990 Cost	FY 1991 Cost
Comm Security Equipment (COMSEC)				
Space Systems (COMSEC)	9.1	16.8	93.2	97.6
Tempest Equipment	.6	.3		
TAC Secure Voice	13.8	3.9		
DCS Secure Voice (COMSEC)	12.9	29.1		
Secure Data	32.1	22.1		
TRI-TAC (COMSEC)	7.8	8.5		
Spares and Repair Parts	6.5	6.1	7.4	7.2
Modifications (COMSEC)	.3	.7	1.8	1.8
Intelligence Programs				
Intelligence Data Handling System	.6		2.6	8.3
Intelligence Training Equipment	8.7	8.8	12.2	12.0
Intelligence COMM Equipment	5.3		2.4	30.0
Items less than $2,000,000	7.2	5.3	8.1	10.7
Electronic Programs				
Traffic Control/Landing	10.2	20.6	4.5	18.7
Tactical Air Control System IMPROVE	126.4	119.0	233.1	264.7
Weather Observ/Forecast	57.4	67.8	55.4	50.6
Defense Support Program	18.4	1.7	89.0	69.4
OTH-B Radar	118.7	159.0	209.5	218.5
SAC Command and Control	17.6	2.4	47.8	49.4
Launch Control Center Communications	8.1			
Cheyenne Mountain Complex	15.7	22.1	36.9	10.9
PAVE PAWS/SLBM Warning Systems	1.6			
BMEWS Modernization	1.4		6.3	.7
Spacetrack	.9		5.4	
NAVSTAR GPS	16.6	12.7	11.5	4.2

Millions of Dollars

Item Nomenclature	(Dollars) FY 1990 Unit cost	FY 1988 Quantity	FY 1988 Cost	FY 1989 Quantity	FY 1989 Cost	FY 1990 Quantity	FY 1990 Cost	FY 1991 Quantity	FY 1991 Cost
USAFE Command/Control System			1.9		1.3		2.5		2.5
PACAF Command/Control					1.3		10.9		1.1
Defense Meteorological Sat Program			10.2		17.7		.8		16.8
Caribbean Basin Radar Network			4.7		28.8		40.0		16.3
MARS/USAF Radar Upgrade			26.4		52.3		67.3		55.9
TAC Sigint Support			28.8		17.5		18.0		14.1
Dist Early Warning Rdr/North Warning			2.8		202.0		195.4		5.2
Tactical Ground Intercept Facility					2.2		6.2		9.2
TR-1 Ground Stations							5.5		
Air Base Operability			2.0		5.3		3.3		3.6
Imagery Trans					1.5				53.7
NUDET Detection System (NDS)			12.4						
Tactical Warning Systems Support			4.7		3.0		1.1		1.7
Special Comm-Electronics Projects									
Automatic Data Processing Equipment			108.0		67.7		78.4		68.7
WWMCCS/WIS ADPE			4.0		12.1		15.6		34.1
MAC Command and Control Support			30.8		20.3		27.8		22.4
MAC Command and Control-SOF			13.1		1.5				
GLCM Communications			2.7						
Air Force Physical Security System			23.9		16.9		21.8		22.8
Weapons Storage/Security			18.4		32.7		36.2		21.3
Range Improvements			175.3		119.5		115.8		114.3
C3 Countermeasures			4.3		5.8		7.0		8.5
Joint Surveillance System			4.0				4.0		
Space Shuttle			.2						
Base Level Data Auto Program			29.7		16.2		28.4		16.5
Satellite Control Facility			101.4		60.7		78.3		50.5
Constant Watch			17.1		5.2		7.3		4.6
Consolidated Space Ops Center			5.1				1.0		1.5
CMD Centre Processing/Display System					23.5				
Hammer Ace			.7		1.4				
SAMTO Test Range I&M			60.6		51.6		72.7		77.2
Air Force Communications									
Program 698AJ			1.7		1.7		1.4		1.9
Information Transmission Systems			11.9		8.1		.3		1.0
Telephone Exchange			30.0		27.7		43.6		54.1
Joint Tactical Comm Program (MYP)			147.7		151.3		126.4		106.0
Joint Tactical Comm Program (MYP) Advance Procurement (CY)									9.3
USTRANSCOM									10.1
USSOCCOM			4.5		5.8		7.4		7.8
USCENTCOM			23.1				9.0		11.1
Automated Telecommunications Program			10.7		4.3		3.9		3.7
MILSTAR					73.1		103.4		227.8

			Millions of Dollars					
Item Nomenclature	(Dollars) FY 1990 Unit cost	FY 1988 Quantity	Cost	FY 1989 Quantity	Cost	FY 1990 Quantity	Cost	FY 1991 Quantity	Cost

Item Nomenclature	(Dollars) FY 1990 Unit cost	FY 1988 Quantity	FY 1988 Cost	FY 1989 Quantity	FY 1989 Cost	FY 1990 Quantity	FY 1990 Cost	FY 1991 Quantity	FY 1991 Cost
Satellite Terminals			6.9		11.8		21.2		42.2
DCA Programs									
Wideband Systems Upgrade			34.1		14.2		47.8		10.8
Minimum Essential Emergency Communications Network			36.1		3.6		3.3		23.3
DCS Secure Voice Equipment			4.6		3.8				
Organization and Base									
Tactical C-E Equipment			51.3		39.9		32.0		49.0
Radio Equipment			41.3		18.0		6.8		3.5
Radio Equipment-SOF							1.6		
Fiber Optics			2.1		1.0				.8
TV Equipment (AFRTV)			4.5		4.1		4.7		4.8
CCTV/Audiovisual Equipment			4.2		3.9		4.0		3.9
E and I Requirements			1.2		.6		1.8		2.5
Spares and Repair Parts			222.4		199.2		253.4		272.5
Cap Com & Eject			.5		.6				
Items less than $2,000,000			8.9		6.2		11.9		16.5
Modifications									
Comm-Electronics Class IV			26.4		19.3		19.9		20.2
Tactical Equipment			26.9		27.2				
Antijam Voice			7.0		8.2		13.2		14.1
Total: Electronics and Telecommunications Equipment			1,899.1		1,909.8		2,387.6		2,374.1

Budget Activity 04: Other Base Maintenance and Support Equipment

Item Nomenclature	(Dollars) FY 1990 Unit cost	FY 1988 Quantity	FY 1988 Cost	FY 1989 Quantity	FY 1989 Cost	FY 1990 Quantity	FY 1990 Cost	FY 1991 Quantity	FY 1991 Cost
Test Equipment									
Base/ALC Calibration Package			55.0		56.1		29.9		31.7
Newark AFS Calibration Package			2.9		2.3		3.0		1.8
Test Equipment-General Purpose			4.5		6.0				
Items less than $2,000,000			40.1		37.3		32.0		36.6
Personal Safety and Rescue Equipment									
Automatic Life Preserver		3373	4.0	1952	2.4				
Night Vision Goggles			10.7		5.6		4.5		4.7
Night Vision Goggles-SOF		309	4.9	166	2.7		1.4		1.4
Chemical/Biological Defense Program			102.2		83.4		70.5		92.6
Items less than $2,000,000			3.8		3.5		3.7		5.5
Depot Plant plus Materials Handling Equipment									
Base Mechanization Equipment			24.6		36.9		28.4		25.9
Air Terminal Mechanization Equipment			6.5		7.0		8.6		7.0
Items less than £2,000,000			12.8		12.4		12.0		13.1
Electrical Equipment									
Generators-Mobile Electric			11.9		13.9		25.9		29.2
Flood Lights									.7
Items less than £2,000,000			4.3		5.5		4.4		5.0

Millions of Dollars

Item Nomenclature	(Dollars) FY 1990 Unit cost	FY 1988 Quantity	FY 1988 Cost	FY 1989 Quantity	FY 1989 Cost	FY 1990 Quantity	FY 1990 Cost	FY 1991 Quantity	FY 1991 Cost
Base Support Equipment									
Base Procured Equipment			26.1		46.9		34.5		37.0
Medical/Dental Equipment			101.0		109.6		124.6		75.6
Air Base Operability			5.0		8.1		36.3		30.5
Pallet, Air Cargo, 108" x 88"	900	2000	1.8	2000	1.8	4132	3.7	4000	3.7
Bladders Fuel		200	1.6						
Photographic Equipment			5.7		6.9		8.3		9.6
Tactical Shelter-SOF							3.6		3.7
Productivity Enhancement			10.1		11.2		10.1		10.8
Productivity Investments			1.6		1.5		5.1		10.9
Mobility Equipment			41.2		29.9		11.7		7.7
Wartime Host Nation Support			8.0		4.5		4.7		8.9
Spares and Repair Parts			5.6		6.1		7.1		5.3
Items less than $2,000,000			19.7		18.6		18.5		21.0
Special Support Projects									
Intelligence Production Activity			112.5		92.1		82.3		81.6
Technical Surveillance Countermeasures Equipment			2.1		1.0		1.0		2.0
Phot Processing and Interpretation System			.9		.3				
Selected Activities			4449.7		4605.8		4901.0		5148.4
Special Update Program			120.6		130.5		217.5		217.8
Special Application Program			.2		4.3				
Industrial Preparedness			2.1		4.5		4.5		4.9
Misc Equipment			10.8		16.6		.5		7.9
Misc Equipment-SOF			1.4		2.5		1.7		1.6
Modifications			5.2		1.0				
Total: Other Base Maintenance and Support Equipment			5,221.2		5,378.8		5,701.0		5,944.2
Total: Other Procurement			**7,941.2**		**8,153.5**		**8,735.8**		**9,256.0**

Defense Agencies
FY 1990/1991 Procurement Program

SUMMARY   **Date: 9 Jan 1989**

Millions of Dollars

Appropriation	FY 1988	FY 1989	FY 1990	FY 1991
Air Force Reserve Equipment	202.1	248.0		
Air National Guard Equipment	341.0	399.4		

Air Force Reserve Equipment

Millions of Dollars

Item Nomenclature	(Dollars) FY 1990 Unit cost	FY 1988 Quantity	Cost	FY 1989 Quantity	Cost	FY 1990 Quantity	Cost	FY 1991 Quantity	Cost
Air Force Reserve									
Miscellaneous Equipment			35.0		10.0				
C-130 Aircraft		8	150.0	6	122.0				
Improved Weather Reconnaissance System		4	4.8						
MH-60G Helicopters				12	74.0				
C-5A Simulator		1	12.3						
KC-135 Modifications					21.0				
Total: Air Force Reserve Equipment			**202.1**		**248.0**				

Air National Guard Equipment

Millions of Dollars

Item Nomenclature	(Dollars) FY 1990 Unit cost	FY 1988 Quantity	Cost	FY 1989 Quantity	Cost	FY 1990 Quantity	Cost	FY 1991 Quantity	Cost
Miscellaneous Equipment			30.0		20.0				
C-130 Aircraft		8	150.0	8	284.9				
MH-60G Helicopters		16	117.0						
HC-130 Aircraft		2	44.0						
F-16A/B MSIP				8	15.0				
ACMI North Tier Flight PH II					16.5				
KC-135 Aircraft					63.0				
Total: Air National Guard Equipment			**341.0**		**399.4**				

APPENDICES

USAF AIRCRAFT TAIL CODES

An A–10 of the 343rd TFW, Eielson AFB, Alabama.

F–15s of the 49th TFW, Holloman AFB, New Mexico.

An A–7D of the 132nd TFW, Grissom AFB, Indiana.

Preceding pages: The end of a day's work for a ground crew of the 1st TFW based at Langley AFB, Virginia.

Code	Aircraft	Command	Unit and Location
AD	Various	AFSC	Armament Division, Eglin AFB, Fla.
AK	F-15	AAC	21st TFW, Elmendorf AFB, Ala.
AK	A-10	AAC	343rd TFW, Eielson AFB, Ala.
AL	F-4D/F-16	ANG	187th TFG, Dannelly Field, Ala.
AR	F-5E, A-10	USAFE	10th TFW, RAF Alconbury, UK.
AZ	A-7D, F-16	ANG	162nd TFW, Tucson IAP, Ariz.
BA	RF-4	TAC	67th TRW, Bergstrom AFB, Tex.
BC	OA-37	ANG	110th TASG, Battle Creek ANGB, Mich.
BD	A-10	AFRES	917th TFG, Barksdale AFB, La.
BT	F-15	USAFE	36th TFW, Bitburg AB, W. Germany
CC	F-111D	TAC	27th TFW, Cannon AFB, N.M.
CM	F-15	ANG	159th TFG, New Orleans NAS, La.
CO	A-7D	ANG	140th TFW, Buckley ANGB, Colo.
CR	F-15	USAFE	32nd TFS, Camp New Amsterdam, Netherlands
CT	A-10	ANG	103rd TFG, Bradley ANGB, Conn.
DC	F-4D	ANG	113th TFW, Andrews AFB, Md.
DM	A-10	TAC	355th TTW, Davis-Monthan AFB, Ariz.
DO	F-4D	AFRES	906th TFG, Wright-Patterson AFB, Ohio
ED	Various	AFSC	Air Force Flight Test Center, Edwards AFB, Calif.
EG	F-15	TAC	33rd TFW, Eglin AFB, Fla.
EL	A-10	TAC	23rd TFW, England AFB, La.
FF	F-15	TAC	1st TFW, Langley AFB, Va.
FL	OV-10	TAC	549th TASTG, Patrick AFB, Fla.
FM	F-4D	AFRES	482nd TFW, Homestead AFB, Fla.
FW	F-4E	ANG	122nd TFW, Fort Wayne MAP, Ind.
GA	F-4E	TAC	35th TTW, George AFB, Calif.
GU	F-4E	PACAF	497th TFS, Taegu AB, S Korea
HA	A-7D	ANG	185th TFG, Sioux City, Iowa
HF	F-4E	ANG	181st TFG, Hulman RAP, Ind.
HI	F-16	AFRES	419th TFW, Hill AFB, Utah
HL	F-16	TAC	388th TFW, Hill AFB, Utah
HM	AT-38	TAC	479th TTW, Hooloman AFB, N.M.
HO	F-15	TAC	49th TFW, Holloman AFB, N.M.
HR	F-16	USAFE	50th TFW, Hahn AB, W Germany
HS	F-16	TAC	31st TTW, Homestead AFB, Fa.
HW	OA-37	ANG	24th COMPW, Howard AFB, Panama
IA	A-7D	ANG	132nd TFW, Des Moines MAP, Iowa
ID	A-10	AFRES	46th TFS, Grissom AFB, Ind.
IL	OA-37	ANG	182nd TASG, Greater Peoria Airport, Ill.
IN	A-10	AFRES	434th TFW, Grissom AFB, Ind.
IS	F-15	TAC	57th FIS, Keflavik NAS, Iceland
KC	A-10	AFRES	442nd TFW, Richards-Gebaur AFB, Mo.
KE	RF-4C	ANG	186th TRG, Key Field, Miss.
KS	EC-130	TAC	7th ACCS, Kessler AFB, Miss.
KY	RF-4C	ANG	123rd TRW, Standiford Field, Ky.
LA	F-15	TAC	405th TTW, Luke AFB, Ariz.
LF	F-16	TAC	58th TTW, Luke AFB, Ariz.
LH	CH-3	AFRES	302nd SOS, Luke AFB, Ariz.
LN	F-111F	USAFE	48th TFW, RAF Lakenheath GB.
LR	F-16	AFRES	944th TFG, Luke AFB, Ariz.
LV	A-7	TAC	4450th TACG, Nellis AFB, Nv.
MA	A-10	ANG	104th TFG, Barnes MAP, Mass.
MB	A-10	TAC	354th TFW, Myrtle Beach AFB, S.C.
MC	F-16	TAC	56th TTW, MacDill AFB, Fla.
MD	A-10	ANG	175th TFG, Martin Airport, Md.
MI	A-7D	ANG	127th TFW, Selfridge ANGB, Mich.
MJ	F-16	PACAF	432nd TFW, Misawa AB, Japan
MO	F-111, EF-111	TAC	366th TFW, Mountain AFB, Idaho

MY	F-4/ F-16	TAC	347th TFW, Moody AFB, Ga.
NA	F-16	TAC	474th TFW, Nellis AFB (TAC)
NF	OA-37	TAC	602nd TAIRCW, Davis-Monthan AFB, Ariz.
NJ	F-4E	ANG	108th TFW, McGuire AFB, N.J.
NM	A-7D	ANG	150th TFG, Kirkland AFB, N.M.
NO	A-10	AFRES	926th TFG, New Orleans NAS, La.
NY	A-10	ANG	174th TFW, Hancock Field, N.Y.
OH	A-7D	ANG	121st TFW, Rickenbacker AFB, Ohio
		ANG	178th TFG, Springfield, Ohio
		ANG	180th TFG, Toledo, Ohio
OK	A-7D	ANG	138th TFG, Tulsa IAP, Pa.
OS	F-4E, OV-10	PACAF	51st TFW, Osan AB, S. Korea
OT	Various	TAC	TAWC, Eglin AFB, Fla.
PA	OA-37	ANG	111st TASG, Willow Grove ARF, Pa.
PA	EC-130H	ANG	193rd SOG, Harrisburg IAP, Pa.
PN	F-4E/G F-5	PACAF	3rd TFW, Clark AB, Philippines
PR	A-7D	ANG	156th TFG, Muniz ANGB, Puerto Rico
PT	A-7D	ANG	112th TFG, Greater Pittsburgh IAP, Pa.
RG	Various	AFLC	Warner Robins ALC, Robins AFB, Ga.
RS	F-16	USAFE	86th TFW, Ramstein AB, W. Germany
SA	F-16	ANG	149th TFG, Kelly AFB, Tex.
SC	F-16	ANG	169th TFG, McEntire ANGB, S.C.
SD	A-7D	ANG	114th TFG, Joe Foss Field, S.D.
SH	F-4D	AFRES	507th TFG, Tinker AFB, Okla.
SI	F-4D	ANG	183rd TFG, Capitol MAP, Ill.
SJ	F-4E	TAC	4th TFW, Seymour Johnson AFB, N.C.
SL	F-4E	ANG	131st TFW, Bridgeton, Mo.
SP	F-4E/G	USAFE	52nd TFW, Spangdahlem AB, W. Germany
SU	A-10	PACAF	51st TFW, Suwon AB, S. Korea
SW	F-16, RF-4C	TAC	363rd TFW, Shaw AFB, S.C.
TH	F-4E	AFRES	301st TFW, Carswell AFB, Tex.
TJ	F-16	USAFE	401st TFW, Torrejon AB, Spain
TX	F-4D	AFRES	924th TFW, Bergstrom AFB, Tex.
TY	F-15, T-33	TAC	325th TTW, Tyndall AFB, Fla.
UH	F-111, EF-111	USAFE	20th TFW, RAF Upper Heyford, GB
VA	A-7D	ANG	192nd TFG, Byrd Field, Va.
VT	F-4D/ F-16	ANG	158th TFG, Burlington IAP, Vt.
VV	OV-10	TAC	27th TASS, George AFB, Calif.
WA	Various	TAC	57th FWW, Nellis AFB, Nev.
WH	OV-10	PACAF	22nd TASS, Wheeler AFB, Hawaii
WI	A-10	ANG	128th TFW, Truax ANGB, Wis.
WP	F-16	PACAF	8th TFW, Kunsan AB, S. Korea
WR	A-10, F-16	USAFE	81st TFW, RAF Bentwaters, GB.
WW	F-4E/G	TAC	37th TFW, George AFB, Calif.
ZF	F-4D, F-16	TAC	31st TTW, Homestead AFB, Fla.
ZR	RF-4C	USAFE	26th TRW, Zweibrucken AB, W. Germany
ZZ	F-15, RF-4C	PACAF	18th TFW, Kadena AB, Okinawa (PACAF)

An F–16A of the 474th TFW, based at Nellis on deployment to West Germany, passes an F–16C of the 86th TFW at Ramstein AB.

The flightline at George AFB with F–4E/Gs of the 37th TFW.

F–15s of the 18th TFW at Kadena AFB, Japan.

GLOSSARY

A-7	LTV Aerospace (formerly Vought Corporation), attack aircraft
A-10	Fairchild, close attack aircraft
AAA	Anti-Aircraft Artillery
AAC	Alaskan Air Command
AAFCE	Allied Air Forces Central Europe
AAM	Air-to-Air Missile
AASM	Advanced Air-to-Surface Missile
AAW	Aeromedical Airlift Wing
ABG	Air Base Group
ABM	Anti-Ballistic Missile
ABW	Air Base Wing
AC-130	Lockheed, fire support
ACM	Advanced Cruise Missile
ACCS	Airborne Command & Control Squadron
ACOS	Automated Commissary Operations System
ACSC	Air Command and Staff College
AEDC	Arnold Engineering Development Center
AEW	Airborne Early Warning
AFA	Air Force Academy
AFAA	Air Force Audit Agency
AFAFC	Air Force Accounting and Finance Center
AFB	Air Force Base
AFCC	Air Force Communications Command
AFCOMS	Air Force Commissary Service
AFCOMPMET	Air Force Comptroller Management Engineering Team
AFE	Alternate Fighter Engine
AFESC	Air Force Engineering and Services Center
AFESMET	Air Force Engineering and Services Management Engineering Team
AFFTC	Air Force Flight Test Center
AFINTELMET	Air Force Intelligence Management Engineering Team
AFIS	Air Force Intelligence Service
AFISC	Air Force Inspection and Safety Center
AFLC	Air Force Logistics Command
AFLOGMET	Air Force Logistics Management Engineering Team
AFMEA	Air Force Management Engineering Agency
AFMEDMET	Air Force Medical Management Engineering Team
AFMPC	Air Force Military Personnel Center
AFMPMET	Air Force Manpower and Personnel Management Engineering Team
AFOMS	Air Force Office of Medical Support
AFOs	Accounting and Finance Offices
AFOSI	Air Force Office of Special Investigations
AFOSP	Air Force Office of Security Police
AFOTEC	Air Force Operational Test and Evaluation Center
AFRES	Air Force Reserve
AFSATCOM	Air Force Satellite Communications System
AFSC	Air Force System Commands
AFSPACECOM	Air Force Space Command
AFSSMET	Air Force Special Staff Management Engineering Team
AFTAC	Air Force Technical Applications Center
AFWMPRT	Air Force Wartime Manpower and Personnel Readiness Team
AGM	Air-to-Ground Missile
ALCM	Air Launched Cruise Missile
AMRAAM	Advanced Medium-Range Air-to-Air Missile
AN/FPS	Search radar series
ANG	Air National Guard
ANGB	Air National Guard Base
ARRS	Aerospace Airlift Wing
ARS	Air Refueling Squadron
ARW	Air Refueling Wing
AS	Airbase Squadron
ASAT	Anti-Satellite
ASD	Aeronautical Systems Division
ASIF	Airlift Service Industrial Fund 96
ASM	Air-to-Surface Missile
ASMS	Advanced Strategic Missile Systems
ATB	Advanced Technology Bomber; see also B-2
ATC	(1) Air Training Command; (2) Air Training Control
ATF	Advanced Technology Fighter; see also YF-22A, YF-23A
AUL	Air University Library
AUTODIN	Automatic Digital Network
AUTOVON	Automatic Voice Network
AUTOSEVO-COM	Automatic Secure Voice Communications Network
AWACS	Airborne Warning and Control System
AWC	Air War College
AW&CS	Airborne Warning & Control Squadron
AW&CW	Airborne Warning & Control Wing
B-1B	Rockwell, multi-role strategic bomber
B-2	Northrop, advanced strategic bomber
B-52	Boeing, multi-role strategic bomber
BMEWS	Ballistic Missile Early Warning system
BS	Bombardment Squadron
BW	Bombardment wing
C-130	Lockheed, Hercules, tactical airlift transporter
C-140	Lockheed, Starlifter, airlift transporter
C-5	Lockheed Galaxy, strategic transporter
C3	Command, Control and Communications
C3CM	Command, Control and Communications Countermeasures
C3I	Command, Control, Communications and Intelligence
CAMNET	Commissary Automated Management Network
CBU	Cluster Bomb Unit
CCTW	Combat Crew Training Wing
CEP	Circular Error Probability
CIDS	Contracting Information Data System
CINCs	Commander-in-Chief of Unified and Specified Commands
CINCAFLANT	Commander-in-Chief, Air Force Atlantic
CINCAFLC	Commander-in-Chief of Air Force Logistics Command
CINCAFRED	Commander-in-Chief Readiness Command
CINCLANT	Commander-in-Chief, Atlantic
CINCNORAD	Commander-in-Chief of North American Air Defense Command
CINCPAC	Commander-in-Chief, Pacific
CINSAC	Commander-in-Chief of Strategic Air Command
COBRA DANE	space surveillance sensor
COBs	Collocated Operating Bases
COMINT	Communications Intelligence
CONUS	Continental USA (excludes Hawaii)
CRAF	Civil Reserve Air Fleet
CSRL	Common Strategic Rotary Launcher
DARPA	Defense Advanced Research Projects Agency
DCS	Defense Communications System
DEW	Distant Early Warning

DMMIS	Depot Maintenance Management Information System	**MAJCOMS**	Major Commands
DMSP	Defense Meteorological Satellite Program	**MAMRC**	Military Aerospace Maintenance and Regeneration Center
DoD	Department of Defense	**MAS**	Military Airlift Squadron
DRU	Direct Reporting Unit	**MATS**	Military Air Transport Service
DSCS	Defense Satellite Communications System	**MAW**	Military Airlift Wing
E-3	Boeing airborne warning & control aircraft	**MIRW**	Multiple Independently Targetable Re-entry Vehicle
EC	Electronic Combat	**MSIP**	Multinational Staged Improvement Program
ECCM	Electronic Counter-Countermeasures	**NAS**	Naval Air Station
ECM	Electronic Countermeasures	**NASA**	National Aeronautics and Space Administration
ECS	Electronic Countermeasures Squadron		
BEEF	*see* Prime BEEF	**NCB**	Nuclear, Biological and Chemical
ELINT	Electronic Intelligence	**NCMC**	NORAD Cheyenne Mountain Complex
ELV	Expendable Launch Vehicle	**NEACP**	National Emergency Airborne Command Post
EMP	Electro-Magnetic Pulse	**NORAD**	North American Air Defense Command
ESC	Electronic Security Command	**NSC**	National Security Council
ESD	Electronic Systems Division	**OL-A**	Operating Location-A
ESM	Electronic Support Measures	**ORI**	Operation Readiness Inspection
F-15	McDonnell Douglas, single-seat fighter	**OTH-B**	Over-The-Horizon Backscatter
F-16	General Dynamics, single-seat fighter	**OTS**	Officer Training School
F-111	General Dynamics, medium-range bomber	**PACAF**	Pacific Air Forces
FAA	Federal Aviation Administration	**PAVE LOW**	MH-53H/J Conversion Program
FB-111	General Dynamics, medium-range strategic bomber	**PAVE PAWS**	Phased-array missile warning system
		PGM	Precision Guided Missile
FEAF	Far East Air Forces	**PRGM**	Program
FEBA	Forward Edge of Battle	**Prime BEEF**	Base Engineer Emergency Force (aka BEEF)
FIS	Fighter Interceptor Squadron	**Prime RIBS**	Readiness in Base Service (aka RIBS)
FLIR	Forward-Looking Infra-Red	**PUP**	Product Upgrade Program
FMETS	Functional Management Engineering Teams	**RAF**	Royal Air Force
FOC	Full Operational Capability	**R&D**	Research and Development
FRP	Functional Review Process	**RDT&E**	Research, Development, Test and Evaluation
FSW	Forward Swept Wing	**RED HORSE**	Rapid Engineer Deployable, Heavy Operational Repair Squadron, Engineer
FY	Fiscal Year (1 July – 30 June)		
GCI	Ground Controlled Interception	**RF-4**	McDonnell Douglas Reconnaissance F-4
Geostationary	Earth orbit maintaining satellite over same point of the Earth	**RG**	Recruiting Group
		RIBS	*see* Prime RIBS
GLCM	Ground Launched Cruise Missile	**R&M**	Reliability and Maintainability
GPS	Global Positioning System	**RMG**	Resource Management Group
HANGB	HQ Air National Guard Bureau	**SAC**	Strategic Air Command
harden	Given protection against nuclear explosion	**SAD**	Southern Air Division
HARM	High-speed Anti-Radiation Missile	**SAM**	Surface-to-Air Missile
HUD	Head Up Display	**SAMTO**	Space and Missile Test Organization
HUMINT	Human-resource Intelligence	**SAR**	(1) Search and Rescue; (2) Synthetic Aperture Radar
HQ	Headquarters		
ICBM	Inter-Continental Ballistic Missile	**SDI**	Strategic Defense Initiative
INCNIA	Integrated Communications-Navigation-Identification Avionics	**SEWS**	Satellite Early Warning System
		SICBM	Small ICBM
IFF	Identification Friend or Foe	**SIGINT**	Signals Intelligence
INEWS	Integrated Electronic Warfare System	**signature**	Electro-magnetic radiation "fingerprint"
INF	Intermediate-range Nuclear Force	**SLAR**	Side Looking Airborne Radar
INS	Inertial Navigation System	**SLBM**	Submarine Launched Ballistic Missile
IOC	Initial Operational Capability	**SMW**	Strategic Missile Wing
IR	Infra Red	**SO**	Special Operations
IRIS	Inferential Retrieval Index System	**SOA**	Separate Operating Agency
IRR	Individual Ready Reserve	**SOS**	Special Operations Squadron
JCS	Joint Chiefs of Staff	**SOUTHCOM**	United States Southern Command
JSTARS	Joint Surveillance and Target Attack Radar System	**SRAM**	Short-Range Attack Missile
		SRW	Strategic Reconnaissance Wing
JT	Joint	**START**	Strategic Arms Reduction Talks
JTF-AK	Joint Task Force-Alaska	**STS**	Space Transportation System, Shuttle
JTIDS	Joint Tactical Information Distribution System	**SUPT**	Specialized Undergraduate Pilot Training
km/h	Kilometres per hour	**TAC**	Tactical Air Command
kt	Kilotons	**TAS**	Tactical Airlift Squadron
LANTCOM	United States Atlantic Command	**TAW**	Tactical Airlift Wing
LANTIRN	Low-Altitude Navigation Targeting Infra-Red, Night	**TCW**	Tactical Control Wing
		TFS	Tactical Fighter Squadron
loiter	Maximum period on station	**TFTS**	Tactical Fighter Training Squadron
MAC	Military Airlift Command	**TFW**	Tactical Fighter Wing
MAG	Military Airlift Group		

TMW	Tactical Missile Wing		**USAFTFWC**	United States Air Force Tactical Fighter Weapons Center
TOSI	Technical On-Site Inspection		**USARS**	United States Air Recruiting Service
TRS	Tactical Reconnaissance Squadron		**USCC**	United States Central Command
TW/AD	Test Wing/Armament Division		**USREDCOM**	United States Readiness Control
TW/ASD	Test Wing/Aeronautical Systems Division		**WRS**	Weather Reconnaissance Squadron
USAAC	United States Air Corps		**WSMC**	Western Space and Missile Center
USAEDS	United States Atomic Energy Detection System		**WWABNCP**	Wordwide Airborne Command Post
USAFADWC	United States Air Force Air Defense Weapons Center		**WWMCCS**	Worldwide Military Command and Control System
USAFE	United States Air Forces in Europe		**YF-22A**	Lockheed, ATF prototype
USAFSO	United States Air Force Southern Air Division		**YF-23A**	Northrop, ATF prototype
USAFTAWC	United States Air Force Tactical Air Warfare Center			

BIBLIOGRAPHY

Books

Aircraft Markings by Barry C. Wheeler, published by Salamander Books Ltd.

United States Air Force (yearly), published by Blackbird Aviation Publications.

The Guide to Military Installations edited by Dan Cragg, published by Stackpole Books 1984.

The Air Force Officer's Guide edited by Lt. Col. John Hawkins Napier III, USAF (Ret.), published by Stackpole Books 1984.

History of the United States Air Force by Bernard Fitzsimons, published by Chevprime Ltd. 1988.

The History of the United States Air Force by Bill Yenne, published by Bison Books Ltd. 1984.

Red Flag by Michael Skinner, published by Presidio Press 1984.

Jane's All the World's Aircraft (yearly), published by Jane's Information Group.

Jane's Weapon Systems (yearly), published by Jane's Information Group.

Nuclear Facts by Christy Campbell, published by The Hamlyn Publishing Group 1984.

Flightplan edited by Christy Campbell, published by Reed International 1988.

Guardians, Strategic Reconnaissance Satellites by Curtiss Peebles, published by Ian Allan 1987.

Magazines

Air Force Magazine (monthly), with special reference to the *Air Force Almanac* (yearly), published by the Air Force Association.

Aviation Week and Space Technology, published by McGraw Hill.

Defence (monthly), published by Whitton Press.

Defense News (weekly), published by The Times Publishing Group.

Flight International (weekly), published by Reed International.

International Defence Review (monthly), published by Jane's Information Group.

Interavia (monthly), published by Jane's Information Group.

Military Technology (monthly), published by The Monch Publishing Group.

US Official Documents

Annual Report to the Congress Fiscal Year 1989 by Frank C. Carlucci, Secretary of Defense.

Military Posture FY 1989 prepared by the Joint Staff.

FY 1989 Air Force Acquisition Statement.

Base Realignments and Closures, Report of the Defense Secretary's Commission December 1988.

The Semiannual Report to the Congress prepared by the Department of Defense Inspector General (various editions).

Fiscal Years 1990/1991 Military Construction Program.

Program Acquisition Costs by Weapon System, Department of Defense.

Budget for Fiscal Year 1989 and Fiscal Years 1990 and 1991.

Procurement Programs (P-1), Department of Defense Budget for Fiscal Year 1989 and Fiscal Years 1990 and 1991.

R, D, T & E Programs (R-1), Department of Defense Budget for Fiscal Year 1989 and Fiscal Years 1990 and 1991.

The United States Air Force Report to the 100th Congress of the United States of America.